Tom Abraham was born in Cheshire, and emigrated to America at the age of nineteen. From 1966 until 1969 he served in the United States Army, including a tour of duty to Vietnam. Afterwards he returned to England, where he made a successful career in the textile industry. He now lives in Walton-on-Thames.

www.booksattransworld.co.uk

The Cage Tom Abraham

BANTAM PRESS

LONDON · NEW YORK · TORONTO · SYDNEY · AUCKLAND

TRANSWORLD PUBLISHERS
61–63 Uxbridge Road, London W5 5SA
a division of The Random House Group Ltd

RANDOM HOUSE AUSTRALIA (PTY) LTD
20 Alfred Street, Milsons Point, Sydney,
New South Wales 2061, Australia

RANDOM HOUSE NEW ZEALAND LTD
18 Poland Road, Glenfield, Auckland 10, New Zealand

RANDOM HOUSE SOUTH AFRICA (PTY) LTD
Endulini, 5a Jubilee Road, Parktown 2193, South Africa

Published 2002 by Bantam Press
a division of Transworld Publishers

A catalogue record for this book is available from the British Library.
ISBNs 0593 049683 (cased)
0593 04973X (tpb)

Typeset in 11/15pt Palatino by Falcon Oast Graphic Art Ltd.

Printed in Great Britain
Clays Ltd, Bungay, Suffolk

1 3 5 7 9 10 8 6 4 2

Dedicated to the men of the 1st Cavalry Division,
United States Army

Contents

Acknowledgements

This book is an account of my tour of duty in Vietnam more than thirty years ago. It is based solely on my memories of what I witnessed, and my subsequent discoveries. It does not purport to be a history book, and I do not claim to have given a complete picture of any of the historical events in which I was engaged. Memory is fallible, and it is possible that a few of the incidents I have described did not happen in the exact sequence shown. Nevertheless, I have tried to provide a faithful picture of events as they occurred within these inevitable limits. Names and certain other details have been changed for the usual reasons.

I should like to thank my agent Mark Lucas for his guidance and support; Lucy and Henry Forwood and Brett Huntley for their valuable comments on the typescript; my ex-wife Debbie for lending me the letters I wrote to her from Vietnam; and my sister Pat and daughters Nikki, Suzy and Jenny for helping me through a difficult period. Most of all I want to thank Sally, for reasons that will be obvious to readers of this book.

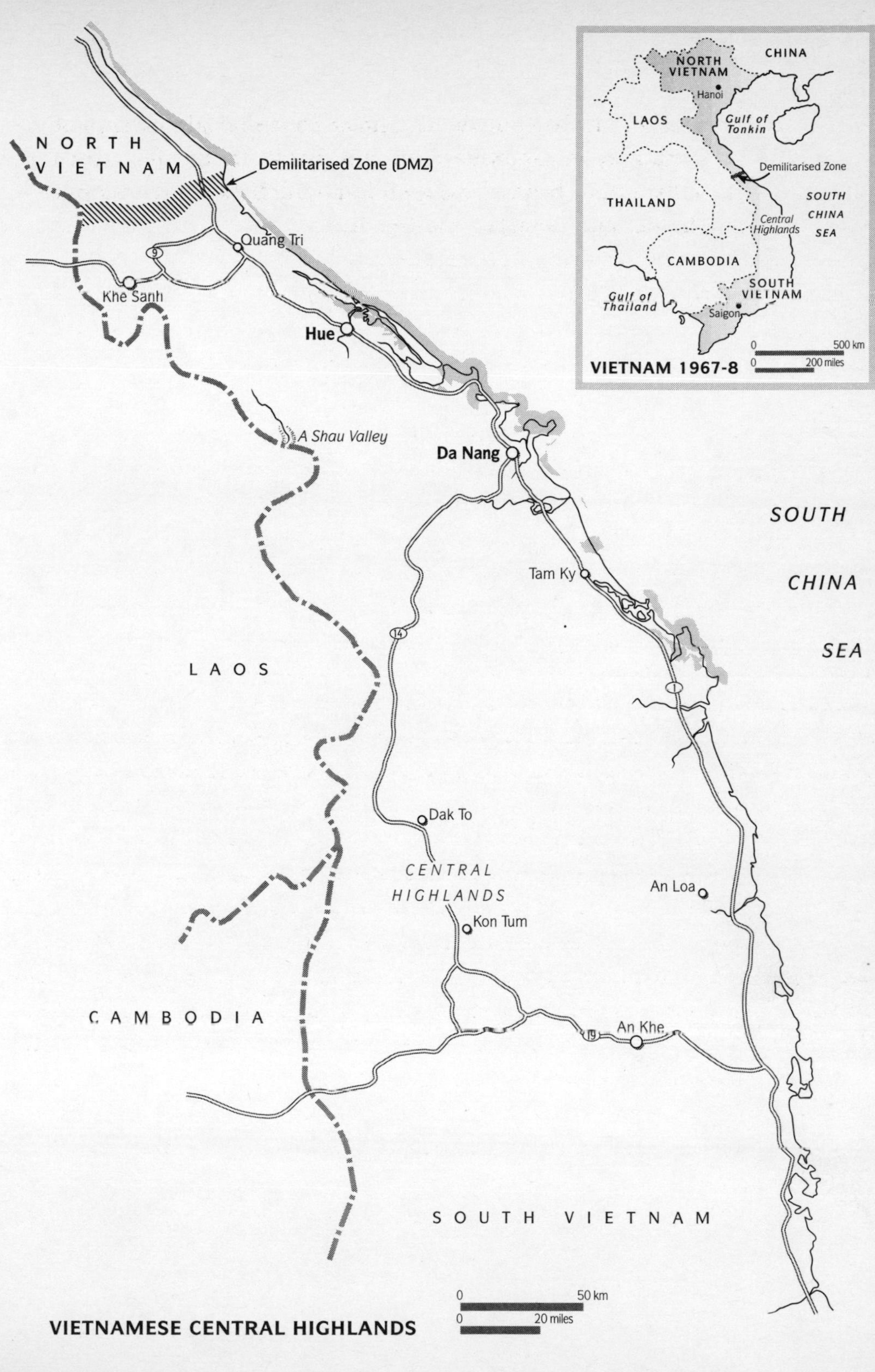
NORTH VIETNAM
Demilitarised Zone (DMZ)
Quang Tri
9
Khe Sanh
Hue
A Shau Valley
Da Nang
Tam Ky
14
1
LAOS
Dak To
CENTRAL HIGHLANDS
Kon Tum
An Loa
CAMBODIA
19
An Khe
SOUTH CHINA SEA
SOUTH VIETNAM
0
50 km
0
20 miles
NORTH VIETNAM
CHINA
Hanoi
LAOS
Gulf of Tonkin
Demilitarised Zone
THAILAND
SOUTH CHINA SEA
Central Highlands
CAMBODIA
SOUTH VIETNAM
Gulf of Thailand
Saigon
0
500 km
0
200 miles
VIETNAM 1967-8
VIETNAMESE CENTRAL HIGHLANDS

The Cage

Prologue

I'm looking at a photograph. That's me, thirty-five years ago, posing for the camera. I crouch with an M-16 rifle in my left hand, wearing fatigues. Round my neck is the neckerchief I always wore to wipe away the sweat. I'm lean and fit. I certainly wasn't overweight when I arrived in Vietnam, but nevertheless the pounds dropped off me as I humped heavy packs around all day in that oppressive heat. Within a matter of weeks, I'd lost about two stone.

Somewhere I've still got a book of photographs I took in Vietnam, including pictures of me like this one that I asked someone else to take with my camera. I used to have a stack of slides as well, but I lost them when they went off to a lab to be made into prints. Over the years I've tried once or twice to show these pictures to my daughters, but they've always resisted it. They don't want to know anything about my time in Vietnam. None of my family does, not even Sally.

I'm living in this horrible bedsit. It's right on the main road. At night, the whole house seems to shake as the lorries thunder past. The cheap curtains over the window are too flimsy to block out the passing headlights. I had to come here after my sister told me it was time to move out. Now my home is this anonymous room, lined with woodchip paper. There's a sink and a two-ring Baby Belling cooker in one corner. A pile of washing-up fills the sink; I don't really have the heart to clean up. To get to the bathroom means leaving my room, going along the corridor and up the stairs. The landlord warned me to lock my door behind me, even if I'm only going for a pee. And then of course I need to take a key. I don't bother: I just take a plastic bottle to bed with me and pee into that.

This isn't how I expected my life would be. When I was a young man living in Pennsylvania, I imagined a comfortable house in the suburbs, a white picket fence, a screen on the door. Perhaps a flag on the lawn. My wife cooking me a meal while I mess around in my den, polishing my knives or fiddling with one of my guns. Or perhaps in the garage, tuning an automobile engine.

I fish around in the supermarket carrier-bag that I use for my personal belongings, and pull out a battered cardboard roll. Inside is my commission, a little creased and faded after all these years. I sit down on the floor against the wall and unroll the piece of card that once made me feel so proud. As I read it here in this empty room, I feel the sobs welling up inside.

PART I: England

1

Surrey, 1999

It's getting dark now, and I'm staring down a conveyor belt of approaching headlights.

I'm driving out of town, on a mild January evening. An ordinary, middle-aged, suburban man, with a house, a garden, a wife and two cats, on his way home at the close of a normal day.

The car radio's playing, not too loud. I'm not really listening, just enjoying the freedom of being out on the road after being stuck inside the auction-rooms with all those people. I'm not comfortable with crowds these days. I suppose you could say I'm a bit of a recluse. Soon I'll be safe home with Sally.

Jesus! What the hell was that bang? I can feel an ugly vibration through the floor. There's a grinding noise coming from the nearside, and the steering-wheel starts pulling to the left. Oh, Christ, a blow-out.

For a few seconds I debate whether to pull over. This is a lonely stretch of road – not the sort of place you want to leave a car. If I abandon it now and come back for it tomorrow morning, I doubt it will still be in one piece. Anyway, I'm reluctant to step out of my nice warm cocoon. There's an isolated twenty-four-hour Shell garage a few hundred yards ahead where I should be able to leave it safely. I drive on slowly, nursing the wounded car forward.

On second thoughts, I tell myself this is silly: you'll damage the wheel if you go on. As my foot moves towards the brake pedal, I glance in the rear-view mirror: a single headlight, coming up fast. A police motorcyclist overtakes, then slows to flag me down. Hell and damnation. I had a bottle of wine at lunchtime.

I pull over and he stops in front of me. He doesn't look back as he dismounts. A gauntlet switches off the engine and a boot kicks down the stand. Then his shoulders push the bike up and forward into a resting position. It's all very slow and deliberate. He turns round, shedding the gauntlets. I can't see his face, just the streetlight glinting off his helmet.

I get out and walk round the Scorpio to look at the damage; both nearside tyres have gone. What a mess. As I'm bending over to examine them, I'm aware of the motorcyclist behind me. I can see his leather toecap out of the corner of my eye, and hear the static from his radio. I straighten up, shrugging my shoulders.

He tells me that I've driven straight across a hole in the road. The visor's up now and I can see his face. He looks sympathetic, but says that he's going to have to conduct a breath test. I suppose he can smell the alcohol. As he fishes in his pocket, I think, Thank you, God, the perfect end to a perfect day.

So I blow into the sodding bag, and of course the result is positive. That's my licence gone, I suppose. The policeman tells me that I'm going to have to accompany him to a station for further tests. He puts me through the usual rigmarole of a caution, and I mumble a reply. I feel a bit stupid – you know, the way you do – but I'm not going to do anything silly. I'm really not going to do anything silly.

He begins to talk into his lapel radio, summoning a car to take me to the station. All this time I'm standing by the side of the road, cars flashing past, feeling a bit of a berk. I reach into my leather jacket for a packet of fags, tip out a Camel and jam it into my mouth, but before I can light it his hand goes up. Sorry, sir, smoking can interfere with the breath tests. The cigarette snaps as I try to stuff it back into the packet.

The policeman isn't unfriendly; we chat while we wait, between bursts of static from his radio. It's not that cold – in fact it's quite mild for a January evening – but all the same I rub my hands together and stamp my feet to keep warm. I'm thinking about when I'm going to get home, rearranging the evening in my mind. It's still only about six o'clock.

A white police Range Rover arrives. There are three more officers inside, and the back is filled with those cones they use to block off lanes of motorways, plus a load of other clobber. A guy inside begins to clear a space for me on the back seat, and the other two get out. One begins talking to the motorcyclist, while the other starts to steer me towards the open door. Suddenly he reaches round in front of me and grabs one of my hands, then the other, yanking them together hard behind my back. Bloody hell, why is he doing this? He shoves me forward, until my face is pressing against the cold metal of the Range Rover. I'm aware of him fumbling behind my back. There's a jangling sound, and then I feel something bite my wrists. A click. The bastard's cuffed me!

'What the hell are you doing this for?' I bellow, outraged.

'I'm not having the likes of you sitting behind me,' he sneers. 'I'm handcuffing you for our protection.'

What in the world is he talking about?

'I haven't given you any reason for this,' I protest, twisting round to face him. Why isn't one of the others protecting me?

Then I look into his eyes for the first time, and see something there I haven't seen for more than thirty years. It's a look that says, 'I'm enjoying this.' He wants to humiliate me, to hurt me if he can. Maybe it's my car, maybe it's the way I look, or the way I speak, or maybe he just didn't get it up last night – I don't know what's eating him, but I can see that he's decided to take it out on me.

For the first time that evening, I start to lose my cool. I wouldn't call it fear that I'm feeling right now, more frustration. If I had a free hand, I would hit something – as it is, I begin banging my head on the side of the Range Rover. 'Oh, my God, it's one of them,' shouts the policeman who has just handcuffed me. 'Call for a van.' He grabs the cuffs and heaves me away from the car.

What the hell does he mean, 'one of them'?

I'm beginning to feel confused. What's happening to me? I don't say anything much, I don't try to escape, I don't struggle, even when the van arrives a few minutes later and that bastard pushes me towards it, although the cuffs are cutting into my wrists.

Someone opens the back of the van. It's the kind they use for transporting dogs: inside is a small caged area with a steel floor. A sense of dread rises within me. 'Oh, no, not again!' I cry, hardly knowing what I'm saying. I'm beginning to panic. They bundle me into the cage, squashing my face up against the ice-cold wire. It stinks of dog. Then they close it, locking me in. I can't stand; I can't even sit straight. Someone slams the door, and I tumble sideways, blind in the dark. There's no sound besides my own frantic breathing and the clinking of the cuffs.

And then the thing I'm always dreading happens. I'm in another place, another time. Bars cut me off from the night sky.

Tepid water laps around my chin; cicadas chirrup on the bank; leeches feed on my flesh.

I am a prisoner once more, in the bamboo cage of my nightmares, back in Vietnam.

2

It's hard for me to describe what happens after that. The memory is very powerful, but of course much of it doesn't make sense. In my rational mind I know that these guys are ordinary British policemen. But I see them as slant-eyed, black-pyjama'd Vietcong. It's as if the past has come crashing into the present, and there's no longer any barrier between them.

For years I've fought against the ghastly images infiltrating my mind. I push them back time after time, but they're always lurking there, waiting for me to weaken. It's been such a long, lonely struggle.

Sally doesn't understand how difficult it's been for me. Even though the evidence is there every morning, when she wakes up to find the sheets soaked in my sweat. Recently it's been getting worse: the hideous pictures keep breaking through, and I'm forced to use more and more effort to drive them back. I've been feeling that one day soon I'm not going to be able to hold out any longer. That's why I've been drinking so much lately: to wash the ghosts out of my head.

And now the battle is over. The enemy is inside the perimeter. My defences are down; my mind has been overrun. It's almost a relief.

Am I going mad?

The lurch when the van starts throws me off-balance. I feel a sharp stab of pain as my weight topples back on to my cuffed wrists. I struggle to brace myself, but I can't stop rolling around helplessly, crashing against the wire. I try to use my elbows and shoulders to protect my face. All the time I'm wondering what they're going to do to me, and whether I'm going to be able to hold out.

The van stops, and I hear the engine die. I feel the bounce as the driver gets out. His door slams. Deep voices, laughter, and the crunch of boots on Tarmac. Then a metallic clunk as the door opens. The inside light comes on automatically and dazzles me. I'm a trapped animal in a cage, terrified.

One of my captors unlocks the cage and opens the door. Then two of them reach in to drag me out by the elbows. I know I'm going to be tortured. I think about resistance, but I see that it's hopeless. My body flops as they pull me out and frogmarch me into some kind of holding pen. I'm aware of bright lights and glossy walls, and another of those bastards behind some kind of counter. None of it looks familiar.

The interrogation begins. By now my Army training has kicked in; I've been taught to adopt a passive-resistance role. I tell them my name and address, but nothing more. I know I mustn't show any weakness – but I mustn't confront them, either, otherwise I may provoke them. Later there may be a chance to escape.

They keep asking me questions, but still I refuse to answer. One wants me to blow into some kind of bag, but I'm wise to that.

After a minute or two they seem to lose interest. The one who was behind the counter leads the way along a corridor and down some steps. I follow submissively, biding my time. Then I hear the jangle of keys in a lock. The door swings open and they push me into a cell. Someone spins me round and unlocks the handcuffs; at last my hands are free. I consider making a run for it now, but I decide that there may be a better chance later. I know I mustn't leave it too long, or I won't be strong enough.

The door slams shut, and I hear the key turn in the lock. I sit down on the bed and try to work some feeling back into my hands. Time passes.

After about two hours they come back for me, the three of them from the Range Rover. They take me up the stairs and along the corridor into an interrogation room. There's a table and some chairs; I'm ordered to sit down facing the door. One leaves and a few moments later he comes back with a woman, a police doctor. But I don't think of her as a policewoman; I think of her as Red Cross, something like that. The others stay in the room with her, as if they think she needs protection. Do they think I'm dangerous?

The stupid fools still haven't searched me. They don't know that I'm carrying a lock knife. I always keep it on me. Just in case.

She wants to examine me. I refuse. I don't want to make it easy for them. OK, she says, we'll do some tests. She drops some coins on to the table and asks me to count them. I can't understand what she's getting at. Is this a trick? Is she trying to communicate something to me without the others knowing?

I decide to do as she says, and we run through a series of 'tests'. At the end she looks at the others and shakes her head. They take me back to the cells.

*

I'm allowed to make one telephone call. I ring Sally and ask her to come and get me. I don't remember too much about what happens after that. I suppose I must have been charged. I know that I'm very, very anxious to get out of there. Eventually Sally arrives and takes me home.

I don't recall what I did that night. I think I hit the bottle.

The next few months pass in a blur. I'm not working, I'm not even going to auction-rooms any more, in fact I'm not doing anything much. I just sit at home most of the time, thinking. The drugs I'm on make it difficult for me to concentrate.

Everything at home is a mess. I hate it like this. Sally sees me sitting in my armchair watching TV. She doesn't know what's going on in my head.

A lot of the time I'm in Vietnam. I try not to think about the cage. It's bad enough being out on patrol in the jungle, trying to fight down the fear that never leaves you. The worst time is at night, knowing they are just outside the camp perimeter, waiting.

I don't tell her. It's difficult to explain to anyone who hasn't experienced it.

I'm watching a war film on TV. Two comrades crouch on the ground, sheltering from a firefight. Suddenly one gets hit. I start sweating, my heart begins to palpitate, and I can't breathe. What's this stuff all over me? I'm desperately trying to scrape it off, this disgusting, horrible gore . . . Then Sally comes running in, and comforts me. She's heard my screams from the garden. I cover my face with my hands and sob.

The doctor keeps prescribing stronger and stronger anti-depressants. I'm not supposed to drink while I'm on these, but of course I do.

She refers me to a psychiatrist, who diagnoses post-traumatic stress disorder. When my case (for 'failing to provide a specimen') comes up in court, the magistrates accept this diagnosis and dismiss the charges against me. I'm not sure what I feel about this. I've seen the movies about Vietnam vets who've gone off the rails, of course, but those guys were all long-haired weirdoes who'd fucked up their heads with too many drugs. I'm English, a respectable married businessman, for God's sake, living in a smart Surrey suburb.

I'm having a struggle with this psychiatrist. He wants me to open up, to 'expose my vulnerable side'. But I'm resisting him. I don't want him probing inside my head. I'm a soldier, not one of those weak people begging for help. I get angry about it and start shouting at him.

The doctors have signed me up for group therapy, which is about the worst possible thing they could have done. It makes me feel nervous to be cooped up with all those people for an hour at a time. I play along, but I despise the others there. They're pathetic.

3

One of the few mementoes I've kept from my Army days is a socking great combat knife, the US M-8 A1 bayonet I brought back from Vietnam, its blade long and very sharp. During my Army training they taught me how to use it to silence a man, approaching from behind and sliding one arm across his throat while the other stabs up from beneath the ribs. Very quick, they said, and very quiet. Since then I've always kept this knife razor-sharp. I sharpen all our knives regularly. I do most of the cooking now, and I can't bear using a knife that isn't sharp.

Sally's been behaving oddly since my arrest. She keeps giving me funny looks. She thinks I don't notice, but I do. The thought crosses my mind that she's been talking to the doctor behind my back.

Then there's the money thing. Before the business went into liquidation, I signed over everything to Sally. The idea was that all the debts would be in my name, all the possessions in hers. (Many of them were hers anyway.) I thought this was very clever at first. Even when the bailiffs come to the door, I am quite relaxed, because I know they can't take anything of Sally's, and everything worth anything belongs to her. But I can't get a bank account or credit of any kind, so I'm completely dependent on her for everything I need. I've been used to living the high life, basically having anything I wanted. I've had a succession of well-paid jobs and then my own business. Now I have to go to her for every little thing, and I resent it. Often she'll give me a hard time, saying that we can't afford what I want. I'll get angry. I throw things at her. Sometimes I reach out to put my hands around her throat.

Sally told me yesterday that she doesn't know me any more.

It gets so bad that I begin to take money from her handbag. Just before we leave to spend Christmas at her mother's place on the Isle of Man, she catches me doing it. It's so humiliating. Over the Christmas period the two of them keep preaching at me. Don't do this. Don't do that. It enrages me that my own wife should speak to me like that. I tell her that I feel like leaving. Her mother says, 'Well, you know, the ferry leaves in the morning.'

Ever since Vietnam I've gone out of my way to avoid confrontation. If a violent situation seems imminent, I just walk away – even if I look like a coward for doing so. I know that I must never get into a fight because, if I do, I may kill someone.

Years ago, I was flirting with an attractive girl at an office party. We were getting on pretty well. Suddenly her boyfriend noticed us in the corner and became very aggressive. He started shouting abuse and pushing me about. I could see that he was wild with jealousy, and he'd obviously been drinking a lot. I just backed off; I actually retreated into the toilets and locked myself into a cubicle when he followed me there. He was still shouting and rattling the door when a friend of mine who knew a little about my past marched in and pulled him away by the shoulders. 'Look, I'm not going to explain why, I'm not going to give you any reason, but please just leave it right there,' my friend said. The jealous guy was still quite drunk, but perhaps he recognized the warning in my friend's voice. In any case, he cleared off.

The point is, I try to stay out of trouble. I'm a decent guy. I've been living a normal life for years. If you met me in a pub, you'd like me. Most people do.

One Saturday evening, soon after we've come home from the Isle of Man, I'm in the living-room with Sally. I'm sitting in the armchair, sharpening my knives. As usual, I've had a bit to drink. Then the arguing starts. There's an old piece of furniture, quite valuable, that we're planning to sell at auction. I tell her I want half the proceeds, to start buying and selling again, and she says no. I begin to get angry. How can she deny me this chance? Doesn't the ungrateful cow appreciate that I need the money? It's just as much my bloody money as it is hers anyway – doesn't she see that?

I hurl a magazine across the room, and it hits her in the face. She starts shouting at me. I'm not going to repeat what she says.

All the frustration of the past few months is boiling away inside me. I *hate* Sally. She is the one blocking me. She is my enemy.

I pick up the knife. I see the flash of fear in her eyes. Good. She backs away, then spins round, looking for an escape, but there's nowhere to go. I grab her by the throat. She's not shouting at me now. I push her down on to the sofa, pressing the knife to her ribs. It pierces her clothes, tearing through one layer and then the next, until it's poking into her soft flesh. Just one wrong move, one tiny little wrong move, and I'll do it.

But she doesn't move, and suddenly I don't want to do it any more. My grip weakens around Sally's throat, and my knife hand goes limp. She tears herself free and runs out of the room. The knife clatters on to the living-room floor. I'm shaking so badly that it takes for ever to light a cigarette. I perch on the edge of the chair. What's happening to me? I rock forward, trying to concentrate.

Minutes later I get up and wander about, and gradually I become aware that Sally has left the house. I don't think too much about it: she's run off a couple of times before when we've quarrelled. Then I hear the doorbell. I open the door to see police officers standing in the driveway, blue lights flashing behind them.

4

Early morning, and I'm lying here in a borrowed sleeping-bag, on the floor of this bare room, wondering how I'm going to fill my day. I've nothing to do and nowhere to go. I'm not allowed to see Sally or to go near the house. I've no home, no job and no money, and it looks as though soon I'll have no wife either. All I have is a criminal record; they've convicted me for common assault. If my sister hadn't agreed to take me in, I'd probably be living on the streets by now. I'm safe here for a while, but I can't spend the rest of my life sleeping on somebody else's floor. Her bloke has made it quite clear that I can't stay here for ever.

I'm still taking these foul drugs, but they're doing me no good at all. However many I swallow, I go on feeling depressed. It's as though I'm not allowed to escape myself. Sometimes I think I'd be better off dead.

I keep looking back over my life, trying to work out where I went wrong. I seem to have made a mess of everything. Time after time I had a chance and blew it. After I left the Army I had one job after another, but I never stayed in any of them. The problem was that I couldn't take orders. It's ironic, really: you'd think that being in the military would teach you to do that if it taught you anything. But I never had much respect for civilians.

When I had my own business I spent money faster than I earned it. Expensive offices, lavish entertaining, unnecessary overheads. I don't know why I behaved like this. Sally tried to stop me, but I just couldn't help myself. What I wouldn't give for some of that money now.

I feel so worthless. Not so long ago, I was chairman and managing director of a company with 3,500 employees, with secretaries and assistants to keep people away from me. Now the phone hardly ever rings. Every week I have to sign on at the Jobcentre . . . I don't care to think about that too much.

And when I think of what a shit I've been to Sally I am filled with shame. I fucked up my first marriage. Now it looks as though I've fucked up my second, too . . .

I've thought a lot about topping myself over the past few months. I go through all the different ways of doing it in my mind. I think I'm too much of a coward, though.

I remember finding my brother. We were living in this rambling great place in Yorkshire, just outside Barnsley. It was a wonderful house, with seven bedrooms, three bathrooms, a library, a cellar, and a coach-house with a stable-block outside in the yard. Best of all, it had three or four acres of garden, full of big trees. It was a boy's dream.

I must have been about thirteen then, and Rick would have been fifteen. We fought like cat and dog, but we were very, very close. I reckon it must have started at birth: apparently, when I was born, my grandfather Mac picked me up and said, 'Here's a little buddy for Rick,' and from then on I was always known as Bud. My sister and my ex-wife call me Bud even to this day.

I looked up to Rick, of course. He was a superb athlete,

especially track and field. I was pretty good at sport, too. I still have a box of the trophies we won up in the attic. In the holidays we'd spend most of the day outdoors, climbing trees, making camp, riding, fishing, all those things boys like to do. We were both Scouts as well.

At that stage we were sharing a bedroom. The house was so big that we could have had a bedroom each, but we preferred being together. It was a huge great room anyway. One morning during the holidays I slept in. When I eventually stirred, Rick wasn't there. Dad had gone out to work, and I knew Mum was around the house somewhere. I stepped out into the garden.

It was high summer. The garden was in full bloom: the trees were heavy with fruit, and flowers sagged on their stems. The early-morning dew had long since burned away. The sun was so bright that when I first stepped outside I was dazzled. It was a beautiful morning. There was no sound but for the murmur of bees, and the occasional drumming of a distant woodpecker. I began to amble down towards the bottom of the garden, out of sight of the house, where most of our adventures took place.

When I found him hanging from the pear tree, I thought at first it was his idea of a joke. It was only when I saw his distorted, purple face that I realized it wasn't funny at all. I shinned up the tree and untied the rope. It wasn't easy. I tried to lower him gently to the ground, but I couldn't hold the weight, and he fell. Then I tried to revive him. I'd learned a bit of First Aid in the Scouts. I remember Jane, our golden retriever, trying to join in the game.

At some point I must have seen that it was hopeless, because I ran back to the house to raise the alarm.

Afterwards, we never talked about why he might have done it. There was no note, nothing. I suppose I convinced myself it was an accident. So far as I was concerned, there was absolutely no reason in the world for him to kill himself.

My brother's death didn't really hit me to begin with. It happened right at the end of the holidays, and I was sent back to boarding-school almost immediately. I don't remember his funeral. Maybe I didn't go.

It was strange going back to school because, of course, Rick had been there and now he wasn't. I'd been the younger brother, and now suddenly I was the only one. It was going to be my first term in the senior school. The silly bastard had left just when I needed him most.

I guess I started to go off the rails a bit then. I was always getting into trouble of one kind or another, always rebelling against any kind of authority. My friends used to joke that I was permanently bent over, ready for the cane. Eventually it became so bad that I was sent home from school, and only allowed to return on condition that I had psychiatric treatment. I was sent to see a shrink, who asked me lots of multiple-choice questions, which might have meant something to him but meant nothing to me. I just told him what I thought he wanted to hear. So far as I was concerned, it was a complete waste of time.

PART II: America

5

Seven years on, and I'm sitting on my bed at boarding-school, wearing the Ellesmere College uniform for the last time ever. My trunk stands on the floor beside the bed, packed and ready to go. It's a sunny July morning in 1964; I'm nineteen years old, and I'm leaving school today. Not just leaving school, but leaving England, leaving my old life behind.

It's unusually quiet. Normally at this time of day the air is filled with the echoing stamp of shoes on the tiled floors. I used to share this dormitory with thirty other boys, but now they've all gone. The school's almost empty. There's just a lawn-mower buzzing outside, and the occasional muffled sound from a distant room.

Each time I hear a car, I leap up and peer out of the window, to see if it's my parents arriving to collect me.

It must have been soon after half-term when my father phones to say that he has been offered a job running a brick-manufacturing company in America. Our new home will be in

York, a historic Pennsylvania town. From what he tells me, it seems too good to resist. Mum was raised in America until the age of eighteen anyway, and she's happy to move back. As for me, there's no special reason to stay. There's my girlfriend Debbie, to whom I've become close, but her parents have sent her abroad to a finishing-school. I'll miss my schoolfriends, but I suppose I wouldn't see much of them after finishing here anyway. My little sister Pat is still only fourteen; it's going to be a big change for her, but my parents are confident that she will settle in over there all right. As a family, we've never stayed anywhere long enough to put down roots. Our home in Yorkshire is fabulous, but none of us can ever forget what happened there. This is a chance for us to make a fresh start. Dad's new salary means that we will be able to live well. The good life beckons.

Of course, leaving England means saying goodbye to everything and everyone I've ever known. It's a wrench. I realize too late that I'm never going to see our old home again. My parents have already packed up the house and sent most of our possessions on ahead.

I got up early this morning and walked all round the school, looking at everything for the last time. The funny thing is that I feel quite sentimental about the old place. I can't resist one last sprint round the athletics track. There is no one else around to see me. I remember holding the Victor Ludorum trophy aloft on Sports Day, catching sight of my proud parents among the watchers.

I hear a horn parping. I jump off the bed and run to the window. A white Ford Consul convertible is pulling up outside. Its red roof is down; there's my father waving up at the window. He's impatient to be going: we've a long drive ahead of us. Tomorrow we arrive at Southampton docks. We'll be crossing the Atlantic by ship, the SS *Mauretania*. I'm quite excited about it, because the only time I've ever been in a ship before was on a cross-Channel ferry, and that wasn't really a *ship*.

I take one last look around, then grab my trunk and head for the door. Outside, my father is standing by the car. The boot is already crammed with luggage, so Dad's fixed a rack on the outside. I heave my trunk on to this, then squeeze into the back alongside Pat as he ties it on. Mum turns round from the passenger seat to talk to me; she's wearing sunglasses and her hair is covered by a scarf. Then my father walks round to the driver's side, flashes us a smile, and climbs in. He starts the engine, and we drive off. I don't look back.

Crossing to America was like stepping into the future. Everything seemed so big compared to what I was used to. The cars were bigger, the roads were bigger, the houses were bigger, even the people seemed bigger. Back then England didn't have shopping malls, supermarkets or motorways. It was all so new, and very exciting. Suddenly I was eating gigantic great steaks (I'd hardly ever seen a steak before) and delicious hamburgers, not the horrible little lumps of grey meat in stale buns that I was used to from English Wimpy bars. Most places in England served only two or three flavours of bog-standard ice-cream; in America you could get twenty – *huge*, delicious ice-creams, drenched in chocolate sauce and covered in nuts. I thought it was all just fabulous.

Our new home was a modern house, built in traditional ranch style, but large and comfortable, with walk-in closets and loads of bathrooms with powerful showers. The kitchen was equipped with the largest fridge I had ever seen. Outside was a double garage, with an up-and-over door; you drove up, leaned out of the window, pressed a conveniently placed button, and hey presto! up it went, all without your having to get out of the car. I was particularly impressed by that.

During my first few months in America I didn't have much to do, so I spent most of my time just goofing around, like a regular teenage delinquent. I was young and fit, and the English accent went down well with the local girls.

Of course, you couldn't do much if you couldn't get about, so one of the first things I did after I arrived was to sit my driving test. I took it in the Pontiac Catalina station-wagon my parents had bought as a family car. It seemed huge: much bigger than any car I'd ever seen in England. Fortunately the test was off-road, where there was no other traffic around to bump into. Once I'd passed, I was able to run around town in Mum's little left-hand drive MG 1100. After a while I persuaded Dad to buy me something a bit more exotic, a beautiful white Ford Mustang: a boy-racer's dream. I think that getting me some wheels of my own was a kind of consolation present for taking me away from England – although, as it turned out, I was more than happy to be there. For me, the whole thing was one big adventure.

I loved that Mustang. It had a V8 engine, which growled when you pressed the accelerator pedal. It was very thirsty, drinking up huge volumes of what I soon learned to call 'gas', averaging about ten miles to the gallon; but in those days a gallon of gas cost only around twenty cents, so I wasn't too bothered. I had it fitted with one of the very first eight-track stereos – the ones that played a huge cartridge, almost as big as a modern videocassette. Every evening I'd head into town and cruise up and down the main drag. Usually it didn't take long before I had a girl next to me in the passenger seat. We'd drive out of town to one of the local beauty spots, or swing by a drive-in movie. Not that we were very interested in what was happening up there on the screen.

Back in England I had managed to scrape one A level, which, as it turned out, was enough to earn me a place in the local university, Dickinson College – not one of the great American universities, but then no one had ever accused me of being a great scholar. Notionally I was supposed to be studying what they called 'liberal arts', but in reality I spent almost all my time partying and playing sports. I mean, here I was, fresh from a traditional, single-sex boarding-school, transported on to an easy-going, co-educational campus. It was just foolish to think I might do any work.

Under Pennsylvania law you weren't supposed to drink until you were twenty-one, but we didn't take much notice of that. Whenever a party was in the offing, a group of us would drive across to Maryland, where the state tax on alcohol was significantly lower, and load up the fraternity car – a huge old funeral hearse – with booze. The danger, of course, was that you might get caught. On the last occasion we found ourselves being chased by the Maryland cops. We tried to outrun them, but we weren't fast enough, and when they caught us they confiscated both the car and its contents: hundreds of dollars' worth. I bet they enjoyed drinking that down at the station.

I'm driving down the freeway in my mother's Pontiac, squinting into the sun, one hand on the wheel and the other on the bare thigh of a girl called Wendy. She's trying to drink a beer, but she keeps giggling – and so do the four in the back, two guys and two girls, all of us dressed only in sheets, with no underwear. It's a Roman toga party. I've got the radio turned up high. Right now we're all nodding along to the Beach Boys.

Wendy leans across the bench seat and offers me the can. The sheet is draped over one of her shoulders, leaving the other – the one nearest to me – uncovered. She smiles beguilingly. I find it hard to drag my eyes away from her body under the flimsy white sheet, secured only with a tuck, liable to come loose at any moment.

I lift my hand off her thigh and take the can. I raise it carefully to my lips and drink.

It's hot and humid in here. I tell the others we need some cool air, and wind down the window. Wendy does the same. The sheets start flapping in the breeze, and she struggles to keep hers down, shrieking all the while. Then the wind catches her sheet: it billows up and seems to fill the car, before the wind sucks it out of the window. For one wild moment it hangs in the slipstream beside us, and then I see it in the rear-view mirror, fluttering back down the freeway. Wendy is writhing beside me, stark naked. I'm laughing so hard that I have to stop the car.

From almost as early as I can remember I've been a firearms fanatic. Even as a toddler I picked up pieces of shrapnel left over from the war. Back in Yorkshire I had learned to use an air rifle, shooting birds and rabbits for the pot. Now that I was living in America where there were very few gun controls, I persuaded Dad to buy me a Winchester bolt-action rifle, a high-velocity, long-range weapon. Near the house I used a .22 semi-automatic rifle to shoot pigeon or anything else that was around, like the squirrels that Mum would make into squirrel pie after I'd skinned them. I was fascinated by everything to do with guns: I cleaned them regularly and I took them apart and reassembled them. I even started to make my own bullets. At Dickinson I joined the rifle club and practised my marksmanship on the range. Later on, when I got to know a bunch of other guys who liked shooting, we'd drive out into the farming country, then cruise along scanning the hillsides through binoculars for groundhogs. Once we spotted one of their burrows, we'd stop and take pot-shots at them from the side of the road, using bipods to rest our rifles on and high-powered telescopic sights to home in on the targets up to a thousand yards away. The farmers encouraged us to do this because to them the groundhogs were vermin, digging holes that undermined their tractors.

Soon I graduated to real hunting, hiking into the woods in pursuit of deer. Occasionally I'd go with other guys, but often I'd go alone, usually driving into the Pennsylvania hills; sometimes I'd make a trip into Virginia, and once I went down to the islands off the North Carolina coast. In the forest I'd look for signs of deer, and then I'd follow them, moving very carefully and quietly as I stalked my prey in thick woodland. There were plenty of bear in those forests, too, and I carried a handgun – a Ruger .44 Magnum, the kind Dirty Harry used – in case one charged me at close range. I manufactured special bullets, which opened up when they entered the body and brought down the target quickly. I saw lots of bear, but luckily I was never attacked by one.

Sometimes I'd stalk deer with just a handgun. The difficulty was to get close enough. I could bring down a deer from a range of fifty or sixty yards, but to get that close you needed to be stealthy. Most skilful of all was to stalk deer with a bow and arrow, crawling though the undergrowth fully camouflaged to get close enough to shoot. I tried this several times, but never managed to make a kill.

The other guys thought I was crazy, but I didn't care.

At Dickinson, I spent much of my time involved in sport of one kind or another. I felt that I was enough of an athlete to become a champion if I put my mind to it, and I had a perfect opportunity because the college offered excellent training facilities. I joined the varsity track team and practised for hours on end, almost every day.

At school I'd been good at rugby, too, and now I took to American football so quickly that I was soon a member of the squad, often playing for the college. One thing I could never understand was why they had so many time-outs interrupting the action. I liked to run with the ball, as I'd always done when I'd been a rugby wing three-quarter.

I was winning trophies on the playing field, but I must have been bottom of the class in school. My grades were about as low as they could be. When my professor found out that I was doing so much sport instead of studying, she went berserk. She read me the Riot Act, warning me that I was in danger of flunking out altogether – but, though I smiled and mumbled a few apologetic phrases, I continued to neglect my work. At the end of my second semester the college decided to be rid of me. I was out on my ear, after just six months.

'What on earth are you going to do now, Bud?' my father asked, when I told him the bad news. I didn't have much of a clue what to do. I was still only a boy, really, living for the moment and hardly thinking about the future. Dad wasn't too bad about it, and he fixed me up with some casual work in a quarry owned by a sister company to his. My job was to dig out the topsoil by hand before the quarrying began. It was hard, dirty work, but I didn't mind that. I was earning pretty good money, and the exercise kept me fit. Every evening I'd come home, shower, get togged up, then climb into the Mustang and head into town.

By this time Wendy and I were 'going steady'. She was pretty – I thought she looked like Jane Fonda – and a little bit naughty, too. She was the first girl I slept with; she was more experienced, and helped me to overcome my initial nervousness. Soon we were making love regularly, whenever we had the opportunity, usually in the back of the car. Without really thinking about what I was doing, I found myself talking about getting married. I didn't give it too much thought. I just knew that I liked Wendy, and for a while I even convinced myself that I loved her.

6

From the moment I arrived in America I knew that at some stage I was likely to be called up for military service if I didn't have a deferment. The immigration people had warned me about the possibility when our ship docked at the Port of New York. I wasn't too bothered about it. For one thing, I thought then that I had four years of college ahead of me. You don't look too far into the future when you're nineteen years old.

I was dimly aware that American troops were serving in Vietnam as 'advisers' to the South Vietnamese army, but that didn't seem anything to do with me, even if I did have to do my military service eventually. After all, there were American soldiers serving in lots of places around the world – in Germany, for example.

I was still at Dickinson when the first US combat troops waded ashore at Da Nang. It didn't seem a big deal. The Marines were going there to protect an airbase – so what? Back then there was no way of telling that this would escalate in the way it did. It was rare to hear anyone criticize America's involvement in Vietnam, even in college. If there were any students at Dickinson protesting about it, I certainly never came across them.

This didn't mean that everyone was keen to join the Army. For plenty of young men, that was just about the last thing they wanted to do.

A lot of the guys I knew were being drafted then. If you weren't at college, you were liable to be called up at any moment. I'd already been for a medical to test whether I was fit enough. They called it a pre-induction physical. An official letter arrived saying that you were required by law to attend at such-and-such a medical centre on a certain day at a certain time. I turned up along with hundreds of other guys. I know it sounds scarcely believable, but some of them were wearing dresses. Pretending to be gay, or transsexual or whatever, was one way of trying to avoid being called up. There were a few titters and maybe some comments when these guys appeared dressed as women, but nothing worse than that. There was a sense that we were all trying to beat the system, and that anything you could do to get out of the draft was fair enough. People tried all sorts of tricks. Some suddenly developed a limp. Another scam I heard about was to chain-smoke, then go for a run just before the medical. Although I was a smoker, I was very healthy, and there was no way I was going to fail on fitness grounds.

Having passed the physical, I knew that my days were numbered. So I wasn't surprised when my draft papers dropped into the mailbox one summer morning in 1965. I didn't open the thick envelope marked 'Department of the Army'. I'd been told that if you left your draft papers unopened you could still enlist, which meant that you had a chance of becoming an officer. I took the sealed envelope down to the recruitment office in the centre of town, and offered my services in defence of my adopted country.

A lot of people still don't understand why I was happy to enlist. Maybe it's harder to explain now than it would have been then. I'm not a political person, I didn't vote in an election until I was in my forties, but I was brought up to believe that if your government says that this is what you must do, then you must do it. I was proud of being British, but I also felt a strong loyalty towards America. So far as I was concerned, this was my new home. At that point I thought I would probably stay there for the rest of my life. It didn't seem right to me to duck out of my responsibilities; twenty years before, my dad had served in the Second World War, and I felt that I should do my bit. And, to be honest, I was excited by the prospect. I needed something to do, and I liked the idea of becoming a soldier. I wasn't afraid of getting hurt. Back then I didn't know anyone who had died in Vietnam, and I couldn't imagine anything like that happening to me. Anyway, it was by no means certain that I would be going to Vietnam. If I thought about what was happening out there at all, I thought that it would be settled fairly quickly. It seemed as though plenty of soldiers served out their term of duty at home, or in comparatively peaceful places like Germany. I think there was a tendency at the time to imagine that serving in Vietnam was only a remote possibility, and perhaps the Army encouraged this illusion so that new conscripts wouldn't panic.

One advantage of enlisting was that I was able to defer my military service by up to six months, rather than heading off almost straight away, which conscripts had to do. I took full advantage of this, carrying on at the quarry, but the day came early in 1966 when I couldn't put it off any longer.

On the last weekend before I left I drove Wendy up into the hills. It was a crisp winter's day, with a dusting of snow on the ground. We got out of the Mustang and walked along the ridge, holding hands. She wore a cute little fur hat, tied around her chin, with bobbles hanging down. At some point we sat down to admire the view. I told her then that I didn't want her to wait for me. She cried for a bit, and I hugged her tight until the cold drove us back to the car.

I'd been told to report to Fort Jackson, near Charlotte, South Carolina, for my induction. It seemed that most of the new recruits would be travelling there by a special train laid on for the purpose. Mum and Dad took me to the station at Harrisburg one cold, misty February afternoon. The platform was heaving with young men and their folks, everyone wearing overcoats and hats and gloves: it was like a scene from a Second World War movie, except that none of the guys was in uniform. People were talking and laughing; quite a few mothers and girlfriends were weeping. It was hard to hear anything over all the noise, and there didn't seem much to say. Mum kept fussing about whether I had everything I needed. She wanted me to open my suitcase to check what was inside, but I refused. I'd packed it myself and knew what was in there. I found myself longing for the train to arrive.

At last it appeared, a seemingly never-ending succession of carriages already almost full of men picked up earlier along the line. It slid to a halt along the platform, with a long, hideous squeal. Suddenly Mum started talking very fast. I put my arm round her, and she made me promise to write as soon as I could. Then I shook Dad's outstretched hand. There was a choke in his voice as he wished me luck. I smiled at them one last time, and turned towards the train. I lugged my suitcase on board, waved at them through the door window, and elbowed my way into a seat. I was lucky to find one, because the train was overflowing – there must have been hundreds of men aboard. Once seated, my suitcase in front of my knees, I stared out of the compartment window, hoping to spot my parents on the platform, but I couldn't see them in the crowd. Someone shouted, and I heard a whistle blow. The train shuddered and began to drag itself forward.

As we pulled out, I caught a last glimpse of them, my mother wiping her face with a handkerchief, my father with an arm around her shoulders. Then the platform disappeared, as the train picked up speed. I sat back and closed my eyes, thinking about Wendy, imagining her as I'd last seen her. The train made its slow way south. The journey lasted all night, and I fell asleep to the sound of long klaxon blasts that seemed to echo through my dreams.

Fort Jackson is a big, anonymous base, with lots of low buildings and masses of flat concrete all around. Everything's neat and anonymous. Tarmac roads wind around the base and head out towards the wire that surrounds a perimeter many miles long, enclosing a rifle range and an airstrip. It's like a small town in a way, where even the centre resembles a suburb and everyone looks the same. It even has its own train junction, and early the next morning there are NCOs waiting for us on the platform in their Smoky Bear flat-brimmed hats. You can see that they're trying to look friendly, though smiling doesn't seem to come naturally to them.

We tumble out of the train, dragging our suitcases down behind us. The NCOs stride up and down the platform, forming us roughly into ranks. 'You, you, and you, over there; you, over here . . .' The atmosphere is relaxed, with quite a lot of laughing and horseplay. Then they march us to our barracks in ragged formation. I feel like a complete idiot, marching along in my civilian clothes, a suitcase hanging from one hand. But the sergeants act as if it's all perfectly normal.

Our barracks are dormitories housing perhaps fifty men each. Bunk beds line each long wall, equidistantly spaced, everything immaculate. At the far end a corridor links the dormitories to an equally institutional block of latrines.

There follows a bewildering few days of standing in one line after another, as the Army processes us from civilians into soldiers. One of the first things they do is scalp me. I have quite a fine head of hair, which I wear Elvis Presley style (it was 1966, after all). Off it goes. They start by shaving my head right down the middle, just out of spite. I feel quite upset as I watch my hair dropping on to the floor in thick clumps. 'I look ridiculous,' I wrote home to my family.

I'm issued with big black leather boots, fatigues and a baseball cap, my uniform for the two-month period of basic training. By the end of my first day in the Army, I look a real hard case. Just another grunt infantryman, Private 05/337/015.

There is a good reason for shaving our heads. Some of the men have lice, some have fleas, some have ringworm. We're going to spend the next three years in close confinement with other soldiers, and it's a good idea to nail any infections at the outset. Along with all the others, I undergo a series of medicals, and am pumped full of inoculations. It's no good saying that you've had this one before. It's as if they're deaf: they take no notice at all.

When we're not waiting in one line or another, we're assigned character-building duties such as cleaning the latrines. It's very hard for those recruits who haven't experienced this sort of regime before. At night you can hear some boys crying into their pillows.

Our induction at Fort Jackson lasts just three days; once we've been processed into the Army, we're due to move on to Fort Gordon, Georgia, for two months of 'boot camp' basic training.

My last night at Fort Jackson is spent on KP detail – meaning kitchen police – from five o'clock one afternoon until four thirty the following morning. Sixteen of us have to eye a ton and a half of potatoes, and peel and chop up another ton and a half of onions. Some of the guys there have never peeled a potato before. It's easier for me because I'm used to mucking in at home and in the Scouts, but by five o'clock the next morning I'm dog-tired and I never want to see either a potato or an onion again.

7

Our train pulls into Fort Gordon, Georgia. This time the drill sergeants waiting for us on the platform aren't trying to be nice; we're in uniform now. Right away they start screaming at us to line up this way or line up that way, bellowing and hollering, calling us cunt-lickers, motherfuckers and other terms of abuse. The blacks are all niggers and the Hispanics spics. 'You fucking bunch of civilians, we're going to sort you out.' It's a shock to be shouted at like this. I'm so bemused, I start to smile.

'You find something I say amusing, boy?'

'No, sir.'

'What kind of a fucking accent is that? Where the hell did you crawl out from?'

'York, Pennsylvania, sir.'

'Don't fuck with me. What's a fucking Limey like you doing in my Army?'

'Enlisted, sir.'

'You're kidding me? They let a fucking English pansy into my Army?'

'No, sir. Yes, sir.'

'I've got my eyes on you, boy. You step out of line and I'll have you licking out the latrines.'

'Yes, sir.'

A guy near me begins to titter, and the drill sergeant punches him straight in the stomach, so hard that he doubles up and collapses on the ground. By this time we're all shaking. Welcome to the Army.

I'm made to get down on the Tarmac and do ten push-ups for having one button undone.

The sergeants form us into lines and march us to our billets, shouting at us all the while. When I glance at the recruit next to me out of the corner of my eye I can see the fear in his face.

It was like that for the whole two-months' basic training. The first few days were purgatory for some of the recruits, particularly those who weren't fit, the great big tubs who'd never run more than a few yards in their lives. Ten days earlier these guys were living high on the hog; then one day their draft papers drop through the letter-box telling them to report to boot camp, and before they knew it they were running up and down outside being shouted at. Plenty of them collapsed.

The sergeants had us doing knee-bends and push-ups; anybody slow was made to do it again. Everything had to be done at the double. They'd march us away from the barracks, then tell us to get back to our billet for an immediate inspection. Everyone would rush back to the barracks, and there'd be a lot of pushing and shoving by the door.

You were given a ten-point Code of Conduct, which you were supposed to learn by heart. The sergeants could come up to you at any moment and ask you to recite it, and if you were not word perfect you'd be in big trouble.

Anyone who questioned what we were doing and why had it knocked out of him. Persistent offenders were sent to the stockade, the Army jail. You soon learned to toe the line and obey orders unquestioningly. A few guys just couldn't take it. They made themselves ill, so that they ended up in hospital. But most kept their heads down and did what they had to.

Gradually we learned basic soldiering: marching in formation, running, parading, how to hold a gun, guard duty – plus, of course, all the usual details such as cleaning floors and latrines and KP.

One aspect of all this was that it brought us down to the same level. The draft scooped up young men of all sorts – black, white, Hispanic, college kids and illiterates, country boys and dudes from the ghettos – and brought us together. No distinction was made between those who had enlisted and those who had been drafted. At this stage we were all part of the training battalion; it wasn't until much later that we would be assigned to regiments. Our training was designed to turn us into soldiers, of course; but, more than that, it was designed to eliminate the distinctions between us. All our peculiarities and all our prejudices were knocked out of us. In a strange way, there's something very democratic about the Army.

Even as an Englishman, I didn't stand out. Every training company had a few foreign nationals, and people seemed to take us for granted. I came across Australians, New Zealanders and Germans, as well as Mexicans, Canadians and South Americans of one sort or another. Being English didn't seem to be a problem.

In fact, I was much better placed than most. To begin with, I was very fit; but, more than that, I'd spent twelve years at a very tough boarding-school where I'd learned to survive in a harsh regime. I was used to sleeping in dormitories, communal showers, never having any privacy. I wasn't shy about shitting in the open. I'd worn a uniform of one kind or another for most of my life, and I knew how to take care of myself. I knew how to make my bed with envelope corners and sheets tight as a drum. Many of the guys there had never made a bed before in their life; their mothers had always done it for them. And now suddenly there's a sergeant shouting at them to hurry up, then telling them to do it again because they haven't done it properly.

I slotted straight in. To me it was normal: I accepted all the rules and revelled in the drills. In the Army everything is run along competitive lines. If your platoon has done well, you'll be awarded extra privileges, like being allowed to eat first, and excused details, giving you more free time. If you do badly, it's the opposite. I wanted my platoon to come out top in every competition. And I was keen to do well for myself, too, because I wanted to be accepted for officer training and I didn't want to blot my copybook in any way.

In some ways boot camp was comfortable compared to boarding-school. We had hot and cold running water, for example, whereas at boarding-school I'd had only cold water and in winter you might have to break the ice before you could wash.

There were some men there who had no idea of personal hygiene. One fellow stank so much that we decided he had to be taught different. A group of us took him into the shower and scrubbed him down with carbolic soap. After that he kept himself clean.

We had a bit of free time at weekends, and when you weren't shining your boots or cleaning your gun you could write letters or join the line to call home. There was always a shortage of coins for the payphone, and often you'd have to queue for half an hour or more to use it.

I'd been at boot camp only a fortnight or so when I received a long letter from my mother. She was worried that I might have found myself in a bit of an uncomfortable situation with Wendy.

In some ways York was still quite an old-fashioned, conservative town. When you picked up a girl from her parents' place you could expect to be invited in so that her folks could give you the once-over. And when you took a girl out for a meal you were expected to wear what they called a coat – a jacket – and tie.

It may seem quaint now, but in those days you could easily find yourself committed to someone on the basis of a rash promise. My mother was anxious that I might have blundered into a situation from which I would find that I could not easily extricate myself. It happened a lot then: love and lust pushed plenty of young people into getting engaged precipitately. Perhaps it still does today.

I was able to reassure my mother that her fears were unfounded. Although I'd been pretty keen on Wendy and we'd even talked about getting married, I hadn't made her any commitment. When I went away I'd told her not to wait for my return. As the weeks passed I found myself thinking about her less and less. Uncle Sam took care of that one for me.

8

My twenty-first birthday fell right in the middle of this two-month period of basic training. As it was a Saturday night, I was allowed to go to the PX – literally, the Post Exchange, but really a sort of superstore, a combined shop/bar/cafeteria – and drink a few beers with some of the other guys. This was the first alcohol I'd touched for more than five weeks, so it didn't take me long to get plastered.

In the third week of basic training I was allowed to start using what the Army insisted I referred to as a 'piece' on the range. The standard issue was the old M-1 semi-automatic rifle, much heavier than the rifles I was accustomed to using and more than twice the weight of the M-16s issued to infantrymen in Vietnam. But my experience on the Dickinson College rifle team stood me in good stead, and I won the marksmanship prize. By this time I'd applied for Officer Candidate School (OCS) and, somewhat to my surprise, my application had been accepted. Perhaps they were impressed by my flawless character.

The basic training finished in mid-April. I was now a GI, Government Issue Abraham. I went home for a week's leave. I flew up to Baltimore, where my dad picked me up from the airport and drove me home. My little sister Pat shrieked when she saw me standing at the door, dressed in a starched khaki uniform, a duffel bag over my shoulder. She laughed and pulled off my hat, then ran her hand across my crew-cut in wonder. My mother rushed out of the kitchen and hugged me tight.

Seven days later I reported to Fort Dix, New Jersey, about half-way between Philadelphia and the Atlantic coast, for a further eight weeks' Advanced Infantry Training (AIT). No longer raw recruits, this time we were treated with a little more respect, and perhaps we were more prepared for what we were about to receive. The training was in advanced soldiering: radio communications, survival skills, combat skills (including unarmed combat), assault course, obstacle course, etc. Even so, a lot of what we were doing was a bit primitive: lunging at sandbags with fixed bayonets, for example. Perhaps this had been relevant in the Second World War, but it sure as hell wouldn't mean a thing in Vietnam.

I was familiar with much of what we were supposed to be learning already, from my experiences in the Scouts and at college. But I didn't want to seem too clever. I found it best to pretend that I didn't know how to read a map or load a rifle. Meanwhile I spent all the time I could out on the athletics track, until I reached the stage when I was regularly competing in events for the Army.

When I had any weekend leave from Fort Dix I often used to go across to Atlantic City or upstate to New York City with some of the other guys. We'd trawl the bars and the strip-clubs, and inevitably I'd end up in bed with some hooker. That was what you did in those days. Nobody thought any the worse of you for it, not even my friend Floyd, whose sister I dated briefly.

A dual portrait of me, in battle fatigues and the smart uniform I wore on my R & R break in Hong Kong.

With my older brother, Rick.

Posing with my parents on our arrival in New York. I was nineteen at the time.

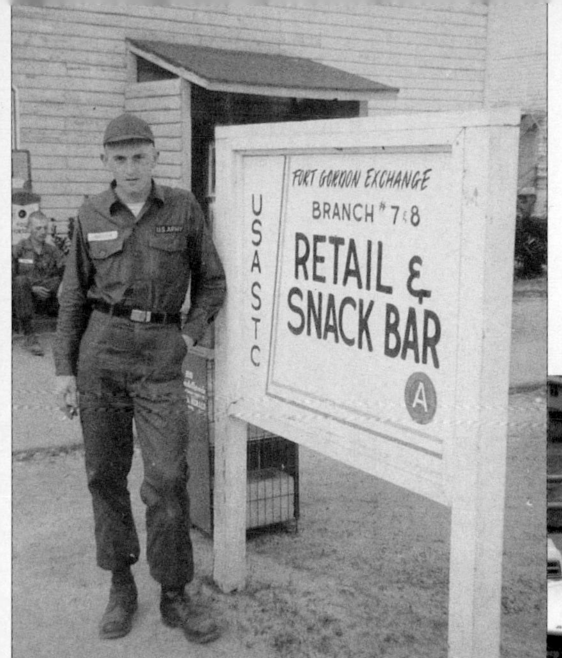

New GI 'Bud' Abraham, freshly shorn.

With my beloved Mustang. I was especially lean, having just finished six months of gruelling officer training.

As Executive Officer (XO) at Fort Dix, I was responsible for doling out wages to the officer trainees. I kept this kukri handy in case of any funny business.

Second Lieutenant Abraham, somewhere in Vietnam.

Posing with one of my squad leaders. He holds a captured enemy AK-47; I have my favourite CAR-15.

On LZ Colt with my commanding officer, Captain Matthews (wearing sunglasses).

Writing a report on a desk we found somewhere; in the background is a hooch, a tent we made from zipping together two ponchos.

Clearing a mortar tube.

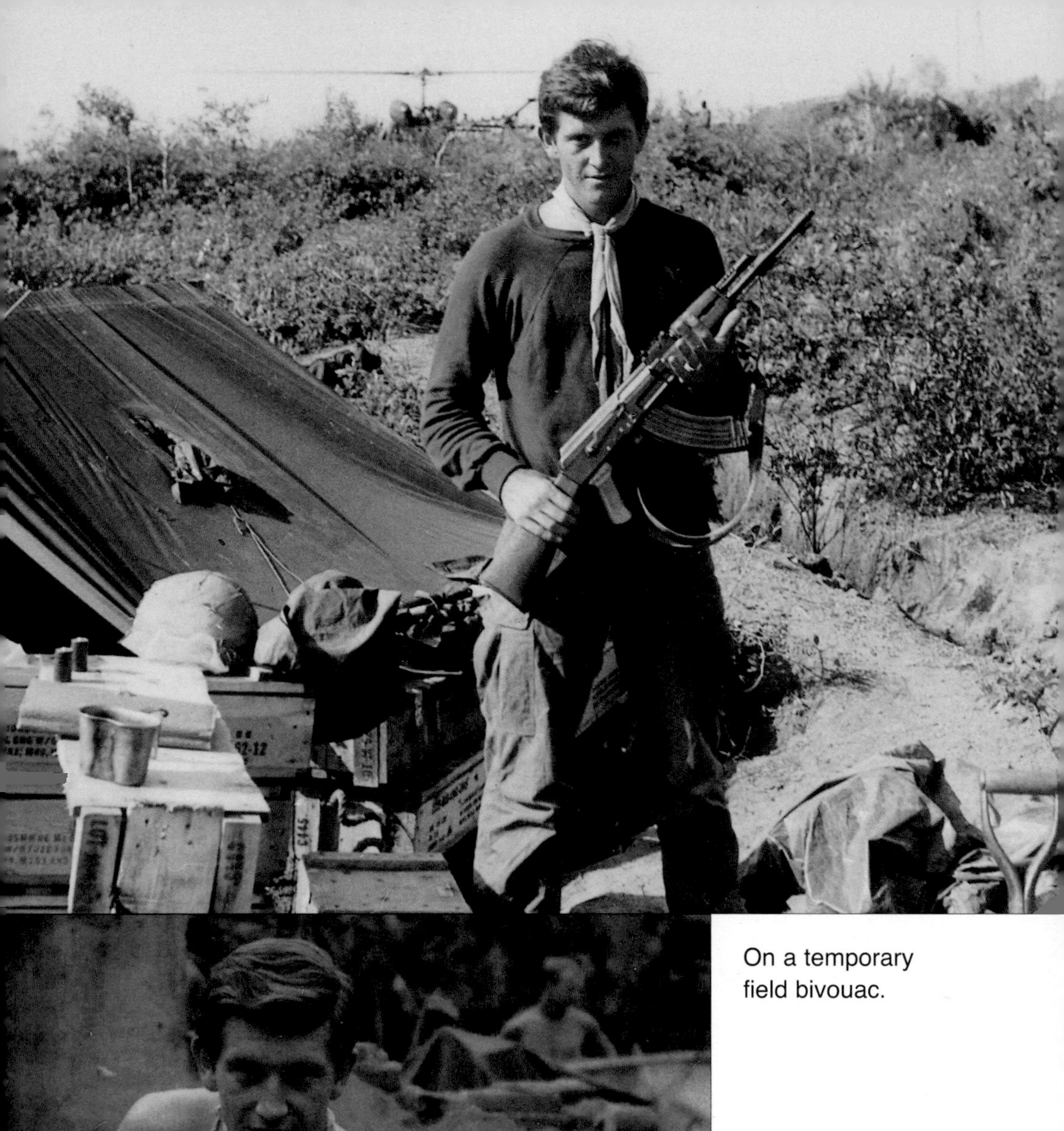

On a temporary field bivouac.

We found this dog in an abandoned village and adopted him as mortar platoon mascot.

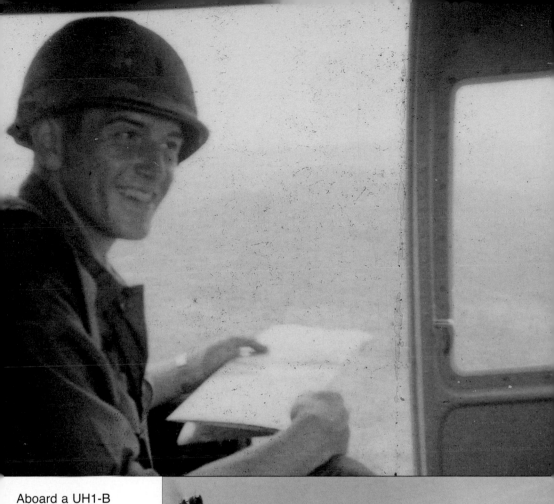

Aboard a UH1-B ('Huey') helicopter.

Helicopter leaves after resupplying a field bivouac; the chopper would try not to stay on the ground more than a minute or two.

With my M-1 sniper rifle. Through this scope I spotted the two USAF airmen, whom we were able to rescue from their Vietcong captors.

I finished my AIT and hung around for a bit as an acting sergeant with the training battalion, carrying out semi-privileged duties while I waited for my officer training to start. I no longer had to do KP or other menial tasks; most of the time I assisted the regular NCOs as they supervised the trainees. Then I had another couple of weeks' leave before reporting to Fort Benning, in the Georgia swampland near the Alabama border, for OCS. I had a friend in York who was due there at the same time – a tall, spindly guy called Curtis who liked bluegrass music – so we decided to travel together, in Mum's Pontiac station-wagon. By this time the family had acquired another car, a great big Buick, so my parents decided they could let me borrow the Pontiac for my six months of OCS. It was a long, long drive, fifteen hours in all. We set off one evening and drove through the night, talking and smoking cigarettes to keep each other awake. Every few hours we'd take a break at a truck-stop café and afterwards change driver. By the time we arrived at Fort Benning it was early afternoon. Amazingly enough, they had a parking facility for officer trainees, though it was hard to see why, as most off us weren't allowed to go off-base while we were there.

Fort Benning was a vast base, even bigger than the others I'd served on. It accommodated the 101st Airborne Division, and one of the first things I noticed as we drove up were the enormous jump towers, pylons perhaps three hundred feet high, which they used for parachute training. On the way in we passed cavernous aircraft-hangars, and beyond the airstrip we could hear artillery fire.

At first it didn't seem too bad. We were shown our rooms – not the long, open dormitories we had slept in during the two earlier stages of training, but smaller rooms, with beds rather than bunks, sleeping three or four men in each – and spent the remainder of the day settling in, finding out which platoon we belonged to, that sort of thing. That evening we gathered in the mess hall for a dinner of welcome. I found it a bit weird that the newly qualified lieutenants who would be training us – known as 'tactical officers' (TACs) – answered our questions 'affirmative' or 'negative' rather than 'yes' or 'no', but otherwise they appeared quite friendly. I was introduced to Lieutenant Raab, the officer in charge of our platoon. He seemed nice enough. As I fell asleep afterwards I thought: This is OK. If it's all going to be like this, I'm on a winner here. Which just shows how wrong you can be.

One moment I'm asleep, the next I'm jolted violently awake. There's a lot of shouting and banging in the corridor. I can't understand what's happening; it's still dark outside. I lift my wrist and try to focus on my watch: four o'clock in the morning. 'Jesus fucking Christ,' I hear someone mumble. Just then Raab bursts into our room, screaming, 'Get up, you lazy bastards.' He thumps the beds to emphasize the order. I roll out of bed and start pulling on my clothes, shivering in the early-morning chill. One guy who is slow to stir gets a kick. There's no time to wash. We stumble out into the corridor like frightened cattle. Other lieutenants are charging through the building, bellowing, 'Move, move, move,' and generally making as much noise as possible. Dazed and battered, we're herded outside on to the parade-ground. We line up as best we can in the pre-dawn gloom.

'All right, dickheads, down on your faces and start doing push-ups. Go on, *move*!'

I lower myself on to the cold, damp ground, forcing my muscles to respond, though every part of my body is longing to climb back into that warm bed. The harsh Tarmac scrapes the palms of my hands as I heave myself up and lower myself down again. Up, pause, down; up, pause, down. A guy in front of me is clearly finding it difficult. Raab starts screaming at him. When he doesn't respond, Raab strides over and kicks him hard in the ribs. The guy buckles up and groans, and then the lieutenant kicks him in the arse, sending him sprawling. The rest of us concentrate on our push-ups.

That's just the beginning. From then on we're harassed morning, noon and night. Everything possible is done to intimidate and humiliate us. We're shouted at and spat at continually, and made to march on the run – 'double timing' – everywhere. Sometimes they wake us at five o'clock in the morning, sometimes at three o'clock in the morning, sometimes at one o'clock in the morning, sometimes all three. We're always herded straight out on to the parade-ground, never given time to shit or shower or shave.

It's hard to explain to anyone who hasn't experienced it just how disorientating this can be. One moment you're in the deep cushion of sleep, the next you're being driven out into the cold and bawled at. I saw some guys wet themselves, they were so shocked by this treatment.

Our rooms opened on to a hall forty foot long, its floor polished until you could see your face in it. There was a black painted stripe along the middle and we were supposed to keep to this; if one of us strayed on to any other part of the floor, even just for a moment, he was made to clean the whole hall. To get into our rooms we had to reach up and grab the top of the door, then swing on to a chair and from this on to our beds – and the same in reverse to go out. If you met someone in the hall coming the other way, you had to lean over at an angle towards one of the walls and support yourself against this while you negotiated your way past each other.

We couldn't even go into the mess hall without first swinging across a row of monkey bars suspended ten feet up. At the far end, of course, there was always a queue waiting for the food, but if you dropped off the monkey bars before the last one you were made to do fifty push-ups, then go back to the beginning and start again.

They harassed us so much that it was hard to get enough to eat. We were not allowed to speak while eating or to look down at our food. Each man was supposed to stare straight ahead and sit bolt upright on the front six inches of his seat. If he leaned back, glanced sideways or whispered to his neighbour, he was made to go outside immediately and do forty push-ups.

We never had any spare time: always polishing, buffing up, tidying or cleaning. Your rooms, your lockers and your kit had to be ready for inspection at any time of night or day. Those TACs delighted in making work for their charges; you might have spent hours spit-shining your boots to a high polish, and then Raab or another of those bastards would come up to you on parade and step on your toe, deliberately grinding his sole across the face of your boot until it was scuffed, while he stared you in the eye, defying you to utter even a squeak of protest.

Just as in boot camp, we were made to run everywhere, and do push-ups, sit-ups and swing from monkey bars, twenty, thirty or even forty times a day. Raab gave us a series of physical tests, and if you failed any of these you were out of OCS. For example, we had to run a mile in full pack, i.e. helmet and boots and carrying a rucksack weighing about twenty pounds, an entrenching tool (a fold-up shovel) and a heavy old M-1 rifle. Anyone who didn't complete the mile in less than eight minutes failed the test. Throughout the training there were further tests: route marches of perhaps five miles along tracks or dusty roads, all in double-quick time. Or low crawl through barbed wire under artillery fire, or quick-stepping between car tyres, all against the clock.

On one occasion they made us crawl through a sewer dressed only in a single boot, a steel helmet and a poncho. Afterwards a man died of blood poisoning.

After only a few weeks, I wrote to my parents that I felt like quitting every hour of the day. The course was much tougher than I had expected, both physically and mentally. Already some of the others were dropping out, unable to meet the required standard of physical fitness or to bear the strain of the relentless harassment. They made it easy for us to quit, because they wanted only the best to qualify.

As time went on, the dropout rate increased. Every day there were more and more empty beds in the billets.

Once a fortnight each of us had to fill in a form rating the forty or so other members of our platoon, and if you came near the bottom of the ratings more than once you were ejected from OCS immediately.

My boarding-school background made it easier for me than for most of the other guys to fall in with such a harsh regime. On the other hand, I was picked on because I was English. Raab especially was always taunting me about the way I spoke.

It's a blisteringly hot day. The thermometer fixed to the wall outside our barracks shows the temperature at 94° Fahrenheit in the shade. Four companies of cadets – more than five hundred young men – are drawn up to attention on the parade-ground, in full pack. I screw up my eyes against the dazzling light. The sun scorches my neck. Sweat stands out all over my body; my hair is dripping; beneath my rucksack my uniform is soaked.

Raab prowls along the ranks, pausing every now and then to lob a question at some poor bastard. Get the answer wrong and you're down on the melting Tarmac, doing push-ups. Or running round the Fort perimeter until you collapse from heat exhaustion.

Utter silence, except for Raab barking questions and cadets stammering their replies. And the crunch of Raab's boots on the Tarmac.

He's approaching now. I see him coming from the corner of my eye. I feel certain that he's going to pick on me. I try to make myself anonymous, invisible, utterly bland.

He stops beside me and leans forward, a leer on his lips. 'Well, well, it's our English gentleman. You think you're better than us, don't you?'

He lifts his head and looks around, as if addressing an audience. Which is exactly what he's doing, of course.

'No, sir.' I stare straight ahead into the distance. I know that I mustn't let him rile me.

'Why don't you learn how to speak right, then?'

'Don't know, sir.'

'You don't know.' He makes an exasperated gesture. 'We're going to teach this Limey bastard to speak American,' he announces to everyone present. Then, just to make it as bad as it could be, he calls forward another of the cadets who just happens to have a particularly strong Bronx accent. The idea is that I should imitate this other guy. 'How do we say "command"?' asks Raab.

'Command,' says the guy from the Bronx, pronouncing the word with a short A, so that what he says sounds to me like 'commay-ind'.

'Command,' I repeat, making no attempt to speak like the other guy.

'Not fucking "commaarnd"!' screams Raab, his nose almost pressing against mine. 'We say "commend". You Goddamn useless Brits, you're so fucking stupid. How do we say "half"?'

'Hay-if.'

'Half.'

'Not fucking "Haarf"! Say "Heff".'

And so on. He goes on trying to get me to 'speak American' for hour after hour, in front of all those men drawn up to attention under the roasting sun. It's as if we're playing a game. He's trying to break me. But I'm damned if I'll give in. I'm not going to change the way I speak, not unless I receive a direct order to do so. And I think even Raab might think that a little excessive.

After perhaps three hours, he relents a little. 'Right, we've been here long enough. I'm sure all these lovely people want to get indoors. OK, Abraham, I'll let you off on this occasion – but only on condition you get your Queenie to write me a letter.'

So I'm forced to send a letter to the Queen, suggesting that she might like to write to Lieutenant Raab. I never had any reply, of course, and so far as I know neither did he – but I had to go through the motions.

As the training continued and more and more of the candidates fell by the wayside, I became increasingly determined not to fail. I'm a stubborn bugger and I've always relished any kind of competition.

I'm lying utterly still in a patch of swamp.

My whole body's submerged in warm, muddy water up to my chin. Only the top of my head is visible above the surface, like an alligator basking in the sun. My face is daubed with mud. I'm wearing a camouflaged helmet. Unless I make a move I don't think anyone could spot me until they were up close.

Enemy soldiers are searching the swamp for our guys. I can see one now through the trees, only about ten yards away. He's wading very slowly towards me, combing the territory to either side of him. I can hear the swish of the stagnant water as he moves. He's so near now that I can make out his finger wrapped around the trigger of his rifle.

Most of my platoon has already been eliminated. I've been hoping that if I lie really still the enemy patrol will pass me by, and then I may just be able to make it to safety. But if he keeps on coming this way, I don't see how he can miss me. I sink still further into the swamp and narrow my eyes to slits so that he won't see the light in them. I'm taking very short breaths through my nostrils, trying to keep my body inert.

The enemy soldier approaches. I can hear his breathing. The water swirls around me as he passes. I can't see him, now that he's behind me. Has he gone?

And then I feel the rifle in my back, and the words telling me to get up slowly, with my hands above my head.

Two hours later, and they're shouting at me in Vietnamese. I can't understand a word, of course. I just keep answering with my name, rank and serial number.

I'm buried up to my neck in wet sand. It's hard to breathe. The sun is burning up the top of my head. I can feel mosquitoes feeding off my face.

The guy who's been doing most of the shouting is dressed in those black pyjamas the Vietcong wear. He's grinning at me now. He's got some kind of bucket in his hands. I don't like the way he's grinning.

And then he upturns the bucket over my head: it's full of snakes. I feel them slithering all around my face in the dark. There's nothing I can do except scream.

In my rational mind I know that they can't be poisonous, but it's a very bad moment . . .

Soon after that they dig me out. It's hard to stand. My head feels dizzy from the sun and my body numb after being buried so long. I don't know what they have planned for me next, but I'm sure it won't be fun.

Two enemy soldiers drag me to a pole staked in the sand. A few yards away a vicious-looking Alsatian dog is tethered to a chain; he starts barking angrily as I approach. They tie my hands and feet around the pole and push me upwards, so that I'm hanging there, my arse sticking out towards the dog, only just high enough to avoid his snapping jaws. It's an effort to hold myself in this position, and I know that I won't be able to stay up for long . . .

I decide to try to escape if I have a chance. When the dog has finished snapping at my rear, they untie me from the post and toss me inside a bamboo hut. So far as they're concerned, I'm too far gone to be worthy of attention for the moment. I lie still, pretending to be in an even worse state than I am. They leave me.

A while later, when no one else is looking, I get up quietly and peep out of the hut. There's a guard outside, but he doesn't seem very alert. No one else around. The guard's sitting on the ground dozing in the sun, his rifle leaning against the outside wall of the hut beside him. Very carefully, I reach for it. My hand closes around the stock. In one quick movement, I grab the rifle and club the guard with the butt, knocking him out. He's going to have a hell of a headache – but I don't feel bad about that, not after what he and his friends put me through earlier today. I kick him, to make sure he's not shamming. Then I prop him up as he was before, his cap down over his eyes, and replace the rifle by his side.

Lurking in the shade at the door of my hut, I take a careful look around the compound where 'prisoners' like me are being held. Twenty or thirty similar huts interspersed with small trees and scrubby grass are scattered around inside a wire fence. Fortunately my hut is near the perimeter wire, well away from the main gate. Most of the guards are amusing themselves with my fellow officer cadets down towards the other end of the compound, about a hundred yards off. So far as I can see, there's only one guard patrolling the perimeter, being dragged along by another of those mean-looking dogs. He's just passing now. I wait for him to come round again, so that I can estimate how long he takes to complete a circuit. About five minutes later I see him reappear.

As soon as the guard is gone, I sneak out of the hut and start crawling towards the wire. It's hot, dusty work. Anyone standing nearby could see me, but I'm hoping that the long grass will conceal me from a distance.

It takes me a couple of minutes to reach the perimeter. Only three minutes remaining to get through the fence somehow and conceal myself on the other side before that guard comes round again. It's a chain-link fence about eight feet high, with barbed wire at the top: a bastard to climb. I crawl along inside the wire, hoping to find another way through. About twenty yards along there's a place where the fence isn't secured to the ground. Lying on my back, I pull the wire up over my head and push myself through with my legs. There's just enough space to scrape under. Once I'm more than half-way, I have to flatten my knees, so I wriggle and push with my heels. Right at the end, I twist my feet to one side and drag them after me one at a time, by bending my knee and then pushing against the wire. I'm covered in dust, but that doesn't matter. I've made it! I crawl for the nearest cover, a bush about twenty yards away. Then I lie flat on my face, watching for the guard through the grass.

There wasn't time to cover my tracks properly. If he notices them, they'll be on to me before I can get clear. I can see him now, his eyes squinting in the sun. He's approaching the place where I crawled under the fence. The dog is straining at the leash and whimpering, wanting to investigate the wire. What will the guard do? It's OK. He doesn't even glance at the spot, yanking at the lead and shouting harshly at the dog to quieten down.

As soon as he has passed by, I rise to my feet and creep forward until I'm out of sight of the perimeter. Then I stand up straight and start walking. About half a mile further on I find a road, and follow it away from the compound. After a while a pick-up comes trundling along behind me; I stick out a thumb and hitch a ride. A couple of hours later I'm back at the Fort.

You're not supposed to do what I've done, of course. It's called 'escape and evasion', but no one really expects you to escape. I report to my commanding officer, who puts me under house arrest. They consider court-martialling me. But when the colonel hears what I've done he just laughs and says, 'Good footwork, soldier.'

By this stage the training was becoming less physical and more academic. They gave us a more elaborate officers' Code of Conduct to 'read, learn and inwardly digest'. I spent much of my time as you would at West Point or Sandhurst, learning about tactics and the underlying principles of weaponry. It's not just a question of pointing a gun and shooting it: you've got to be able to set the azimuth and the elevation and all the rest of it, and to do that you need to understand the principles of geometry and trigonometry involved.

We were also carrying out role-playing exercises, taking the part of battalion commander, platoon leader, or whatever. I began to contemplate what I would be doing after OCS finished. Vietnam was always in the background, a prospect that came nearer and nearer as the training advanced. I was forming a picture of what the war in Vietnam would be like. By late 1966 it was becoming impossible to avoid the disturbing images that appeared daily on the television news and in the pages of every newspaper or magazine: wounded GIs on stretchers, their faces contorted by pain; terrified villagers fleeing along roads; bombs tumbling out of aircraft bays; rows of fiery explosions over what looked to be virgin jungle; impassive Buddhist monks immolated in front of horrified spectators. And, back at home, long-haired protesters chanting and burning the American flag.

I never questioned whether the war in Vietnam was worth fighting. It was obvious to me that serving there would be unpleasant, and if I could avoid it with honour, I would probably do so – but that was because I didn't want to get killed, not because I thought it was a bad thing to do.

One morning I was detailed to serve breakfast to those attending the career officers' course at Fort Benning. Among the guests was a British officer, a captain in the Scots Guards; he seemed somewhat taken aback to be asked by the cadet serving him whether he wanted tea or coffee in a soft but nevertheless distinct Yorkshire accent. We started chatting and I explained to him what I was doing there. I learned later that he subsequently asked my commanding officer to keep him informed of my progress.

By now I was getting a bit more time to myself. Every other Sunday I managed to escape from the base for a few hours, when I drove a Mormon friend into town so that he could attend church. This gave me a few precious hours of freedom, before I picked him up and drove him back again.

The training was still very hard, but from here on in they were trying to develop and harden us as potential officers, rather than trying to break us and prevent the weaker candidates reaching the end of the training. Those of us who remained in OCS were now permitted to wear the blue hat of a senior candidate, and allowed certain privileges like not having to run everywhere and being able to sit and talk in the mess hall.

At last, at the end of six months, the course was over. Of the original class of six hundred trainees, fewer than half made it through to the end.

I'm sitting rigidly upright in my smartest uniform, in a big hall full of people. I'm in the front row. The first few rows are occupied by cadets dressed like me, and behind us are many more rows of civilians. If I crane my neck round, I can see my parents at the back, and next to them my date, a girl called Libby. My sister Pat is there, too; she's sixteen now, and she's come as my roommate's date. After the ceremony there will be a dinner and dance at the officers' club.

We've been listening to a pep talk from a four-star general up there on the stage. Of course, I take what these brass hats say with a large pinch of salt, but it's hard not to feel a lump in the throat when he tells us that we are the very best young men in America, and that he's proud to be here with us today. He talks about the challenges that await us in the years ahead: the need to resist the Communist threat to the civilized world. He doesn't mention Vietnam.

He concludes his peroration and we all clap. The presentations are about to begin. I see the general glance down at the lectern and pick up the list of those who are about to receive their commissions. I know that I'll have the honour of being the first to be called, because my surname comes at the beginning of the alphabet. I run my finger nervously around the inside of my collar where it's chafing my neck. I hear the general read out my name, and I stand up to the sound of applause, with some whistling and hilarity from the other cadets in my platoon. I look back and catch a glimpse of my parents beaming proudly. Chest out and shoulders back, my arms swinging, I approach the steps and climb up to the stage, marching stiffly across to the waiting general, who stands clapping. He and I exchange salutes. Then he shakes me by the hand and presents me with a scroll informing anyone who cares to read it that the President of the United States reposes special trust and confidence in my patriotism, valour, fidelity and abilities.

I feel pretty proud at this moment. I am one of the élite who has stayed the course. I am now Second Lieutenant Bud Abraham, US Army. I am ready for anything.

I walk off the stage and out into the hall, clutching my commission. Raab is waiting there and, even more alarming, he has a smile on his face. He offers me his hand! 'Well done, Abraham,' he says. 'You'll make a fine officer.' I take his hand and stammer out some thanks. Thinking about it later, I reckon that in his peculiar way Raab quite likes me and has been trying to ensure that I succeed. Maybe he reckoned that all the taunting would help to harden me.

I continue into the billeting hall, where our new orders have been posted on the noticeboard. It's a bit of a surprise. I find that I've been posted to the Old Guard, the regiment based in Washington, DC, assigned to escort the President on ceremonial occasions, the American equivalent of the Household Cavalry. It's also the outfit that buries the dead at Arlington and guards the tomb of the Unknown Soldier.

Of course, I have no idea of any of this as I stare at the noticeboard. But when I find out more about it later that day, it sounds like a cushy number, especially as I discover that one of my duties will be to act as escort for the wives or daughters of visiting dignitaries.

Anyway, I didn't have long to contemplate this new challenge, as my orders were changed the very next day. The authorities had twigged that it might not be a very good idea to have an alien citizen guarding the President. Much later I found out that I should never have been allowed to become an officer at all. Apparently it's against the Constitution for an American soldier to be under the authority of a foreigner.

9

My next posting was as executive officer (XO) – meaning second-in-command – of a company of basic trainees back at Fort Dix, New Jersey, where I'd done my AIT. By this point I knew that I was likely to be posted to Vietnam in due course; and, since I also knew there was a possibility that I might not be coming back, I thought that while I had the chance I might as well use up the three weeks' leave I had accrued.

I was hanging about at home when the idea popped into my head to go over to England for a week or two. It was very much a spur-of-the-moment decision. The thought occurred to me, and later that same day my dad was driving me to Baltimore airport.

This time I had decided to fly across the Atlantic. Today flying is cheap, but back then it cost more to go by plane than it did by sea. I didn't mind: I'd saved plenty of money after six months' OCS with nowhere to spend my pay and I wanted to make the most of the time I had available.

I changed planes at Heathrow and flew on to Manchester, where I hired a car at the airport, a great big flash Ford Zephyr 6, with American-style wings and masses of chrome. Then I drove across to my grandfather's place in Llangollen, North Wales. In so far as I had a plan, it was to base myself there for a few days while I visited some of my old haunts.

Grandfather Mac was a widower, still upright and dignified in his seventies. As a young man, he'd gone out to America and worked on a ranch in the prairies; later he'd made a successful career in British industry, and had been awarded the MBE in recognition of his achievements. Mac still spent six months each year in America, and the other six months back in Wales. He and my grandmother had always been very much part of our immediate family; during my childhood we often stayed with them for substantial periods, as my father moved around from job to job. I was fond of him, and he of me. That night he took me out to a local restaurant. As we shared a bottle of wine, he asked me how I felt about the possibility that I would be going to Vietnam. For some reason I didn't want to talk about it, to him or anybody else. It may seem strange, really, but that's how I was. Whenever the subject came up, I'd start talking about something else. If anyone persisted in asking me what I felt, I'd get quite irritable. I just didn't want to think about it.

My old school was only thirty miles or so away, and the next day I decided to drive over there. I couldn't resist showing off my new uniform. It was more than two years since we'd left England on the *Mauretania*. Then I'd been a boy of nineteen, just out of school; now I was coming back as an officer, as a man.

When I turned up at the school, the Combined Cadet Force (CCF) just happened to be on parade, ready to begin an exercise on what we used to call the top golf course. The corps commander, a retired Army officer called Major Sutterby, did a double-take when he saw me. 'Abraham?' he said, not quite believing what he saw. I had never had much time for the CCF while I was at school – I thought it was stupid, playing at boy soldiers – and I suppose I had regarded him then as a bit of an old fart. He probably hadn't thought much of me at the time either. But now, seeing me in uniform, he must have thought, This chap can't be all bad, and then and there he invited me, as a visiting American officer, to review the troops drawn up on parade.

I played along with the whole thing and took the salute. Afterwards I watched the exercise. Of course, they made a complete hash of it, letting the muzzle of the howitzer drop into the mud.

Later on I bumped into Simon, Debbie's younger brother. She and I had never really broken up: she'd been sent off to Switzerland while I was still at school, and then my family had emigrated to America before she came back. We wrote to each other for a while, but the correspondence had tailed off. It's hard to sustain a romance when you don't know if you're ever going to see each other again. And there had been plenty of other girls in York to help me forget about her.

Debbie was a tall, well-endowed blonde, an affectionate, straightforward girl, whose sweet nature and English-rose looks attracted dozens of admirers. Back in the old days we used to hang around in coffee-bars, with a gang of other teenagers, feeding coins into the juke-box. It must have been back in 1963 when I'd taken Debbie one evening into Liverpool to the Cavern Club, to see the Beatles. All I remember is that it was very hot and rather smelly. We had snogged on the train home afterwards.

I got talking to Simon, and he urged me to give her a call. 'She'd love to hear from you,' he said, as he scribbled down her number. Apparently she was in London, training to become a nurse. So I called Debbie, and we chatted as if we'd never been apart. It turned out that she was due to come up north, to spend the weekend with her parents in Southport. She invited me to come, too. She had a boyfriend at the time, one of my contemporaries from school, and he was staying there as well – but fortunately he had to leave the same day I arrived.

I phoned Mac from the school to tell him that I'd changed my plans. He sounded disappointed that I wasn't coming back, and I felt a twinge of regret. But I was excited at the thought of seeing Debbie again. I drove up to Southport, still wearing my uniform. I knew the route well enough: I'd often visited her house back in the old days. I parked the car in the road outside, and sat there for a moment to compose myself. I hadn't seen Debbie for two and a half years. There was no reason to think that anything was going to happen – but I felt a sense of anticipation none the less. I straightened my tie in the rear-view mirror, then stepped out of the car, strode up to the door, and rang the bell.

Debbie opened the door, looking even more gorgeous than I'd remembered. We shook hands awkwardly. Her parents welcomed me as an old friend of the family. I took her to the cinema that first evening, and it seemed the most natural thing in the world to put my arm around her as we sat there in the darkness. We drove back to her house afterwards, but neither of us wanted to get out of the car. Soon we were kissing. It was hard to stop and go inside.

I spent almost every waking moment of that weekend with Debbie. We talked easily, without any restraint. When she had to go back to London to carry on with her nursing I offered to drive her. I felt so happy having her beside me on that long journey south. Late that afternoon I dropped her at the nurses' hostel. I couldn't stay with her there, of course. The plan was for me to go and find a hotel and for us to go out together in the evening.

I checked into a hotel near Piccadilly, the Regent Palace. Later that day I went back to pick up Debbie from the hostel. She was all dolled up in mini-skirt and leather boots; I thought she looked wonderful. I took her out to dinner at the Talk of the Town, the smart dining club off Leicester Square frequented by pop stars and millionaire playboys, where we saw Dusty Springfield. I'd managed to get tickets through the hotel concierge. It cost the earth, but it was worth it. We didn't talk much during the concert; most of the time we just sat there, holding hands under the table.

After the show I sneaked Debbie up to my hotel room. We'd never made love before. Debbie asked me to wait in the bathroom while she undressed, then slipped under the bedcovers. The room was dark when she called me in. I climbed into bed beside her, as shyly as if it were my first time. We embraced with a tenderness I'd never felt before.

Early the next morning I smuggled her out, because in those days you couldn't share a room in a respectable hotel unless you were at least pretending to be married. She came back the next night, too, the last before I was due to fly back. Those were some of the happiest days of my life. I thought about Debbie all the time. I was intoxicated by her, and I couldn't bear the thought that soon we were going to be separated. Having found her again, I didn't want to let her go.

In fact we'd begun to talk about getting married. We arranged that Debbie would fly over to the States to see me during the summer, towards the end of my posting at Fort Dix, so that I could take her with me back to Pennsylvania to meet the family.

I'd fallen in love with Debbie, and I wanted her to be my wife. But, if I'm honest with myself, I'm forced to admit that there was another motive. I was feeling twitchy about Vietnam. It was frightening to think of going out there without anybody back home caring whether I lived or died. Of course, there was my family – but somehow that wasn't enough. I suppose that I wanted someone to be proud of me, someone to make it worthwhile. And I didn't want to be alone in Vietnam. Debbie would be coming with me – not literally, of course, but I could cherish the memory of this beautiful girl while I was away, knowing that she was mine and that she would be waiting for me when I came home. It would be something to hold on to.

While I was staying at the Regent Palace I left the car in the street outside. Back in 1967 there were far fewer cars on the roads, and fewer parking restrictions, even in central London. When I went out to collect the car on the morning I was due to leave, I couldn't find it. For a moment I thought that it had been stolen. But the hotel staff explained that I had parked it illegally, and as a result it must have been towed away. They helped me to find out where it had been taken, and I took a taxi down to the pound, a great big multi-storey just south of the river, to reclaim it. By this time I was in uniform once more, because I was on my way back to Fort Dix. The guy manning the pound must have been around in the Second World War, as he helpfully remembered a law dating from then to the effect that American servicemen could not be fined or prosecuted for common traffic offences. Apparently this law was still on the statute books; perhaps it still is today. Anyway, I filled in a form and he let me have the car without paying a fine. I drove back to Heathrow and dropped off the car before flying back to America.

Months later, back at Fort Dix, I was ordered to report to my commanding officer. 'What the fuck is this?' he said, waving a piece of paper in front of me.

It was the report I'd filled in back at the pound. 'Oh, shit,' I replied.

'Aw, take it away; I don't want to know about it.'

10

The six months I spent at Fort Dix were pretty relaxed, compared to what had gone on before. For one thing, I was now an officer, and officers didn't have much to do with the trainees. When I'd been doing basic training myself, officers were remote figures whom we regarded with awe. Whenever we saw an officer, even passing in his car, we were duty-bound to salute. Now I had blue stickers on the bumper of my car indicating that I, too, was an officer, which meant that any serviceman on the base had to stop what he was doing and salute the car – no matter who was in it at the time. (Later in the summer, when Debbie came over to stay, I was living off base, and she would drop me at the Fort in the morning before taking the car on. She was astonished to find soldiers saluting her!)

Now that I was an officer, I was allowed to grow my hair back to a reasonable length, which meant that I no longer looked like a skinhead.

As executive officer, my duties were mainly administrative.

My responsibilities encompassed all but the training itself, which by and large we left to the NCOs. My job was to provide everything for the 640 men in my training battalion: the food, the accommodation, the quartermaster's stores, even the payroll. I still have a picture of myself sitting behind a desk covered with piles of coins and notes in various denominations, as I dished out their weekly pay to the men, kukri in hand, a loaded revolver lying on the desk as back up, in case anyone took it into his head to rob me.

Every day I'd pick up a stack of mail from my cubbyhole and carry it into my office. Then I'd sit down behind my desk and start going through it, just like any other office worker.

One fine spring morning, I'm just collecting my mail, when the sergeant who sorts it walks past. 'I see your number's come up,' he remarks casually. He doesn't look straight at me, but I can sense his smirk. I have a sinking feeling that I know what he's talking about. I mutter some noncommittal reply, and take the mail through to my office, closing the door behind me. I'm still on my feet as I start riffling through the pile, and suddenly there is the news that I've been dreading: my orders to Vietnam. I've been assigned to the 1st Air Cavalry Division, a helicopter-based force. Oh, Christ, this is it.

I collapse into my chair and lean forward with my elbows on the desk, hands folded under my chin. I'm staring out towards the wall opposite, but I don't see the framed pictures hanging there. I sit motionless for several minutes, trying to take it all in.

I'm lying face down on my bunk, reading a letter from my mother. I sense that she's found it difficult to write. She tells me that Walter, a guy I knew back in York, has been killed out in Vietnam. I can't believe it at first. I've never known anyone my age who's died – except my brother, of course.

I used to play football with Walter at Dickinson. If I close my eyes, I can see him now, grinning under his helmet, as we lean forward together. I remember the way he used to laugh, throwing his head back so that you could see his Adam's apple. He seems so familiar to me – I can just imagine the kind of conversation we'd be having now if he were here. But he won't be here, not ever again. I imagine his body lying stiff inside a coffin, lowered into the ground by solemn soldiers in full-dress uniform as his family stands beside the grave.

My mother writes something about duty and sacrifice, but I can tell that her heart isn't in it. I know she's thinking that I could be next.

I'm standing in shorts and US Army vest, trying to stay focused on what I'm about to do. I've already warmed up, and now I'm shaking my arms and legs to keep my muscles toned. It's a beautiful spring morning here in Washington, DC, without a cloud in the sky.

Lots of people are milling around nearby, but I don't allow that to distract me. I can hear the occasional starting-pistol, and the odd burst of cheering. Words crackle from the Tannoy, but I don't notice them. I've been here several days, and I'm used to it all by now. Besides, I must concentrate. It's the 1967 Mid-Atlantic Championship, and I've reached the final of the triple jump.

I shouldn't be nervous, because I've been to these championships before. Last year I won medals in this event and in the high jump, and I was Mid-Atlantic Champion in the javelin. I sailed through the heats. But earlier this morning one of the other contestants gave me some disturbing news. Apparently scouts from the American Athletics Union are here, strolling around making notes on their clipboards. It's a big thing for me, because I'm on the fringes of selection for the American

Olympic team in triple jump. And, if I'm selected for the Olympics, I won't be going to Vietnam.

All I have to do is jump the qualifying distance: fifteen metres. That shouldn't be a problem. I regularly jump fifteen metres in training.

On my first attempt I jump 14.85. No problem: I'm just getting started. My second attempt is a no jump.

Now it's my third and final attempt. I take a deep breath, duck my head, and get set on the starting-line. The approach to the take-off board stretches out a hundred feet before me. I stare at the ground, trying to concentrate. Fifteen metres. Get a grip!

I stand in a crouched position, swinging my body back and forth to gain momentum. When I feel ready, I start pounding down the track, arms balanced, head still, strong legs driving me forward. I'm accelerating all the time, reaching maximum speed as my right foot hits the board. I kick hard, climbing through the air until I land on my right foot and stretch out in a stride, not so far this time; then the final spring from my left foot, soaring through the air again, dragging back my arms to catapult my legs forward for the landing, then swinging my arms up again as my heels touch the sand, so that my momentum will carry my body on beyond.

As both feet hit the sand, I know that I haven't given my best. A few seconds later the result is confirmed: 14.97 metres. I've missed getting out of going to Vietnam by three centimetres.

Just before I left, I received an air-mail letter from Mac. He recalled the time when I had been to visit him, six months earlier, and explained how he had not been able to find the words then to say what was on his mind.

> It may be difficult to understand how it comes about that you – an Englishman – are caught up in an American war. So far as I am

> concerned this is not just an American war but another phase in the age-long struggle for the preservation of liberty and other priceless gifts handed down from past generations. These cannot be defined or enumerated in this letter, but they are real and must be fought for by each generation. England is not fighting in this war, mainly because she has been terribly weakened in earlier phases. Have no doubts about it, you and your kind are fighting for mankind and its future. Let us hope that the present phase will soon end in victory and that America will then turn to the social injustices crying out for solution at home. In future years you will hold your head so much higher for having done what you see to be your duty.

I refolded his letter and placed it carefully in my wallet. I remembered how Mac had tried to talk to me while I was staying with him, and how I'd avoided the subject.

I could picture him sitting down to write to me at his Victorian roll-top desk, his hand trembling a little as he unscrewed his fountain-pen. I imagined how carefully he would have chosen his words, writing them out in draft beforehand. I could see the moisture in his eyes as he picked up the letter and checked it through one final time, before pressing it against his blotting-pad, folding and sealing it.

A few days before my time at Fort Dix was up, Debbie flew out to join me. It was wonderful to see her again, after six long months of separation. I'd already written to tell her about my being posted to Vietnam. I was sharing a house with three other piss-head lieutenants, so she was able to stay there with me. It was a bit of a shit-heap, but we were so absorbed in each other that I don't think she minded. One Saturday we drove over to the Jersey coast and walked for hours along the sands, hand in hand. By this time we were in effect engaged, though I hadn't yet given her a ring. We decided to get married as soon as possible after I returned from Vietnam. If she wondered then whether I might not be coming back for the wedding, she kept it to herself.

My posting at Fort Dix came to an end late in July 1967. I had a fortnight's leave remaining before I was due to fly out to Vietnam. Debbie and I drove up to New York, where we had a look around town and spent a night at the Sheraton Hotel. Then we went home to spend a few days with my family. There was a strange atmosphere in the house. That first evening we all gathered downstairs for a drink. My dad didn't say very much, but Mum talked all the time, lots of inconsequential gossip about neighbours I barely knew. She seemed very fidgety, and kept getting up and fetching things we didn't really need.

Even at this late stage, my mother was trying everything she could think of to prevent me having to go. She wrote letters to our local senator, the President, the Prime Minister, the Queen, anybody who might be in a position to get me out of it. I think she was more anxious than I was. She'd already lost one of her sons; she couldn't bear the thought that she might lose the other.

I found out later that she and Debbie had held a private discussion in the bathroom about whether they could persuade me to make a run for it.

The next day we went into town together, and I bought Debbie an engagement ring, a big sapphire surrounded by diamonds. We arranged to have her name inscribed inside my fraternity ring from Dickinson College, and I promised her never to take it off until we were man and wife. We fixed a wedding date, a couple of weeks after my tour of duty in Vietnam was due to end. My parents held an engagement party for us, and together we were photographed cutting the cake.

Debbie had to fly home a few days before I was due to leave. I drove her to the airport at Baltimore. She sat very still and solemn on the journey. I thought that she looked more beautiful than I'd ever seen her, a simple headscarf covering her hair.

I parked the car, then took her hand as we walked through the airport. We paused at the departure gate. It was very difficult to say goodbye, knowing what lay ahead. I put my arms around her and hugged her tight. I was too choked to be able to say how I felt. She pressed a St Christopher medallion into my hand, before tearing herself away and disappearing through the barrier.

It was a bleak drive back from the airport. I kept thinking about Debbie on the plane; I wanted to turn back and run after her. I couldn't bear the thought that we might never see each other again. As soon as I reached home, I wrote her a letter, and during the week that followed I wrote to her every day. I had this sense that doors were slamming shut on me, one after another. It was almost as though I was under a death sentence.

By this time I was counting the hours I had remaining before I had to go. I spent some of this time talking to a friend's cousin who had just returned from a tour of duty in Vietnam. Somehow he reassured me and boosted my morale. 'It does not sound half as bad as it is made out to be,' I wrote to Debbie.

On the day before I left I went to see the rector of our local church in York. I was not particularly devout, but I was lonely and frightened, and I suppose that I was in a very vulnerable state of mind. I was desperately trying to find a way out, like a fish in a net that is closing around him; and yet at the same time I felt guilty about thinking this way and selfish for trying to avoid the burden that other men were shouldering. The rector took me into the church, and asked me to kneel down beside him before the altar to pray. Then he turned to me and anointed my head with oil. I found this oddly comforting.

The next morning my parents took me to Baltimore, and I caught a plane to California as the first leg of my journey. As soon as I was on the plane I felt less nervous. From this point on there was nothing I could do but accept whatever was coming to me.

I had a few days in San Francisco before I was due to report to Oakland Air Force Base for my onward flight to Vietnam. My father had arranged for his company agent to meet me there and show me around. Luke was a bachelor, only a few years older than me, and a bit of a raver – what we called then a 'swinger' – who had a circular bed fitted with black satin sheets. There was a sense that I might not have too much time left, and I wanted to pack in as much experience as possible in the days that remained to me. Luke fixed me up a date with Christine, a friend of one of his regular girlfriends, and the four of us hit the town together.

The next morning I took a taxi to Oakland Air Force Base and boarded the plane for Vietnam.

Many years later, when both my parents were dead, I found a letter my mother had written to Debbie after I had gone. I could hear her voice in my head as I read her words on this faded piece of writing-paper, now more than thirty years old. She described my father pacing the room, endlessly repeating, 'If only I could have gone in his place, I would have wanted nothing more, but what can I do, what can I do?' I had no idea at the time how upset he was.

I have a picture of Dad in his RAF squadron leader's uniform, the Distinguished Flying Cross ribbon pinned proudly to his chest. During the Second World War he had served as a Pathfinder pilot, flying Mosquitos, the wooden planes that served as the vanguard of Bomber Command, showing the way to the target zones. All my life I have admired him for his heroism – but it never occurred to me until the moment I first read her letter that Mum had needed to be brave, too.

> It is going to take all our efforts to stop Bud knowing how worried we all are, but that is the only way we can help him for the next year, to keep him looking forward to the end of his tour and your future happiness together. My heart goes out to you both. I know what your position is from my own experience of the last war (as I expect your mother does too), and I knew then that the only way I could help was to never let Geoff know of my fears and grief but only to try to buoy up his belief in his own ability and positive talk of our future after the war. Next year this will all be like a nightmare, unbelievable in our joy at your wedding time.

PART III: Vietnam

11

Day 1 (365 days short): 7 August 1967

We fly out of Oakland in a Boeing 707 specially chartered from TWA to carry officers to Vietnam. The atmosphere isn't particularly tense. It's just like a scheduled flight, with meals served by air stewardesses and film showings. The main difference is that all fifty or so passengers are in uniform.

Our route takes us via Honolulu and Okinawa to Bien Hoa, just outside Saigon. It is an overnight flight, and we cross the dateline *en route*, so that the date when we land is two days later than when we take off. 'Thank Christ for that,' someone says. 'That's forty-eight hours less we've got to be in this fucking place.'

'Don't forget you've got to add twenty-four hours,' someone else says sourly. '1968 is a fucking leap year.'

As we fly in over Vietnam from the South China Sea, the countryside looks peaceful at first. I can see mountains, and rivers snaking through green jungle. Then, as we descend, I notice that the pattern of paddy-fields along the coast is pockmarked with what look like meteor craters. I learn later that these are the so-called 'arc-light strikes', where B-52s have dropped hundreds of thousand-pound bombs, illuminating the ground like a floodlit stadium.

The plane lands. As we taxi to a halt one of the stewardesses makes an announcement over the PA. 'Welcome to Vietnam,' she says. 'We hope you boys have a good tour. We'll see you back here one year from now.'

The engines die away to the sound of clicking seat-belts. Men begin to stand up and retrieve gear from the overhead lockers. After a frustrating delay, I can see through the window some steps being wheeled towards us. A few moments later, the doors open, and I join the file towards the exit. A stewardess gives me a last sympathetic smile. Behind her I can see bright sunlight shining through the exit door. Outside is all the paraphernalia of a typical military base: rows of combat aircraft, all positioned at exactly the same angle; big heavy transport planes; helicopters and military vehicles of various shapes and sizes; stores in neat piles; hangars, warehouses, and other plain concrete buildings. Though this is nominally a civilian airport, the Boeing 707 feels oddly out of place, like a man in civilian clothing in a uniformed group.

As I step out of the air-conditioned plane, I feel a blast of humid heat. It's like walking into a Turkish bath. The air smells of sweat, excreta, rotting vegetables and petrol fumes.

I walk across the runway towards a waiting bus, blinking in the bright sun and still unsteady from the long flight. Behind a wire fence I can see a crowd of GIs, cheering and celebrating as if their team has just won a big football game. They must be on their way home, probably going back in our plane. In a year's time, I think, that'll be me. Unless I'm coming back in a bag, of course.

From Bien Hoa we are transported by bus a few miles down the road to Long Binh, a huge base holding perhaps 25,000 men at one time. We're housed in single-storey barracks, thirty or so men to each room. The heat is unrelenting, and the humidity often up around 100 per cent. It's so hot at night that it's hard to sleep. Mosquitoes are everywhere.

At the base, we form a line and wait our turn to see a surgeon-captain, who warns me of the dangers of heat stroke and issues me with a packet of salt tablets, telling me to take two daily. He also issues me with anti-malarial pills, informing me that failure to take these regularly is a court-martial offence – because otherwise, I learn afterwards, some men will deliberately allow themselves to contract malaria in order to avoid active duty. I have two little tablets to take every day, plus a great big horse pill, as big as a gob-stopper, to swallow weekly. Hours after you've swallowed the damn thing, you still have the unpleasant feeling that it is stuck in your throat.

Long Binh is like a city in itself, with all the amenities you'd expect to find in one. We are to stay here for a few days acclimatizing and learning something about this country we've come to defend. Most of us haven't much of a clue where we are, except that it's a long way from America.

The next morning our lessons begin. At 8 a.m. sharp we new arrivals are required to attend the first in a series of talks, most of them given outside, on what Americans call 'bleachers': tiered seating, facing a podium and a display board. We are given a rousing homily by a lieutenant-colonel. Like all the rest of us, he's dressed in green fatigues and a baseball cap. He tells us that the war is almost won. From what he says, we'll be lucky to see any action before the end. Then a captain takes over. He uses a drill stick to point to the map pinned up on the display board behind him. It shows Vietnam to be shaped like an S, with weird dimensions: around 1,600 kilometres from top to toe, but never more than 200 kilometres wide – long stretches in the middle are only fifty or sixty kilometres wide. 'This narrow strip contains the Demilitarized Zone, or DMZ, which separates North and South Vietnam,' the captain explains. 'For reasons best known to our politicians, we are not permitted to conduct operations above the DMZ – though the North Vietnamese do not have the same inhibitions about coming south.'

It soon becomes apparent that all the maps we will be using in Vietnam measure in kilometres – known to soldiers as 'klicks' – although, of course, we're all more familiar with miles.

The captain describes the country we will be fighting in. South Vietnam is shaped like a banana, with Saigon, the capital city, near the widest bit at the bottom, in the lowlands close to the Mekong Delta where the majority of the population lives. A coastal highway runs north up to the city of Da Nang, home to a big Marine base, and on further north, to the old imperial capital of Hue, less than a hundred kilometres south of the DMZ. All along the coastline is a fertile plain, often no more than twenty or thirty kilometres wide; inland are the jungle-covered hills, which cover three-quarters of both North and South Vietnam. The Central Highlands, a range of mountains often more than two thousand metres high, stretch up along the border with Cambodia and Laos towards China.

'The threat to South Vietnam is twofold,' he continues, 'from the so-called National Liberation Front [NLF], that is South Vietnamese Communist irregulars or Vietcong, and from regular North Vietnamese Army [NVA] units coming south along the Ho Chi Minh Trail, which snakes back and forth across the borders with Laos and Cambodia. For reasons best known to our politicians, we are not permitted to conduct operations across those borders.'

I'm conscious of a murmuring among the audience. This is beginning to sound like an unfair contest. I hadn't appreciated before that we're going to be fighting with one hand behind our back. It seems that in some areas we can't even return fire without authorization.

Once you get to look at the map, you can see that South Vietnam is almost impossible to defend against infiltration from the north. According to what we've just been told, the North Vietnamese can move freely in Laos and Cambodia, and they can choose from some 1,500 kilometres of border where they want to cross into the south – most of it jungle-clad highlands, inaccessible by road. The speaker voices the thought forming in my mind. 'We have to accept that they can enter the country freely, and somehow deal with them here.'

Of course, as the captain goes on to outline, we have a whole bag of tricks to help us deal with the enemy: overwhelming firepower in almost every department of the war, plus complete supremacy in coastal waters and in the air. 'And we have a new weapon, one hardly used in any previous war: the helicopter. This can act as a platform for devastating fire, and as a supremely flexible form of transport, taking troopers quickly into any region, however remote.'

He talks at us for a couple of hours or more. Then he asks for questions. A freckled, red-headed guy a few rows back from me sticks up his hand. The captain indicates that he should speak. 'Uh, sir, what I don't understand is this – where on this map is the front line?'

The captain gives a grim smile. 'The front line? That's hard to answer. I'd have to say that there is no front line – or maybe I should say that the front line is everywhere.'

That same afternoon we begin a 'jungle screening' course, led by a grizzled old sergeant, a veteran of the Korean War, on his second tour in Vietnam. This is my introduction to the booby-traps that 'Charlie' leaves everywhere – hidden on paths, in ditches, on bodies, anywhere an American soldier might be expected to go. They didn't tell us anything about these back in the States.

It seems that the enemy has a whole bunch of such nasty surprises waiting for us out there in the field. The sergeant holds up a bamboo stake, its upper end needle-sharp. 'This little motherfucker is a punji stick,' he tells us. 'It's sharp enough to pierce the canvas boots you'll be wearing on patrol and penetrate the flesh right through to the bone.' Apparently the enemy likes to place these sticks anywhere an American soldier might tread. 'Can you believe what those fucking gooks do?' asks the sergeant, his lip curling with disgust. 'Well, I'll tell you. They smear the end with shit, so that wounds will be infected.'

A ripple of revulsion passes through the audience.

'Charlie sure plays dirty,' some wag chirps up.

The sergeant continues his talk; I have the impression that he enjoys making our flesh creep. He tells us how the enemy will dig a pit and fill it with punji sticks, then cover it over with leaves and branches, so that anyone stepping on these will drop through. The sergeant goes on to describe what happens next. Typically, the sticks drive deep into both legs as you plunge through the camouflaged covering; then your momentum carries you forward on to the other sticks, your own weight tearing them through the flesh of your legs as you fall.

'Holy shit!' exclaims one of the lieutenants sitting next to me.

It seems that Charlie has plenty more sophisticated booby-traps, too, such as the 'Bouncing Bettys', which fly up into the air when disturbed and then explode, scattering shrapnel in all directions from head-height. 'They use every kind of booby-trap you can imagine and plenty that you can't,' explains the sergeant. Often they adapt our own Claymore mines, which they obtain through various underhand methods, then use against us.

By the end of that day we all have plenty to think about. The general feeling is one of increased hostility towards such a sneaky enemy. 'I can't wait to get out there and whip Charlie's butt,' declares one of the guys as we walk back to our barracks.

In the evenings there's a lot of hanging about in the officers' club, drinking, gambling, just killing time. I get to know a few of the other guys superficially, but we all know that in a few days' time we will be heading off in different directions, and the chances are that we will never see each other again. There are Vietnamese around, of course, 'mama sans' and 'hoochgirls' who do much of the domestic work, living in squalid hovels just outside the base. Even in those first few days, I see enough of the conditions in which the people live to be shocked by the poverty. Just like a tourist, I take some photographs to send to the folks back home.

A lot of the talk is about the nightlife in Saigon. Everything I hear makes it sound a pretty sleazy place. One guy tells me about the rats. 'The rats in Saigon are like nowhere else in the world,' he says. 'The biggest rats you've ever seen, and not afraid of nothing. One time I went out the back of some restaurant and saw one of those fuckers with a kitten between its jaws. A *kitten*, for Chrissake! Can you imagine that?'

One night, after I've had a few beers at the club, I'm walking back along the path to my billet in the dark when I feel a crawling sensation just inside my collar. I flick my neck with my fingers and touch something hard. I feel it run down my chest, and I hold my shirt open to try to see what it is. As it moves into my sightline, I glimpse it in the gleam from a nearby porch: a cockroach, as big as a matchbox. Revolted, I start tearing at my clothes, stripping off my shirt, before I hear the click as the roach drops on to the Tarmac and the sound of it scuttling away in the darkness.

At Long Binh there is little sign of the war, except the odd thump of a distant artillery shell and the constant drone of helicopters. Sometimes at night we see the sky lit up by illumination flares.

'Darling, this does not look like being a very good assignment,' I write to Debbie, sitting in the officers' club on my last day at Long Binh, a beer near at hand. The 1st Air Cavalry was the first Army division to go to Vietnam, and, as it will turn out, will be the last to leave. The 'Cav' has a reputation for seeing a lot of action. It's based at An Khe in the Central Highlands, an area where the Vietcong have been particularly active in the past: one in which they are able to move freely, because the hilly, jungle-covered terrain provides them with plenty of cover. Until this last moment I've been hoping that I may be reassigned to administrative work behind the lines. I'm still in a very volatile mood, veering between the hope that somehow there may be an eleventh-hour reprieve and going crazy with boredom.

I've been assigned to the 5th Battalion of the Seventh Cavalry, known as the 'GarryOwen Brigade'. I'll be entitled to wear the crossed sabres of a cavalry officer on my lapel, and the much respected 'Cav patch' sewn on to my left shoulder – a yellow shield with a diagonal black stripe and the silhouette of a horse's head. Apparently the Seventh Cavalry has a proud history. Almost a century before, under the command of General George Armstrong Custer, the regiment was cut to pieces in a heroic last stand against overwhelming Sioux odds at Little Big Horn. It doesn't sound like a very good omen.

I fly up to An Khe in a Hercules C-130 transport. It's very different from the flight into Saigon. Sixty-two of us, all second lieutenants, are herded up a ramp into this warehouse of a plane, along with any other cargo that happens to be going north. The difference is that the cargo is secured: we are loose, squatting among the hard metal racks and the rollers that make it easier to shift the pallet-loads. The noise of the engines drowns any conversation. I find myself looking at the faces and wondering how many of these men are flying to their death.

Those great big transports fly very low, so low that they're vulnerable to small-arms fire from the ground. That's one reason why they aren't pressurized. They're very slow, and they don't have air-conditioning. The journey north seems interminable: hot, sticky and uncomfortable.

An Khe is another huge base, with a perimeter many miles in circumference, protected by multiple layers of barbed wire. It's so big that you can't easily see from one side to the other. Most of the buildings have wood floors and walls, with sandbag reinforcements on the outside, and tent roofs. There's constant activity, with helicopters taking off and landing all the time, heavy transports lumbering along the airstrip, and every now and then a Phantom screeching into the sky. Lines of trucks rumble into the base, and jeeps rush to and fro at alarming speeds, throwing up dust from the dry brown earth.

A sergeant is waiting for us as we stumble out of the rear of the C-130. He escorts us towards our billet, rows of single-storey barracks, each housing perhaps twenty newly arrived officers in a single dormitory. Only twenty yards away is the perimeter wire. 'That is what we call the Green Line,' says the sergeant, pointing towards the perimeter. 'Out beyond the wire is Charlie's domain.'

I stare out past the bunkers and rolls of wire. The land beyond has been cleared of trees and other cover; all that remains is scrub. Beyond I can see fields, and beyond these foothills, with higher mountains visible in the far distance. I imagine enemy soldiers coming down from those hills and creeping up to the perimeter at night. For the first time since I arrived in Vietnam, I feel vulnerable.

The billet is quite comfortable, nicer in many ways than some of the accommodation we've got used to back home. Each of us has our own bed and locker, where we can store our khaki uniforms, personal effects and valuables including, in my case, my British passport. A group of us find our way to the officers' club, trying to look as if we know where we are and what we're doing. As we stand at the bar, I remark to the others that this is OK, I could get used to this. I was expecting something much worse. Another officer standing nearby laughs into his drink. 'Oh, baby, hasn't anyone told you? You're not staying *here*, for Chrissake!' I offer to buy him another drink and ask him to join us. 'Listen, man,' he says, 'this place is just a staging-post. You fucking new guys are heading out there into the boonies, where there ain't no showers and there ain't no sheets. You boys are going to get shot at. You're all going to be platoon leaders, the cannon fodder of the US Army.'

That night is punctuated by heavy artillery fire. I'm puzzled by this at first, because I can't figure out what the hell our guns can be targeting in the dark. Our new friend explains that this is 'H & I' – harassment and interdiction – basically just blasting away at areas where Charlie might be lurking. It doesn't sound very scientific.

The next morning we assemble at another bleacher to begin 'orientation school', learning officially what we are supposed to be doing – the Standard Operating Procedures (SOPs), general guidelines rather than specific instructions, because no two situations encountered in the field are ever the same. School begins with an introductory talk by a lieutenant-colonel, again dressed informally in fatigues and cap. He tells us that the 1st Air Cavalry Division is a helicopter-based force. 'This doesn't mean that you will be spending every day flying around in the air, firing down on the jungle. On the contrary, most of your time will be spent on the ground, hiking through it.' The enemy is capable of living off the land, being more or less permanently on the move and very difficult to detect from the air. Locating the enemy is more than half the battle. 'Charlie is a coward,' says the colonel, his jaw jutting out aggressively. 'When we advance, he retreats.' To counter this, our strategists have developed an airmobile concept of anti-guerrilla warfare. The Cav is a 'ready reaction force', operating right up to the DMZ. We will be flown into areas where Charlie is known to be active, then patrol these areas looking for signs of enemy activity.

The colonel outlines an impressive-sounding theory to explain the purpose of what we were doing. The South Vietnamese government is trying to establish control over the countryside by winning the loyalty of the local population. They have a policy of placing agents in each village: teachers, social workers and suchlike. But this can only work if the villagers are free from Communist intimidation. The enemy usually moves around in small bands, ranging in size from two or three up to a dozen or so. The villages are always vulnerable if Charlie is around. 'Your job will be a cleansing operation, patrolling into the surrounding country to find the enemy and eliminate him.

'I want you gentlemen to appreciate something,' he says in conclusion, his gaze sweeping across the tiered rows facing him. 'To fulfil this task you are about to undertake will require outstanding qualities of leadership and initiative. I am confident that you will rise to the challenge, because you have already shown yourselves to be among the finest young men of your generation. Leading a platoon is a lonely job. Sometimes you are going to feel isolated out there in the field. You will wonder why you are there and what you are doing. But let me assure you: your patrols are essential to our strategy for defeating the enemy. I would even say that platoons like those you will be commanding are the spearhead of the Army here in Vietnam. This is a lieutenants' war.'

A senior NCO conducts the next lesson. He explains that the

Division consists of three brigades, of something over 1,500 men each. Most of the time, we will be operating in battalion strength, five or six hundred men moving into a designated Area of Operations (AO). 'As you gentlemen will be aware, each battalion is made up of four companies, designated A, B, C and D, each of which is subdivided into four platoons, thirty to forty men strong. Your task as lieutenants will be to lead one of these platoons. Under your command will be a platoon sergeant and four or five NCO squad leaders – corporals or sergeants – each leading a squad of eight GIs.'

At the battalion Command Post (CP) – also known as the firebase – is an artillery company, equipped with heavy guns of 105-mm calibre. These can bring down devastating fire anywhere within a radius of perhaps 10–12 kilometres, over an AO of perhaps 400 square kilometres. Each firebase is fortified with semi-permanent sandbag-and-earth bunkers and perimeter wire. The other three companies operate from less fortified Landing Zones (LZs) somewhere within this area, with a weapons platoon defending each LZ and the other three platoons from each company out on foot patrol. If any of them is attacked, they can call down artillery fire in support. 'These foot patrols are sweep search-and-destroy missions, generally of several days' duration. Your men will be carrying their own kit, but you will be resupplied twice daily by helicopter whenever weather conditions permit.

'This is a hit-and-run enemy,' concludes the sergeant. 'He spends most of his time in hiding. You gentlemen are here to flush him out.'

I remember a scene from my childhood in Yorkshire, of putting ferrets down burrows to flush out a rabbit warren. We're going to be like those ferrets. Only these rabbits can kill.

The same afternoon, another senior NCO briefs us on the enemy's weaponry. We see captured mortars and a big, heavy

.50-calibre machine-gun on wheels – how the hell do they pull this around in the hills, I wonder. But obviously they do. The sergeant then hands round a captured enemy rifle. 'This piece is an AK-47, a Chinese copy of the Russian Kalashnikov. It's Charlie's main weapon: well made, reliable, practically indestructible. Much lower maintenance than the M-16. It fires a conventional 7.62 round, like our machine-guns – a bigger and more destructive round than the M-16. Plenty of experts think it's a better rifle.'

The orientation-school briefings continue throughout the next two or three days. We endure seemingly endless lectures, talks and briefings. By the end of it all I am longing to get out of the base to a place where people aren't talking at me all the time. I discover that I can expect to be out in the field for perhaps ten months of my twelve-month tour. The remainder is likely to be spent on guard duty here, in and around An Khe.

A captain from intelligence warns us to expect increased Vietcong activity over the coming weeks in the run-up to the South Vietnamese elections. Charlie will be doing what he can to disrupt them and intimidate the local population into voting against the Government, or not voting at all. Our units are on alert throughout the country in expectation of this. Moreover, we are on the verge of the monsoon season. During this period before the rains, the Vietcong will be trying to infiltrate South Vietnam and set up supply caches to sustain them through the coming year. Part of our mission will be to locate and destroy such caches.

There is a constant succession of officers flying into the base and flying out again, and whenever I get the chance I question them about the conditions I can expect out in the field. Of course, experienced platoon leaders like to make fun of green lieutenants like me. 'Oh, man, you are *dead*!' is a typical response. But, from what I can gather, there doesn't seem to have been too much contact with the enemy recently, beyond the occasional sniper who is often more of a nuisance than a real danger.

As well as our own boys, there are loads of South Vietnamese soldiers around the base, known as ARVNs (Army Republic of Vietnam). I'm not too impressed by what I see of them. They don't seem very well trained. From what I'm told, their senior officers seem to be appointed because of their contacts rather than on merit. The talk among our guys is that the ARVNs stay close to the rear, and when they move up to the front line they desert at an alarming rate.

While I wait for my orders to go out into the field, I assemble my kit from the commissary: compass, maps, binoculars, flashlight, entrenching tool, canteen, helmet, helmet liner and cloth camouflage cover, fatigues, flak jacket, poncho, webbing, canvas boots, pack, mattress, combat knife, Colt .45 cavalry pistol and holster and, of course, rifle. The standard issue is the M-16; I choose a snub-nosed version known as the CAR-15. According to the commissary sergeant, this combat assault rifle is often issued to officers. About a foot shorter than the M-16, it will be much handier in the confined conditions in which we will be patrolling, although of course it's bound to be less accurate at long range than a weapon with a longer muzzle. It isn't always easy to get what you want: more a case of 'grab what you can' when you can. I've been advised that it's worth crossing the palm of the commissary sergeant to get the right kit, because if he's inclined to be cussed he can hide behind enough red tape to make it almost impossible otherwise – so I slip him twenty bucks.

Both the M-16 and the CAR-15 have a very fast rate of fire, faster than the AK-47. Neither has much recoil, so they can be fired straight from the hip.

One of the sergeants warns us not to load up our packs with anything that we won't need. Even the minimum is quite heavy enough, given the conditions we'll be patrolling in. Apparently some guys start out carrying around lots of personal stuff, heavy transistor radios and so forth. They soon discard all but the most essential items once they begin humping them around all day long in the field.

After we've sorted out our weapons, we're each given a hundred rounds and encouraged to head for the wire and blaze away at anything we like, provided it's outside the perimeter. Once everybody starts firing it's like a madhouse; the noise is unbelievable. I just hope there aren't any civilians hanging around out there.

I've started thinking about what it must be like to kill someone. I keep imagining armed Vietnamese in the sights of my rifle. I see them trying to rush the wire, carrying rifles with fixed bayonets, shrieking fierce slogans as they approach. I have one in my sights now. I squeeze the trigger, and he throws up his hands in horror, falling backwards under the impact of the bullet. The body rolls in the dirt, twitches, and then is still.

It's my turn tonight for a spell of night-time perimeter defence. As darkness falls, two of us relieve another pair of soldiers manning a bunker a few yards inside the wire. I have my CAR-15 and a bunch of flares, plus rations and a drink. A sergeant explains the drill. Our job is to stay awake, and to raise the alarm if we see anything suspicious. Anyone approaching should be challenged to produce the password. If in doubt, shoot.

I settle down inside the bunker. It's dug chest-deep into the soil, the sides supported by sandbags that project above ground level another two or three feet. There's a side entrance, and a slit window facing out. Above our heads is a roof of corrugated steel, covered with more sandbags. This is a permanent bunker, as big as a small room and well drained. There's one of these every forty or so yards along the perimeter, so that you can maintain visual contact and communicate from one to the other by shouting. Each sector of the perimeter is controlled from a command-post bunker.

The other guy in the bunker with me is an experienced trooper. Though I'm an officer and he's not, I don't feel superior to him – quite the contrary, in fact. His experience – 'in-country' – gives him an authority over anyone just arrived. You ignore that rule at your peril.

It's obvious he doesn't want to chat. We agree to maintain watch in shifts of a couple of hours each. I will take the first watch. The other guy slumps on the ground, his helmet tilted forward over his eyes. I think he's asleep.

I peer out through a gap in the sandbags, my CAR-15 propped up in the bunker beside me. Immediately in front is a zone fifty or sixty yards deep, filled with row after row of razor-sharp concertina wire. Then beyond there's a further thirty or forty yards littered with booby-traps: mines, trip-wires, flares, and fifty-gallon oil-drums buried in the earth facing outwards at an angle of 45°, filled with what we call 'fugas' – a mixture of diesel and napalm, ignited electrically. I've seen a demonstration: it's quite impressive. When the drum explodes, pieces of burning napalm are hurled all over the place. Napalm is nasty stuff: it goes on burning after it sticks to the skin. That's why the drums face outward.

By now it's completely dark. I can't see anything further than the first few rolls of wire, except when artillery fire lights up the scrub outside the perimeter for an instant. It's an eerie experience, looking through the wire and knowing the enemy may be out there, watching us from only a hundred yards away. Strangely, all these defensive barriers don't make me feel especially secure. I can't help thinking that Charlie must be pretty formidable if we need so much protection to keep him out.

*

Early afternoon, and I'm strolling around the base without much to do. I've drunk a few beers; perhaps I'm a little the worse for wear. A jeep with a flat-bed back drives slowly past, and I decide to jump aboard, just for the hell of it. I grab hold of the upright bar as it passes, but I mistime my spring, and my legs trail in the dirt behind the jeep. I don't think the driver has noticed me; in any case, he doesn't slow down or stop. I try to let go of the bar, but my ring is trapped in the metalwork and I find myself being dragged along for several yards before the ring breaks, releasing me. As I get up, I'm already furious with myself for my stupidity. I could easily have broken my finger. I search for the broken pieces, but it's obvious that the ring can't be repaired. The more I think about it, the more depressed I feel. Debbie had that ring inscribed for me on our last full day together. It was a token of her love. And now it's destroyed, before I've even gone out into the field. If I were a superstitious man, I'd say that was a bad omen.

It's the evening before I'm due to fly out by helicopter into the field. All the other guys in my billet have gone to the PX for a drink, but I've stayed behind to write a letter to Debbie. I find myself having to fight down a sense of panic. I'm very restless: I sit on my bunk, then get up again and walk around. But I know I haven't much time if I'm going to get this letter off to Debbie before I leave. I sit down again on the mattress, lean forward and start to write. 'I ask myself: what am I doing here? Why am I here? What do I owe the USA? Certainly not enough to be doing this. If I could leave right now, I would not hesitate.'

12

Day 11 (355 days short): 17 August 1967

It's a hot, steamy, overcast morning. I've been told to report to the helicopter pad at 8.30 a.m. A couple of replacement NCOs are coming along, too. The chopper waiting for us is a 'Huey' – a standard UH1-B helicopter, the workhorse of Vietnam. There's a crew of four: two pilots and two gunners manning big M-60 machine-guns. My attitude to them is similar to that of a guest. These helicopter crews are like cowboys, very much a law unto themselves. We will be riding out about fifty klicks to the battalion's forward supply base, a place called LZ English: funny, that. Besides the three of us, the chopper is carrying the day's supplies to the battalion firebase: food, mainly, and ammunition.

The starter whines, the rotors begin to move slowly, and then they accelerate into a blur. The air is filled with their thudding whoop-whoop-whoop sound. The chopper lifts. In a matter of seconds we've crossed the Green Line. Soon we're cruising, at a height of perhaps two thousand feet. Looking down I can see we're flying over dense jungle, broken here and there by shell-holes and bomb craters like a moth-eaten carpet. Mist hangs off the tops of the trees. Gradually the foothills give way to jungle-covered mountains, their steep sides sliding down sharply into ravines, with trees and bushes poking out at crazy angles. Great boulders litter the flanks, as if temporarily pausing during their tumble into the gorges below. In the clefts I can glimpse the odd glint of water through the canopy. In between the mountains is the occasional high plateau, where I recognize signs of abandoned plantations. Except for the peaks, where the trees surrender to scrub, and the ugly shell-holes, the landscape is an unbroken green, stretching to the horizon. In the distance ahead I can see still higher mountains.

We don't talk much in the chopper. It's too noisy.

As we're riding out, it starts to rain, just a few heavy drops at first and then a downpour. Inside the chopper we're getting wet, so one of the NCOs slides the door closed. Normally the doors are left open all the time, and pretty soon I find out why. It's stiflingly close without the breeze.

After about half an hour we arrive at the firebase. It's located on a hilltop; the trees all around have been flattened by daisy-cutter bombs and bulldozed out of the way. From the air I can see a heavily fortified perimeter and the big artillery pieces in their huge sandbag emplacements, their muzzles pointing into the sky. I can see several vehicles, too, and a road leading into the firebase. As we come in to land at the helipad I put on my helmet and poncho to keep out the wet. I duck out of the chopper and begin looking for the CP, where I'm due to report to the battalion commander. It's hard to see anything much through this torrential rain. Droplets run down my helmet and fall on to my poncho, while more rain collects on my face and drips down over my eyes. The earth beneath my feet is sodden, and the mud clings to my boots. One of the GIs points towards a semi-fortified bunker with a tent roof. I make my way over to it, slipping and sliding in the mud, and give my name to the sentry outside. After a minute or two, I'm invited to step inside. There's the colonel sitting behind a primitive desk. I can see that he's a full colonel – what we call a 'bird colonel' – by his eagle insignia: as opposed to a lieutenant-colonel, who has just a silver leaf cluster. I'm amused to see an ivory-handled Colt .45 pistol poking out from the holster on his hip: clearly a lovingly customized weapon, more for ornament than for use. Like me, he's wet, and my nose tells me that he hasn't washed recently.

I salute, and he gestures to me to sit down. At his prompting I remove my helmet and poncho. 'OK, Abraham, you're Company B,' he tells me. He gives me what the Army calls a 'personal orientation'. Apparently my predecessor was killed in a firefight. I don't say anything except 'Affirmative, sir,' and 'Negative, sir,' from time to time. There isn't much else I can say.

My next stop is to find Company B. I fly out to LZ Sandra with the evening supplies. For short hops like this we fly much lower, just above the treetops. That way the gooks can't see you coming until you're right on top of them. It's still raining.

LZ Sandra is on a much more modest scale than LZ English; if the firebase is like a village, this looks a mere hamlet. There are no permanent fortifications on the perimeter that I can see from the air, just a few rolls of wire and foxholes at regular intervals around the perimeter. The ground has not been scraped clear of boulders and bushes, as it had at LZ English. Beyond the perimeter the jungle seems threateningly close. I can see tents beside the foxholes, and more in the middle of the LZ. The company CP is the only bunker, with just a few simple sandbag emplacements for the mortars, much smaller than the massive fortifications around the artillery pieces on the firebase. The helipad is just a patch of cleared ground.

On my arrival at Sandra I ask for the company commander,

and one of the men points out Captain Matthews, a black guy who seems a little older than most of the men – about thirty, I reckon, as I look at him more closely. Like everyone else, he's dressed in fatigues; there's nothing about his uniform to distinguish him from any other grunt on the LZ. I march up and announce myself with a salute. 'Jesus, don't fucking salute me,' he says, looking worried. 'You'll get me killed.' I glance round at the perimeter, suddenly conscious that there could be snipers out there, just waiting to pick off any officers they can identify. The captain smiles, as the water drips off his helmet. I observe that he's not showing any rank. 'Out here in the field,' he says, 'we don't wear any insignia of rank, and there's no saluting. OK?'

'Yes, sir.' I fight down the impulse to salute again.

Matthews unclips the gold lieutenant's bar from my own helmet and hands it to me. 'Now, you put that in your pocket, and don't put it on again until you're back in some nice safe place like An Khe.'

We find another little tent to shelter in while we talk. As the rain drips off us both, he briefs me on the local situation. It seems that Charlie's been pretty quiet lately. He profiles the other officers in the company, as well as the guys in my platoon. Under my command will be Schroeder, a junior sergeant acting for the moment as platoon sergeant, and four squad leaders, another junior sergeant and three corporals. While I'm listening a stray round pierces the tent and buries itself in a box. I'm startled, but Matthews pulls a face and carries straight on.

The captain seems OK – which is just as well, because he's going to be my direct boss from now on. I like his relaxed, authoritative style. It's obvious that he knows what he's about, but he doesn't rub my nose in it. He answers my naïve questions politely. I find out later that he's on his second tour; on his first tour he'd been a platoon leader like me.

When we've finished the captain takes me outside to

introduce me to another of the platoon leaders in B Company, a quiet Virginian called Phil Schwarz. I see that he isn't wearing a lieutenant's bar, either: just a faint smudge of inked-in black in the middle of his helmet, which can't be seen except from close up. I make a mental note to do the same.

Schwarz offers to show me the ropes, and I spend the rest of the day observing him as he organizes his platoon on perimeter duty. He's been in-country three months. I like the careful, low-key way he handles his men. He's a little older than most of us, which may enhance his authority. I gather that he's married, with a young family back home.

That evening I lie on a blow-up mattress in a tent as the rain buckets down outside. It's so hot in here that I'm sweating freely. I'm trying to write a letter to Debbie, but the paper keeps getting soaked. The thought of Debbie stops me feeling too sorry for myself. Back there in the civilized world is a beautiful girl who loves me more than anyone else. That's something to hold on to out here.

Eventually it gets too dark to continue writing. I could go on if I used a torch, but I've been warned not to show a light after dark. I don't want to provide Charlie with an easy target.

Next morning it's stopped raining. I'm flown out in another chopper to take command of my platoon in the field. They've moved in and secured this location the night before, so it should be a relatively safe LZ. I can see coloured smoke ahead, indicating their position. As usual they've chosen a piece of high ground, which has been cleared of trees and undergrowth in the immediate vicinity to provide a clear field of fire. From the air I can see men in foxholes guarding the perimeter and a dozen or so 'hooches' – ponchos studded together down the middle and stretched over bamboo poles to form a kind of makeshift fly-sheet tent – in the centre. It's a typical field bivouac.

The chopper circles the camp and begins its descent. I scarcely feel the impact as it touches down and bounces gently on its skis. I grab my kit and jump out, half running, half walking towards the main camp while some of the men standing by unload. The air is full of leaves and other debris sucked up by the updraught. Then the chopper lifts into the air again. He can't have been on the ground for more than thirty seconds. The throbbing sound of the blades dies away.

I'm alone with my new platoon. Thirty-two men, some of them scrutinizing me curiously as they munch their breakfast. The acting platoon sergeant steps forward to introduce himself. I remember his name: Schroeder. We don't salute. Like all the others, he looks weary and dishevelled, his fatigues stained and torn. There's a strong scent of male animal pervading the camp, like the smell of a menagerie. I feel suddenly self-conscious about my relatively clean fatigues. I scan the men's faces, trying to form some sense of my first command. A few appear friendly; some look hostile; most seem indifferent. I find myself wondering how my predecessor died. 'Oh, my God,' I hear one of the NCOs mutter, 'another fucking new lieutenant – and he's a Limey, too.'

I know that it would be stupid to arrive there and start telling them what to do on day one. All too often a green young lieutenant walks into a new command and starts throwing his weight around. They're bound to resent you if you behave like that. Worse still, it can be dangerous. There's an expression they use out here in Vietnam: FNG, meaning Fucking New Guy. I'm that FNG, and I know there's nothing the men dislike more than a newly arrived gung-ho officer with a map and a compass.

So, once they've finished eating I call together the squad leaders and the platoon sergeant for a talk. 'From what I've heard, you're obviously doing a pretty good job,' I tell them. 'I want you to carry on just as you were while I look, listen and learn. Make no mistake, I'm in command here, but unless I see something going wrong I'm not going to start exercising any control until I have a better understanding of what's going on.'

I can feel the atmosphere relax. I've done something right. It's a start.

Later that morning I begin my first patrol. While the men have been packing up the camp I've been on the radio to my company commander, Captain Matthews. I call him 6; since I'm leader of the second platoon he calls me 2/6. My platoon sergeant is 2/5, and the squad leaders are 2/4 down to 2/1. The leader of the first platoon is 1/6, and so on down the line.

The captain has given me a six-figure map reference to reach by the evening. After studying the map, I gather all the squad leaders together and brief them on the route I've decided upon. At last we're ready to go. Each man has loaded up his pack, with his rifle at the ready. One guy has an M-60 machine-gun over his shoulder, and several others carry M-79 grenade-launchers.

The point man sets off first, and the others follow one by one. Each man stays back ten or fifteen yards from the man in front of him, so that by the time we've all got going we're strung out over perhaps a quarter of a mile. I'm about two-thirds of the way back; directly behind me is the radio operator (RTO).

Within a few hundred yards we leave the cleared area and descend into thick triple-canopy jungle. It's dark, like entering a dimly lit tunnel. From ground level you can glimpse only the occasional small patch of sky. I've never been in country like this before. The tallest trees can be more than a hundred feet high; most of the time their tops are invisible from ground level. There's another layer of smaller trees, and then plants like bamboo, man-high or a little taller. There are plenty of banana plants, with big drooping leaves, and masses of stuff called elephant grass, which looks like reeds but which I find is razor-sharp when I cut the side of my hand on it. Sometimes there are giant herbaceous plants, like a monstrous mutation of something you might expect to find in an English garden. Plenty of the trees are leaning over at crazy angles; all their trunks are covered in sinewy creepers that trail down to the jungle floor. The ground is carpeted with rotting vegetation and fallen trees, some so big that you can't see over them. Where a big tree has fallen recently, there's sometimes a much lighter clearing, and often a grove of saplings already forcing their way upwards to begin the cycle again.

There's so much growing here that most of the time it's difficult to see more than a few yards in any direction. Often you lose sight of the man in front of you. The dark, leathery leaves rustle a protest as you push your way through.

Down here under three layers of foliage the air is even more hot and humid and, of course, there's no breeze. Within minutes the sweat is pouring down my back and running down the side of my face. My new canvas boots chafe my feet, and the pack bites into my shoulders. Mosquitoes dance around my face.

The forest is full of the background noises of birds and insects; every now and then there is the rustle of something bigger in the undergrowth. There are supposed to be all sorts of animals here in the jungle: from little flying squirrels right up to elephant and rhinoceros. It's hard to distinguish anything clearly because the foliage breaks up outlines. I keep expecting an ambush at any moment. The first time I hear a monkey moving in the trees, I dive for cover. The men near enough to see try not to laugh.

It's very slow going. When there is any form of trail it winds around natural obstacles, fallen tree trunks and big boulders. At one point we follow the edge of a gorge, high above a fast-flowing river. Much of the time we're moving uphill, hauling ourselves forward and slipping in the mud. Next moment we'll be swinging from branch to branch, trying to stop ourselves crashing down a steep ravine. When we're not following an established trail, the point man hacks away the undergrowth with his machete. The rest of us can't move forward until he's cleared a path for us. And we keep halting. Whenever the point man sees anything suspicious – anything out of the ordinary, even the slightest thing – he drops down into a low-profile position and signals the man behind to stop. The same thing happens right along the line, the men going down like a row of dominoes. Then his squad leader goes forward to investigate. Crouching low, he asks the point man, 'What do you see?' It could be a slight movement in the undergrowth up ahead, or maybe he's heard something. If the squad leader agrees that it's significant, then he'll pass the word back down the line for me. 'Send up the LT.'

I make my way up the line, not knowing what to expect. The squad leader and the point man are waiting for me. The point man uses his rifle to push aside some leaves and undergrowth strewn over the trail and there it is, a pit six feet deep, bristling with punji sticks.

I stare down, imagining what it would be like to fall into this pit. The sudden alarm of vertigo as the ground beneath you gives way, then the crunch as the stakes drive deep into your legs, snapping bones as they tear through the soft flesh. The sense of helplessness as you lie there impaled, your hot blood sinking into the earth. The hideous pain as you try to move. The growing despair, as the realization dawns that you're going to die.

I feel a rush of anger against this cruel trap. I tell one of the men to destroy it with a white phosphorus grenade, a 'Willie Peter'. The intense heat this throws out will burn all the stakes. I make the men stand well back. These grenades explode with a pop rather than a loud bang; they scatter pieces of burning phosphorus, which sticks to your skin and burns straight through your flesh. We wait until the white smoke has cleared. Then we move on, more carefully than before.

There are dozens of such alerts that first day. Sometimes there's something to investigate, sometimes nothing at all. One time I'm called forward, and when I reach the point man he gestures towards a large animal about fifty yards off the trail. It's a water buffalo. The Vietnamese domesticate buffalo, so perhaps there's somebody around. The sergeant and I decide to send out a handpicked squad to reconnoitre. An hour later they're back again. No sign of anyone.

By now it's raining heavily. Soon we're squelching around in mud up to our knees. It's almost a relief when we reach a river and have to wade through waist-high water, carrying our weapons high above our heads. I see now why the men wear their fatigues tucked into their boots: the water's full of leeches. I find one on the back of my hand, about three inches long, and shake it off in disgust.

The rain stops around five o'clock that evening. Half an hour later we reach the destination designated by the company commander. This is on a small hillock, so it's comparatively clear of jungle. Immediately the platoon sergeant organizes a defensive perimeter, setting the men to dig a ring of perhaps a dozen foxholes about ten yards apart. I can see that it's not easy. The ground is a tangle of roots, and full of stones. An entrenching tool doesn't make an ideal spade. Some of the other guys are clearing the brush, and a small group sets to work felling any trees, wrapping white detonation cord round the trunks and then blowing them up with C-4 plastic explosive. Within half an hour or so we have a makeshift LZ. Three areas of ground have been completely cleared as potential helipads. About fifty yards outside the perimeter a squad places mines and flares, some rigged to trip-wires. Other guys set up hooches close to each foxhole, one for every two men. Half the platoon will be on watch at any one moment, and this makes it easy to change over. I tell the sergeant that I want to do my share of watch duty, though as the platoon leader I'm the only one who doesn't have to do this.

The hooches keep the rain off, and we sleep on blow-up mattresses. It's pretty damn luxurious, really. Mind you, there's no pillow, no sheet, no blanket, and no netting to keep the mosquitoes off.

While the sergeant organizes the watch rosters, I radio the command post to say that we're ready to receive a chopper. A few minutes later they radio back to tell me one is on its way. I order the men to pop smoke canisters, to indicate our position to the approaching helicopter. Soon red, white and blue smoke is pouring into the air, from canisters scattered around the LZ. Of course, the smoke also advertises to any enemy troops in the vicinity that a chopper will be arriving here soon. In the early days in Vietnam, before we started using coloured smoke as a code, Charlie had been known to decoy helicopters by sending up his own smoke. Now the main danger to the choppers is from attack while they're hovering stationary above the ground, when they're at their most vulnerable to incoming fire. The reason for releasing several different-coloured smoke-canisters around the LZ is to confuse any watching enemy soldiers, so that they won't know where the helicopter will be landing until the very last moment.

Minutes later I can hear the throb of the rotor blades. Suddenly he's here, scudding across the tops of the trees. I call the pilot on the radio: 'Identify smoke.'

The pilot's voice comes in clear over the radio: 'I identify red, white and blue.'

Looking up, I can see him in the cockpit. 'Go for blue.'

Now there's a man standing beside the can of billowing blue smoke, waving him in. The chopper hovers overhead like a predator. Then he descends slowly, scattering dust and other debris across the campsite. The downdraught is wonderfully refreshing in this sticky heat. As the chopper hovers over the LZ just off the ground, several of our men run forward to unload the supplies. Within less than a minute, the chopper is airborne once more, tilting forward and accelerating until he disappears over the trees.

We're on our own again. When the throbbing of the helicopter blades fades into the distance, the jungle seems suddenly very quiet, ominously so.

But at least the chopper's brought us some chow. On the menu tonight is beef stew, eaten straight out of the can. Sadly no vegetarian option tonight, boys.

By the time we've finished eating it's getting dark. The sun goes down very fast out here. Above the low sound of talk and occasional laughter I can hear the chirping of the cicadas and the croaking of the frogs. Every few seconds I hear the whine of a mosquito coming close and I swat it away. The men finish their preparations for the night, because once it's dark you've got to maintain light discipline. Some are writing letters, others cleaning weapons, yet others just smoking and staring into the distance. The musky smell of marijuana drifts across the campsite.

'They seem like a pretty square bunch of men,' I write to Debbie. 'I am not scared yet. The only thing that frightens me is that I do not know if I am man enough to lead them and care for them in the way I know I must.'

By seven o'clock it's pitch-dark. Those who aren't on guard duty in the foxholes have settled down for the night in their hooches. I share mine with my RTO. We don't undress, we don't even take off our boots. No one wishes me good night.

And that's what it's like, day after day. Humping that damn pack up and down hills, scrambling up riverbanks and across boulders. Trying to avoid becoming entangled in the vines that lurk around my ankles. Just existing is a trial. Feeling like a blob as the rain drips down my nose. Or sweltering in the heat, sweating from every pore. If I put my rifle down in the sun, it's too hot to pick up again. Always tired, because I can't sleep properly in this heat. Wearing the same clothes for weeks on end, and hardly ever taking off my boots. Socks rot on my feet, and briefs bring me out in jungle rash. I'm covered in mosquito bites and welts left by leeches. My hands are lined with cuts and punctured by thorns. When we're ordered back to the CP after a week's patrol I haven't had even a glimpse of Charlie or heard a shot fired in anger. I'm beginning to wonder what this war is all about.

13

Day 20 (346 days short): 29 August 1967

My platoon has made camp for the night. Everybody's wet; it's been raining all day. The sky is darkening fast. I'm lying in my hooch, trying to read a letter from Debbie that came in with the evening chopper. I hold it up to catch the last light from outside, and a large raindrop falls on the paper, smudging the words. With a sigh, I fold it up and put it carefully into my pocket, then turn over on to my back and stare up at the canvas. I light a cigarette and draw deep, blowing out the smoke in one long exhalation. A moment later the man lying on the mattress next to mine speaks. 'It must be nice to have someone back home who cares about you, huh?'

It's Bruce Schroeder, the acting platoon sergeant, the nearest thing I have to a friend out here. A tall, gangling guy with buck teeth. A bit green, but game for anything. From a little town somewhere in southern Illinois.

'Yes, it's nice.' I'm thinking about the letter from Debbie, when she said she'd been invited to a party. All the guys will be after Debbie; she's so pretty. I imagine her drinking cheap wine, and giggling as a boy puts his arm round her. But it's no good worrying: the party will have happened by now anyway. The rain drums down outside.

'I don't have anyone,' Schroeder continues. 'There was a girl back home, but she found some other guy.'

'That's too bad.'

'Yeah, ain't life a bitch?'

Debbie has a flatmate called Anthea, a very pretty nurse, who for some mysterious reason doesn't have a boyfriend. I tell Schroeder about her. He seems interested. I suggest to him that he should write to her. At first he shies away from the idea, but the next evening he shows me a letter he's written to Debbie, asking if Anthea would like him to write. He tells her what a fine chap I am. I enclose his letter with one of my own, and a photograph showing the two of us together.

The next day I get another letter from Debbie with the evening chopper. She describes the party. Everybody drinking and having a good time. She keeps thinking about me, wondering if I'm safe. She can't help imagining my body lying cold and pale, being zipped into a black bag. Suddenly she can't bear it any more. She runs into the kitchen and starts crying her eyes out.

It's tough for her, too.

It's our turn to spend a while here at the CP on LZ Sandra. Each platoon rotates around the CP, patrolling a different area in turn, then spends a while defending the CP while the others are out on patrol.

We're extending our perimeter defence, clearing jungle and building new bunkers. It's hard physical labour, made worse by the rain and the mud. I'm with some of my men in the woods, cutting support beams for the bunkers with chain saws, when suddenly I'm poleaxed from behind. It's like being attacked by a giant wielding a huge club. I lie stunned for a moment or two. I'm face down. I feel scratches on my face and neck, and I'm aching in various places. Have I been shot? Something is pressing down on top of me, and there's a heavy smell of damp earth and leaves. I hear anxious voices. Twisting my head, I can't see anything but branches on either side. I remember lying on my face in the tree-house in our Yorkshire garden, with Rick holding me down, his knee in my back.

I feel the weight on me ease, and I close my eyes as branches brush across my head. Someone is asking me if I'm OK. I roll over stiffly and groan. Then I stagger to my feet, piecing together what's happened. An engineer bulldozer has come rumbling up and pushed a tree over on top of me. Fortunately its branches cushioned its fall; otherwise I'd certainly have been killed. As it is, I'm able to walk away with nothing worse than bruises and scratches. I didn't mind these so much as the fact that the St Christopher medallion Debbie gave me is damaged. I can't help feeling superstitious about this. I take the medallion off its chain and attach it to my dog tag.

A few days later I'm whacking away at the scrub with a great big Bowie knife, its blade about twelve inches long. The knife glances off a tree and gashes me on the forehead. There's quite a lot of blood, and my head needs to be stitched up at the aid station. Some facetious debate ensues about whether I should be put forward for a Purple Heart, the award given for wounds received in action. 'I don't think I can recommend you for one on this occasion,' says Captain Matthews, grinning.

I'm lying in my hooch, writing another letter to Debbie as the rain drums down on the canvas. It's been raining incessantly for the past two days. The ground is soaking; it's impossible to keep anything dry. 'I have been here nearly three weeks and I have not even seen the enemy yet,' I complain. 'Meanwhile

I have nearly been hit by a stray round, I have had a tree fall on me and now I have cut myself on the head with my own knife. It all seems like such a waste of time and effort. What am I doing here, I ask myself.'

Phil Schwarz flies into the LZ for a few hours, leaving his platoon in the field. He spends some time with the company commander. Afterwards, we sit on the ground talking while he waits for a chopper to take him back. It's good to be able to chat to another platoon leader: we can discuss problems that I can't share with any of the men, not even Schroeder, and that I wouldn't feel comfortable raising with one of the more senior officers. I tell him how frustrated I am. It seems crazy that we should be slogging through the jungle like this every day. When are we going to see some action? I've been out in the field for a month now, and I still haven't seen anything of the enemy. Occasionally someone takes a pot shot at us from the hills, but these aren't serious snipers, probably just a small cell of two or three gooks who happen to be passing. We never see them, and so far they haven't hit any of us. Of course I'm glad that no one in my platoon has been hurt, but I can't see the point of patrolling like this. The only 'Vietcong' I've actually seen are a middle-aged woman and her six-month-old baby whom we picked up and brought back to the company CP. They're lucky to be alive, because we found them wandering about in what we call a 'free fire' zone, where anyone who moves is assumed to be Vietcong and is liable to be shot on sight.

As I pour out my frustrations, a wry expression creeps over Schwarz's features. When I'm finished, he begins to speak. His quiet Southern drawl seems to put all my problems into perspective. Relax, he says. I should be grateful not to be shot at all the time. And it's the same for everyone. Very few patrols report confirmed kills. The average kill rate for a whole battalion is less than one gook per day. Charlie is keeping low. But don't be fooled, he says. Charlie's around, and he's almost certainly watching you. Stay alert. He pats my arm, gets up and heads for the helipad.

It's ten thirty one early September morning. We're moving out.

We flew into the firebase yesterday, up to ten men crammed into each Huey. Now the whole battalion is getting ready to fly down to the lowlands, to forestall Vietcong activity nearer the population centres in the week running up to the election.

It's an awesome sight. There are dozens, no, scores of helicopters lined up, ranging from Hueys to Chinooks, the long choppers with two main rotor blades fore and aft used for transporting artillery pieces, through to the really huge ones I know only as 'Cranes', which can pick up pretty much anything. Guys on the ground use hand-signals to shepherd these big brutes into the correct formation. All these choppers, filling the air with the thudding sound of their blades. When you see something like this, you can't believe that Charlie has a chance in hell.

We're still out on patrol every day, just as before, only now we're not having to hike up and down hills all day long because the terrain here is pretty flat. Lots of paddy-fields, many of them flooded, separated by high dikes, with occasional ridges and patches of woodland. Every now and then a village.

We're all a bit jumpy here because we know that more of the enemy are around. But the first day passes without incident. On our second day of patrolling we come across a mud hut that has been occupied very recently by Vietcong. There's still some of their stuff strewn around. Among the debris we find a quantity of opium. Afterwards we set light to the hut and burn it to the ground.

A mile or so further on, we're moving cautiously along a trail through thick woodland when the men in front of me stop. I'm towards the rear of the patrol. Word comes back down the line that I'm needed up ahead. I make my way forward. There's an expression of disgust on the point man's face, and when I reach him I understand why: the stench of rotting flesh hangs in the air. He shows me the body, a few feet off the trail. It's swollen to the size of a cow; the flesh has blackened; the legs project stiffly into the air. As we approach the smell becomes almost overpowering. I take shallow breaths, stifling an impulse to retch. It's my duty to investigate, though my instinct is to turn and get away as quickly as possible. At least it's not a woman or a child. From the length of the hideously bloated corpse, I would guess that the man was Vietnamese, though the flesh is so blackened that it's hard to be certain. The body's been stripped of clothing and equipment. I approach warily, knowing that these corpses are often booby-trapped. Crawling things feast on a wound beside his ear. His hands are tied. An execution, then. Using a stick, I poke around for his dog tag, but if he ever had one, it's gone. There's nothing to identify this dead man: all I can say for certain is that he wasn't American.

I walk back to the trail. I'm not going to put my men through the horror of burying this revolting piece of rotten meat. We pass by, leaving the body to the flies, which have already devoured much of the face. In a matter of days it will disappear, becoming one with the jungle.

A black night, not even the stars to see by. So dark that I can't even see my own body in the foxhole. I try to fix the memory of the ground in front of me, but it's hard to hold it in my mind when it's no longer visible. Distances expand and contract, shapes alter, and the ground ripples in the dark.

The rain stopped about an hour ago. The dripping slows and

eventually ceases. Now there are just the usual night sounds: croaking, chirping, rustling.

Fork lightning flashes on the horizon. Several seconds later, a distant rumble of thunder. More lightning, moving ever further away. Then nothing.

I'm suddenly alert. A primitive sensation of imminent danger crawls across my skin. What is it? I peer out into the darkness, sniffing the air, straining to catch the slightest sound. And then I realize what has been nagging at the corner of my mind: the animals have fallen silent.

Very carefully, I slip off the safety catch and lift my rifle to my cheek, cramming the stock into my shoulder. And wait.

If I were to start firing into the blackness, the muzzle flashes could reveal my position to anyone watching. Almost worse, it would wake the whole platoon and send every man running for cover. I don't want them to think I'm nervous. They're beginning to accept me, but I'm still on probation.

The dark seems to intensify. I keep thinking that I hear movement. The idea grows in my mind that a fanatical VC is creeping towards me, now almost within touching distance. I have to fight down a sense of panic.

A low, mocking laugh from beyond the perimeter, shockingly close. I can't stand it any more. I unclip a grenade, pull the pin and hurl it out into the dark. As the explosion illuminates the scene, I'm both relieved and humiliated to see nobody there.

While we've been here in the lowlands I've been assigned a new platoon sergeant. Maybe the company commander feels that I need a more experienced man than Schroeder to help me, I don't know. These things are not always spelt out. This new guy McCoy is regular Army, and regular Army NCOs often look down their noses at draftees and rookie lieutenants like me. I don't take to him, and I don't reckon he thinks much of me, either. His whole manner suggests that I don't know what I'm doing. I can see that I'm going to have to prove myself worthy of his respect.

We're conducting push operations, sweeping though the AO and rounding up any suspicious-looking civilians, ready to be handed over to the South Vietnamese police for questioning. Most of all, we're here to reassure the civilian population, to protect them from VC intimidation in the run-up to the elections.

We've just entered a village, perhaps twenty buildings, all hovels made of mud and straw on a wooden frame. A couple of the squads have circled it beforehand and secured the perimeter. Now the rest of us are moving in, weapons at the ready.

There aren't many people about: hardly any men between fifteen and fifty, just a few old guys with wispy beards, and more women, all wearing black pyjama-style trousers and sandals. Most also wear shallow conical hats made of reed. Half-naked children run around, getting under our feet and chattering excitedly. My men search each hut one by one, herding the people out into the open, then checking for hiding places or caches where food or weapons might be stored. So far we've drawn a blank. The people seem friendly, smiling or grumbling in what sounds to be good-humoured Vietnamese. One beautiful young woman smiles at me, and I smile back.

The squad leaders report that the village is 'clean', so we begin to move out. As we leave it behind, we pass several small plantations of sugar cane. I'm standing on the edge of the trees, looking back along the line towards the village, when I notice one of the men towards the rear of the patrol leave the track and enter one of these plantations. I know all the men by name now; this one is King, a big, slow-talking Southerner, with a quiet, gentle manner. He must have decided that he's going to hack off a stem of sugar cane and suck it for a bit of sweetness. You'd often see guys on patrol do this. It's such a common sight that I don't give it a second thought. Then the plantation explodes.

The first thing I know is that I'm lying on the ground face down, the palms of my hands covering my ears. The roar of the explosion is still echoing through my brain. I look up carefully. I can see flames and smoke swirling from where the plantation used to be. I hear screaming. Are we under attack? The guys nearby shelter on the ground, weapons at the ready, scanning the surrounding cover anxiously. I crawl across to the nearest squad leader, and order him to organize the men into taking up a defensive position. But after a minute or two it's clear that there's no incoming fire. A booby-trap, then.

I make my way back down the line to the now devastated sugar plantation. Several wounded men lie on the ground groaning; one receives emergency treatment from the platoon paramedic. It's pretty obvious by now what's happened. The poor sucker with a sweet tooth must have detonated a mine when he entered the plantation. I turn away in disgust from the sight of his entrails hanging from a stump of sugar cane, and radio to the CP to request emergency medical assistance. The chopper's already in the air by the time I've worked out our co-ordinates and radioed them in. Then I tell the squad leader to clear up the mess. I find it hard to keep the shakiness out of my voice.

All day long I keep thinking about it. Charlie's a crafty bastard. I reckon that he's been watching American soldiers leaving the trail for a taste of sugar, and worked out that this habit presents an opportunity for a booby-trap. A trip-wire, just inside the plantation, all the way around, linked to a Claymore mine or maybe a group of mines in the middle. I could see the remains of the wire afterwards. When the mine detonated, King must have been shredded by hundreds of pellets half a centimetre in diameter, at point-blank range.

What gets me is thinking of that smiling girl in the village. She, like all the other villagers, must have known that the mine was there but, like them, she was quite happy to let us go and blow ourselves up. Nobody gave us a hint, not even the slightest warning. And these are the people we're here to protect.

That night one of the booby-traps outside the defensive perimeter detonates. The men send up flares and fire dozens of rounds towards the place where it exploded. In all the noise and confusion, it's hard to be sure whether there's any fire coming back. We don't see anyone moving out there, and we don't take any casualties. For the rest of the night the whole platoon remains on high alert. Dawn comes up very fast; one moment the sky is glowing red, the next moment the sun has risen over the horizon. I take a squad out to investigate. We search all around, but we find nothing, nothing at all.

As usual, I plot the route to the destination the company commander's given me before we set out in the morning. Then I brief McCoy and the squad leaders. McCoy favours another, more direct route. I say no, that route means following a trail likely to be booby-trapped. In addition, it means exposing us to the risk of ambush as we pass through a ravine. I've chosen this route to avoid such unnecessary risks to the platoon.

McCoy persists with his objections. His way will be quicker, he says, and he doesn't want his men to be patrolling longer than they have to be. I don't want *my* men to get killed, I snap back. In my view, a good patrol is a patrol on which none of my men gets hurt. Like the guy with the sweet tooth? McCoy asks sarcastically. For a moment I can't find a reply: he's got below my guard. Then I cut him short. I've decided on the route I want us to take, and that's the end of it.

He's not happy, but I can't help that. The safety of the men is my responsibility, not his.

The rest of the day passes without incident. That evening I'm sitting alone eating my chow, gazing out at the sun going down over the hills, when one of the men strolls over to join me. It's Ehrlich, one of the freakier characters in the platoon. He wears a bandanna tied round his head, and he's stoned a lot of the time. Schroeder told me that before Ehrlich was called up he lived in a hippie commune in San Francisco's Haight-Ashbury district. I'm a little wary of him; but, according to Schroeder, Ehrlich's a good man to have with you in a fight: cool under fire, with the highest number of confirmed kills in the platoon.

I gesture for him to sit down, and he lights a cigarette. We talk about nothing in particular for a few moments, and then he suddenly starts speaking, as if there's something he's been brooding on all day.

'LT, what happened yesterday, that wasn't your fault. Shit happens. There's something you should know. Morale in this platoon has improved a hundred per cent since you took over.

'The lieutenant we had before, he was an asshole. Going out on patrol with him was fucking bad news. One time we couldn't even find the LZ, we were jerking around in the boonies, and we all knew that he was fucking lost. It got so dark that we had to camp right there in the middle of the jungle, with no perimeter or anything, just hoping that Charlie wasn't in the AO.

'The men are happy serving under you. You're organized, and you know what you're doing – that's what the men like. That's what *I* like. Most of us just want to make it through our tour of duty and go home in one piece. We want a lieutenant who looks out for us.'

I turn to look at him in the gathering gloom. Finally I smile. 'Thank you, Ehrlich.'

I'm dreaming about Debbie, remembering her face when we said goodbye at Baltimore airport. How she broke away and disappeared behind the barrier without looking back.

'LT!'

Someone is shaking me. Price, one of the squad leaders, a coloured guy from the Bronx.

I'm lying in my hooch, still half asleep. 'What is it?' I groan.

'LT, wake up.' Price is an easy-going fellow. Most of the time he has a rich, relaxed voice. Now he sounds anxious.

I sit up. It's still dark. What's happened?

'It's McLellan. I can't find him. I think he must have gone outside the perimeter.'

I'm pulling on my boots now. 'How long ago was this?'

'About half an hour.'

Jesus, doesn't the guy know any better than to go wandering around at night? I picture McLellan, a tubby Irish boy with laughing eyes. The life and soul of the platoon. It seems that he was on guard duty and told the other guards he was going for a crap. He said he'd be back in five minutes. Fuck, fuck, fuck. I suppose it's quite easy to get lost in the dark, but how on earth did he get out without triggering off the perimeter defences?

I ponder the alternatives. Either he's lost, or he's been captured. If we send out a search party, we could be walking straight into an ambush. If there are VC around, he's probably dead by now; if he's just lost, we've more chance of finding him in the morning. Then I imagine a naked McLellan, tied to a tree, hot blood bubbling from his throat and flowing down his body into the earth. I know we can't leave him out there.

Just then I hear a shout from the perimeter. I make my way over there, picking my way across the camp in the dark. One of the men shines a flashlight out from his foxhole towards a trembling figure, about thirty yards beyond the wire: McLellan. Together we guide him in, past the mines and the trip-wires. It's some time before he can speak. It seems he became disorientated when he couldn't find his flashlight. The poor boy is terrified.

A few days later the battalion is flown up to the vicinity of An Loa, at the foot of the hills north of An Khe. It seems that Charlie has been very active in this area lately. Our platoon is going in first, to secure a new LZ. We're riding there in seven helicopters. This is what we call a 'combat assault', because we know there's a possibility of coming under fire as we land. There's a sick feeling of fear in my stomach at the prospect.

The choppers approach in arrowhead formation, like a gaggle of geese, so that the door gunners on the outside have a clear field of fire. Each chopper comes in low and fast over a paddy-field, and remains hovering several feet off the ground as we all pile out at the double. We hit the ground running: as the choppers leave, we make for the nearest cover as quickly as we can, splashing though the shallow water and spreading out as we do. There's a dike round the field. It's tempting to dive on to the slope of the embankment when you're landing in a 'hot' LZ, but we've been warned not to do that. The enemy's seen us do it too many times, and the insides of the embankments are often festooned with punji sticks. Landing on one of these wouldn't be fatal, of course, but in some ways Charlie prefers injuries to kills. A wounded soldier needs other soldiers to care for him. From their point of view, the more Americans they can take out of the front line, the better.

This time there's no enemy fire as we land. While some men remain on alert for any possible attack, the others begin to prepare a defensive perimeter for the new LZ. The day passes without any contact with the enemy. In the morning we'll be setting out on patrol.

We're following a trail upriver along the left bank. The water runs fast and dark, forcing its way through the boulders scattered across the riverbed. Its banks are more than man-high, and in places heavily undercut; it must flood later during the monsoon. To the left of the trail are open fields; the far bank is thickly wooded. I'd like to send a squad across the river to sweep through the woods and flush out any gooks that might be hiding there. But the river's too deep to cross.

Ahead the river curves round in a bend to the left, so that here the other bank is facing us. I've halted the men and moved up to the front of the platoon. Something about this place makes me uneasy. I scan the opposite bank through my binoculars. Nothing. So what is it? Am I getting too jumpy? Trust your instincts, Abraham. I glance down, and notice that the left-hand edge of the trail is slightly darker. Looking closer, I see that some of the vegetation has been flattened, as if people have been leaving it here. And maybe those are faint traces of a path through the field, rejoining it another fifty yards or so further on. Perhaps there is a booby-trap up ahead? I tell the men that we're leaving the trail here. I can see that not all of them are convinced of the need for this detour, but I'm not going to let that worry me.

Later in the day, we leave the riverbank and follow another trail south. Right now we're advancing though a field of elephant grass towards some trees.

There's a whooshing sound in the air and then the heavy thump of an explosion. Mortar attack! The air is full of smoke and flying debris. I shout to the men to start pulling back. Another whoosh, another thump, closer this time. There's smoke from the trees up ahead where the enemy must be. Bent low, McCoy comes running up. He wants us to split the patrol into three and advance in the direction of the mortar fire. I say no, we have no idea what we're facing up ahead. For all we know, in those trees could be an NVA company with dug-in machine-gun posts. I tell McCoy I'm calling in artillery support. I can see he doesn't like it. Another mortar explosion. I can hear someone screaming. The radio operator is kneeling beside me. I grab the handset and start speaking to the firebase, while with my other hand I fumble with the map, trying to work out exactly where we are. Another explosion. It's hard to concentrate in this shitstorm. When I'm confident of our co-ordinates, I give them to the firebase over the radio, speaking slowly and deliberately despite the chaos all around, and making the guy at the other end repeat them back to me. I tell him I want smoke rounds to begin with. Within ten seconds the first smoke round arrives and drops short, slightly to the left of where the mortar fire seems to be coming from. 'Up one hundred, right one hundred,' I shout into the radio. Another smoke round explodes, much closer this time. 'Up fifty, right twenty-five, then fire for effect.' Ten seconds later shells arrive, pounding the trees up ahead with heavy explosions that make the ground shudder even where we stand. The mortar fire has stopped.

If the co-ordinates had been even slightly wrong, those shells might have been landing on us. It's a good illustration of why accurate map reading is a very important part of my job here.

Price reports one man wounded by mortar-fire; I radio for a medevac chopper. Meanwhile the platoon medic administers emergency first aid. The artillery fires another salvo before I call them off. Then I tell McCoy he can go in, warning him to proceed with caution.

A chopper arrives and takes the wounded man away. McCoy calls on the radio to report that he's found nothing but shell-holes. Whoever was firing at us has gone, leaving no trace.

Tonight we're going to play a little trick on Charlie. We know that he's watching us from the hills above the battalion LZ, so we've been making it look as if we're pulling out, apparently dismantling the perimeter, packing up and loading stuff on to helicopters. Meanwhile we've been camouflaging our bunkers.

As evening falls the choppers leave an apparently deserted LZ. Our men are all hidden in the bunkers. It's very quiet. We're under strict orders not to speak or show ourselves. A deer emerges from the woods and strolls across the LZ, stopping to graze every now and then.

It's now almost dark. I'm in a bunker with my radio operator and one other infantryman. The radio is turned down very low.

Suddenly there's an explosion as something hits one of our trip-wires. A flare ignites, showing dozens of figures just outside the perimeter. Then everyone opens up, and all hell breaks loose. The noise is terrifying. Grenades and rockets rain down on the area where the silhouettes appeared, while machine-gun tracer cuts through the darkness. I'm firing like all the others. In this darkness it's hard to tell whether you've hit someone or not; figures disappear, but whether they've fallen or taken cover is hard to tell.

The firing continues for about five minutes. There doesn't seem to be any incoming. Then another flare goes up. Nothing. The smell of cordite drifts across the camp.

We don't move that night. At dawn we send out a patrol to explore the perimeter. There's plenty of blood about, but not a single body. It seems that we've been firing at ghosts.

14

Day 30 (336 days short): 5 September 1967

A dark, moonless night in the jungle. I sit upright against a huge tree-trunk, a few yards off the trail, my rifle cradled in my arms. I peer through a fringe of leaves, which I'm relying on to conceal me from anyone coming down the trail. Right now it's so dark that I could be sitting right in the middle of it and nobody would see me. A couple of yards behind me one of my men is dozing: I hear his breathing become heavier, and I reach across to nudge him awake. Beyond there are three more, one with a machine-gun. Although they can't be more than a few yards off, I can't see anything of them except the occasional silhouette of a helmet.

An owl hoots in the canopy above, and something small scurries for safety across the forest floor. The jungle goes about its business, as it has done for millions of years.

I'm very tired, but I'm determined to stay awake. Anyway, I'm too terrified to sleep.

Earlier today, we received intelligence reports that enemy

forces were present in this area in considerable strength. Anticipating that they would be moving by night, the colonel ordered us to send out this ambush patrol. The company commander has given me a map reference for the ambush, and that's where we are now. As an officer, I'm not supposed to take part in these ambushes – but it seems to me that I can't order other men to go out time after time without knowing what it's like myself. It's important to set an example. Although I can't prove it, I strongly suspect that a lot of these ambush patrols never go anywhere near the designated ambush site. I think that many find a nice safe place to bunk down and spend the night there instead.

McCoy has handpicked four other men to accompany me. After the evening chow, I gather the ambush party together for a briefing. If anything happens to put me out of action, they'll need to know what to do. The men listen, but they don't say much. All of us are preoccupied with checking and rechecking our kit, making sure that we haven't forgotten anything important. Once we've left the LZ, there'll be no going back until morning.

The five of us leave the camp just before dark, hoping not to be seen. I feel a strong psychological reluctance to venture outside the safety of the perimeter. It's as though this arbitrary line around every campsite has acquired talismanic significance. Inside is home. Outside is . . . outside.

This place is only about half a mile from the camp, but if we do get into a fight there's not much the rest of the platoon can do to help us. We might as well be in a different country.

We arrive just as it begins to get dark. I arrange the men in a standard L-shaped ambush, with the machine-gunner facing up the trail and the others spaced out in a line alongside it, towards the way we expect the enemy to come. The idea is that each of us has a clear line of fire. Of course, it's just too bad if the enemy decides to come the other way.

While the others dig in, I scout round the immediate area – I can't rid myself of the sense that we're being watched. But I don't find anything. I return to the ambush site, and talk to each man individually to make sure he's comfortable and knows what's expected of him. Then I settle down. I have the radio beside me on the ground, the volume turned to the lowest setting. It has an attachment like a telephone that you can speak into and hear messages through. To activate it you click on a rubber-coated bar. I've arranged a code with McCoy that means I don't have to speak: one click means everything OK; two clicks means we're in position; and three clicks danger. I click the bar twice.

In a very short time it's completely dark. I can never get used to how quickly the sun goes down in the tropics. The evening lasts only a matter of minutes. Half an hour ago it was late afternoon and we were still at the camp; now it's night, and we're out here on our own. There's no light in the sky, there's no moon, and cloud covers the stars. At first I can hardly see anything. Gradually, my night vision begins to distinguish details: a tree-trunk, a bush, a rock, the edge of the trail. If he's coming, that's where the enemy will appear. I find myself hoping that he won't come.

For the first few minutes there's a bit of whispering between the men. Then silence descends on the site. Or, rather, other sounds emerge, because the jungle is never quiet. Leaves rustle in the canopy; small creatures scamper through the undergrowth; insects drone relentlessly. Occasionally there's the sound of something larger on the move – a monkey, perhaps – up above.

A toad begins to croak, absurdly loud.

About an hour after nightfall, it starts raining heavily. My poncho is tied tightly round my neck and spread out around my knees, covering my rifle. Soon the earth is running wet. I try to sit on my cape to keep dry. Rain courses down my helmet and drops off on to my poncho. Eventually it stops. The forest is full of the sound of dripping.

As the night deepens, it becomes colder. Fog curls around the trees, concealing outlines, teasing the watcher. I shiver, and huddle within my poncho to keep warm.

I remember hearing some of the guys talk about the creature that lives in the jungle that nobody's ever seen. The Vietnamese have a name for it. It's like a man, but it's not a man, it's an animal with sharp teeth and claws, and it preys on men. It moves at night, stealthily, walking mainly on all fours. Sometimes it comes into villages when everyone's asleep and drags away children. I tell myself that the creature is a myth. But somehow it's not so easy to be certain of this when you're out in the jungle at night.

Fear isn't a logical emotion. It doesn't increase or decrease in proportion to the danger you're in. When you're most at risk, there often isn't time to be afraid. Your mind is bound up with doing what you have to do, and the intensity carries you through. In most of the firefights I've been in, it wasn't until afterwards that I'd feel a reaction. Then, sitting in the chopper back to the LZ or resting at the camp, you'd often see guys staring blankly, appalled by thoughts of what they'd just been through and what might have happened to them.

You're most vulnerable when you've nothing else to think about. Sitting here in this alien place, with nothing to do except wait, I can't subdue the fear lurking at the back of my mind. I try to analyse it, to break it down into components, but it's too primitive. I am alone in the dark, and the terror rises within me. The silence of the jungle becomes increasingly oppressive. I have to resist the urge to spring to my feet and shout.

Looking down the trail, I imagine NVA soldiers appearing out of the mist. After a while the image is so powerful in my bleary head that I'm almost seeing them there. Although I've never actually seen an NVA soldier, alive or dead.

Worst of all, I cannot rid myself of the suspicion that someone – or something – is stealing up on me from the blind side, creeping up behind me just out of sight. I keep wanting to turn round to check that no one is there. I know this sensation isn't rational, so I force myself not to look, but I feel a rising sense of panic. I take a quick glance: nothing. Relief floods through me. But then the fear starts mounting again, and I have to steel myself not to take another glance.

What was that? There's something moving in the trees. I point my rifle towards the place, my finger curling on the trigger. Another movement. Then I see it emerge from the undergrowth: a small dark bear, about as big as a wolf, with a light-coloured muzzle. The creature steps out on to the trail and stops, lifting its head and turning it this way and that, as if suspecting that someone is near. Us? Or someone else?

The bear lowers its head, and lumbers forward into the undergrowth. My trigger finger uncurls. I start breathing again.

Time passes. I realize with a start that I've been dozing. I look about me. The sky is becoming light; dawn is not far away. Already the first few birds are singing. I look at my watch: nearly four o'clock. Nothing's going to happen now. I call the other men and tell them it's time to be going. Then I get up stiffly and stretch.

There's a village up ahead, just around the next corner. I order the platoon to halt. Taking Schroeder with me, I leave the trail for the woods and climb to the top of an incline, from where there should be a vantage point. You can't be too careful. We keep low as we reach the top – and, sure enough, there is the village below us, a few hundred yards away.

I get out the binoculars for a closer look. It's a typical 'ville': a couple of dozen huts, arranged higgledy-piggledy, with animals scratching away in the mud. I can see a group of people, men, women and children, all standing around a hut near the centre of the village. Jesus Christ, one of them's armed! He's holding a rifle, facing the other villagers, keeping them away from the hut. A young man, dressed in black pyjama-like clothes: almost certainly Vietcong. It's startling to see an enemy soldier at last. Another comes out of the hut, gesticulating, dragging an old man with his hands tied behind his back, and then another VC with a rifle. The one doing all the talking is waving a pistol about. This looks bad: maybe an execution. I'll have to act fast. Quickly I scan the rest of the village. Nobody else visible.

I tell Schroeder to wait there and scramble down to find the rest of the platoon. Calling the men together, I explain carefully what I want them to do. If we just burst in shooting there's a danger of getting ambushed, or of hitting innocent civilians in the mêlée. I want to surprise the enemy: my orders are to move silently, communicating only by hand signals.

I send McCoy with one squad to join Schroeder, with orders to cover us as we move in. Then I take the rest of the men up the trail. Soon the woods give way to a series of small plantations. We're very watchful, knowing we may come across a villager at any moment. But we must press forward.

We reach the edge of the village without encountering anyone. The trail leads between two huts, then bends round to the left. I send a squad round the side, while the rest of us cautiously approach the centre, where everybody is gathered watching the show. The men scan the inside of each hut as we advance. Up ahead I can hear shouting; the guy with a pistol must be working himself into a frenzy, ready to shoot the village elder.

We creep into the village. The crowd of villagers is only about thirty yards away. Still nobody seems to have noticed our presence. The others should be in position by now. I gesture to the men to wait, keeping down. I slip the safety catch off my rifle, stand up and walk forward. As the hut comes into view, I fire a round into the air and shout the Vietnamese phrase for surrender, '*Chieu hoi!*' Everyone spins round to look at me and, as they do, my men appear from all around.

The VC who has been haranguing the crowd flings down his pistol, exclaiming angrily. The other two drop their rifles and raise their hands. The watchers hover nervously, not wanting to miss the action. The platoon moves in to secure the village, kicking away the weapons and pushing the gooks down on their faces, while others herd the crowd to the edge of the village. One of the guys unties the old man, who is almost crying with relief and starts thanking us effusively. He spits on the VCs, who by now are lying face down, hands and ankles bound. I gesture to him to join the others outside the village. My men start to search the village hut by hut, bayoneting the walls and pulling up the matting floors to look for concealed weapons or food supplies. The villagers wait, watching impassively. When I'm sure the village is secure, I gesture to McCoy to bring the rest of the men down to join us. Then I get on the radio and order a chopper to take the prisoners out of here. I can't help stealing glances at them. They seem much smaller than I expected.

I'm crouching at the edge of some trees, scanning another village through my binoculars. It looks quiet enough. But I don't want to take any chances. I creep back to the platoon and tell the squad leaders what I've decided. I plan to take one of the squads and work my way through the woods around to the other side of the village, before moving in cautiously from there. The rest of the platoon should wait here, ready to deal with any gooks flushed out during our advance. I'm leaving McCoy in command.

Half an hour later, we've reached the far side without disturbing anyone. I climb a tree and take a look. The village still seems quiet. I climb down and make sure the men know what I want them to do. Then we advance back towards the village. We're maybe half-way there when I hear shouting up ahead. What the fuck's going on? I signal the squad to move in, and a few minutes later we arrive in the village to find it in uproar, already occupied by McCoy and the rest of the platoon, rounding up the civilians and searching the huts for hidden weapons. I walk straight up to McCoy and ask what the hell is happening. He pretends not to understand: he's relying on my not wanting to make a scene in front of the men. But I'm incensed that he should have disobeyed my instructions. Nothing could be more stupid than to approach from opposite sides unawares: we might easily have found ourselves shooting at each other.

I don't say anything then, but afterwards, once we're clear of the village, I take McCoy aside and tell him how furious I am at his stupid behaviour. His response is almost insolent, claiming that my orders hadn't been clear.

I've been having more trouble with McCoy. He's been ordering the squad leaders around without consulting me. I was quite happy with Schroeder as acting platoon sergeant: he used to come to me with his thoughts about what we should do next for my approval, and that seemed to work well. In a relatively short time I feel that I've built up a relationship of trust with my men. But McCoy has been trying to cut me out of the process altogether. I've caught him doing it once or twice and tried to straighten him out, but he doesn't seem to listen.

One day it all comes to a head. McCoy wants to take one particular trail and has already given orders to that effect. I don't agree, so I countermand the orders he has already given. I can see he doesn't like it. Later in the day I find that we're following the wrong trail. While we're making camp I take Schroeder aside and ask him what the hell is going on. He looks embarrassed. It turns out that McCoy has told him not to pay any attention to what I say.

I know that I've got to deal with this situation. If I let it continue, I won't have any authority over my platoon. You can't have two people running one show. I'm responsible for their safety, and I can only be responsible if my orders are carried out unquestioningly. I've got to get rid of this man.

When the patrol returns to the CP, I go and have a talk with the company commander. I explain the kind of difficulties I've been having, while he looks at me sympathetically but without committing himself. 'Look, 6, I can't live with this man,' I tell him. 'I've no doubt that he's a fine sergeant, but I want you to take him back. He's causing strife within the platoon. If you make me keep him, I won't be able to vouch for our safety.'

Matthews is OK about it. He says he trusts me to make the right decision. 'Speak to McCoy, then have him come and see me,' he says. I tell him that I'm grateful to have his support, and he smiles before asking, 'So who's going to replace McCoy?' I realize that it's a mark of his confidence in me that he asks my opinion. I reply that I'd like him to promote Schroeder to full sergeant, and to promote one of the men to squad leader to take his place. So that's what we do. Once my interview with the company commander is over, I ask McCoy to come and see me in my hooch. I tell him that I'm relieving him of duty, effective immediately. He doesn't like it, but he's too professional to argue when he knows he can't win.

I can see the difference next time we're out on patrol. The men seem happier, now that we're all working together as a team once more.

Early morning, and we're waiting for the chopper. The men

have packed up the hooches and dismantled the perimeter. I'm trying to shave for the first time in a week, using my upturned helmet, filled with water from a stream, as a bowl. I've a little mirror I keep just for the purpose, but I'm getting more and more lax about shaving regularly. Though it feels refreshing when I do.

The mirror is propped up against a stone while I lean forward, scraping my skin. Suddenly I stop concentrating on my chin and examine the face reflected back at me. My cheeks are hollowed; my eyes are sunken and wild; my hair is matted and filthy. What would Debbie think if she saw me now?

My radio operator is cooking the breakfast, heating up a can of C-rations with a thumbnail-sized block of C-4 plastic explosive. It burns with a high heat, but it's quite safe without a detonator.

Later that day, I'm called up to the front of the patrol. Sergeant Price is the squad leader on point; he looks shocked. He shows me what the point man has found. There's a little clearing up ahead. Tied to the stump of a tree is something that was once a human being: a corpse, the skin cut and peeled back while the man was still alive and writhing in his terror, before they shot him and left this stinking mess for us to find. Impaled on his forehead is a brass pin: a pair of crossed sabres. I feel the nausea rise within me, and suddenly my stomach heaves.

Now it's the evening bivouac, and I'm trying to write another letter to Debbie. I'm running out of things to say. Much of my life here is too horrible to describe, and the rest is boringly repetitive. I haven't been anywhere or done anything I want to tell her about. I feel contaminated by the things I've seen. My whole existence seems to have shrunk to this waking nightmare, hacking through a landscape of death and decay. The evening chopper brings us magazines full of news and glossy pictures, but even the pin-ups fail to stir a response in me. I feel less and less connected with what the men call 'The World'. The things Debbie writes about in her letters seem increasingly remote to me. Already I'm beginning to feel distanced from her.

A week later we're pulled back to An Khe for Green Line duty. It's a huge relief to be out of the field for a while. For the first time in a month we can relax. I shower and put on some fresh clothes, then I join some of the other guys over a crate of beer, and by the end of the evening we feel no pain, no pain at all.

15

Day 42 (324 days short): 17 September 1967

There's fighting on Highway 19, about twelve kilometres north-west of An Khe. Apparently a bulldozer clearing the verges has come under attack. Its Military Police escort is returning fire, but they're pinned down; it seems that the enemy may be present in strength. One of our platoons, the one on fifteen-minute standby, has already been airlifted into the area. The rest of us follow, air-assaulting on to a small hill about one kilometre south of the highway. The men are tense and excited. We're now sweeping through thick woodland towards where we think the enemy must be. I'm just behind the point man. Up ahead we can hear sporadic firing and the sound of air rocket artillery (ARA). Two Phantoms are peppering suspected enemy positions.

We burst out of the jungle on to the open verge of the highway. It's such a contrast from the country we've been forcing our way through that we stand there dazed for a moment. Like reaching the summit of a mountain and finding a dirty great warehouse on top. A strip about a hundred metres wide has been cleared on each side of the road, so there's a wide area of open ground in front of us, littered with tree-stumps and fallen tree-trunks. The sun is setting; soon it will be dark.

Firing breaks out, some way up the road to the right. Across the other side of the highway we see an NVA man running for cover. A guy beside me starts firing. The running figure freezes, then falls.

A helicopter gunship comes throbbing through the air and lands on the far side of the road. We start moving out from the trees towards the chopper. Suddenly there's the shockingly loud crackle of machine-gun fire. The first few seconds are completely chaotic. We're taking casualties. Guys are shouting and scattering in all directions. It's hard to know where the fire is coming from. The chopper bursts into flame, exploding a moment later in a huge fireball.

As I lope forward, keeping low, I realize that I'm being shot at from almost point-blank range. I can see muzzle flashes from what looks like a pile of old logs just a few yards ahead. Green tracer fire passes between my legs. Shit! An inch or two to the left or the right and I'd have been lucky just to lose a leg.

We've blundered into the back of an NVA ambush. They were dug in, waiting for a convoy of thirty petroleum tankers to come up the road, sheltering behind fallen trees in improvised bunkers, their machine guns and rocket launchers at the ready. Instead they've become involved in a pointless skirmish with a bulldozer. And suddenly we've crashed out of the jungle behind them. There's a moment of confusion on both sides. Then they've swivelled round and turned their weapons on us.

The din of gunfire is almost continuous now. Smoke drifts across the highway. The sharp smell of cordite fills my nostrils.

Out of the corner of my eye I see one of our men chasing an NVA soldier down the road, tearing at his shirt to try to stop him. Neither man appears to be armed. It's a surreal sight.

Two of my men are exchanging fire with soldiers concealed in some kind of bunker. The machine-gun fire has ceased: maybe they've taken out the gunner. I creep up from the side, keeping low. As I reach the bunker I rise, lifting my weapon to begin firing. A young enemy soldier spins round and looks straight up at me. For a moment I see another human being, an expression of terror on his face. I don't hesitate, I just fire from the hip. Then his body jerks as the bullets rip into him, and he's just a target again.

There's no more movement from the gooks inside the bunker. But now we're coming under fire from further up the road. All three of us hit the deck. More men begin to join us, darting out from the edge of the jungle in the fading light. My radio operator is here. I hold a brief conference over the radio with Captain Matthews. We're too close to the enemy for air support to be effective. He orders me to take eight men and move east along the highway, attacking any enemy positions we find, leaving the rest of the platoon here with Schroeder.

I radio to the firebase, giving them a map reference and requesting illumination. Within a few seconds the gloom is lit up by the first artillery flare.

We move along the flank, parallel to the road, tackling one bunker after another, using grenades when we get close enough. There's plenty of incoming, so we can't move too fast. Ehrlich is with me, ahead of the rest. It's becoming too dark to see where we're firing, so we just aim at the muzzle flashes. The enemy seems to be very close, sometimes only about ten feet away.

After a while I can hear a chopper approaching. Another artillery flare, and I can see him hovering overhead. It's a spy helicopter – what we call a 'Snoopy' – and he's telling me over the radio what's happening on the ground in front of me. Those Snoopy helicopters are just glass bubbles; he doesn't have any firepower to speak of, but it's an enormous advantage to us to know where the enemy is, and in what strength.

By the time we reach the last bunker, darkness is falling fast. Every two minutes or so the sky is lit up by another flare. I'm up in front of the others, with Ehrlich a little to my left. I'm aware that somebody is firing a pistol at me, because instead of the steady sound of automatic fire I can hear distinct shots, crack-thump, crack-thump: 'crack' as the bullet passes over your head, and 'thump' as it is actually fired. You'd think it should be the other way round, but in fact you hear the bullet passing over your head first, because the bullet travels faster than the sound.

I get down on one knee and peer forward, trying to spot the silhouette of whoever is shooting at us against the horizon. It seems to me that I make out a figure peeping from behind a tree up ahead. I always keep two magazines taped together, so that I can reload simply by ejecting the old magazine and, while it is still in my hand, turning it over and locking it back into the CAR-15. I empty both magazines at this tree in two bursts that together last not more than a few seconds. Then the tree begins to fall. 'You've fucking felled that tree!' laughs Ehrlich.

There's no more enemy fire coming in. The sky is now completely dark, and the Snoopy has left. It's too dangerous to continue, so I pull the men back. Astonishingly, my squad hasn't taken any casualties – though we lost some men at the start of the action, and there were some other men down from the bulldozer escort and the destroyed chopper. The guy who went tearing off down the road has caught his gook and made him prisoner. I radio the firebase and cancel the illumination. We start moving back along the highway, our eyes gradually adjusting to the dark. As we approach the rendezvous I get on the radio to Captain Matthews to tell him not to shoot, we're coming in. It's just as well I do this because they've been involved in some more action, too, and a few of the guys are a little trigger-happy.

We'll bivouac tonight a few hundred yards up the road, where D Company, responsible for road security in this area, has established a secure camp. By the time we reach it, I'm exhausted. The sheer intensity of the firefight has drained me. Jesus Christ, I could have been killed! I'm trembling and chain-smoking to try to calm down. It's all I can do to make my report to Matthews. He tells me just to give him the bare essentials: the rest can wait until tomorrow. Somehow I do what I have to do, and then I collapse. Tonight I'll be sleeping in the open, as there's no time to blow up a mattress or put up a hooch. I wrap myself in my poncho and lie on the bare ground. The fierce exhilaration of the fight lingers as I drift off to sleep.

The next morning I learn that I've been put in for a citation. I'm given the privilege of leading my platoon back along the highway towards where the fight took place. It's important to try to establish how many gooks we killed: the Army lays great emphasis on 'body count'. We're all on edge, given what happened the evening before. To be honest, I don't expect to find anything, because the enemy normally collects his casualties and their weapons during the night. This time, however, we're lucky. Maybe the firefight was so close to the camp that the enemy didn't feel it was safe to come out that night. Maybe they feared an ambush. Maybe there weren't any others. Whatever the reason, they haven't taken away their dead. We spread out, counting the bodies. I can't believe how many there are. Twenty of them, to our six dead and seven wounded. Of course, we don't know how many of their wounded men have got away.

We don't pick up the enemy bodies or bury them; we just leave them for the jungle to reclaim, or for their friends to collect. I'm still not used to the sight of corpses. As I'm standing over one, Ehrlich strolls up beside me. He rips the Cav patch off the left shoulder of his fatigues and jams it between the dead man's teeth. Then he turns to me and grins. I'm bemused, not knowing how to react to this macabre behaviour. 'Relax, LT, it's SOP,' he says, laughing at my shocked expression. 'We like to leave the gooks a calling card, in case one of their friends comes past and wants to know who dropped by.'

We gather their weapons and pile them in a heap: six AK-47s, two 57-mm recoilless rifles, two carbines, various light machine-guns – plus maps and documents and half a mile of communication wire.

One of the last bodies we find is that of the guy who was firing from behind the tree. He was an NVA lieutenant: my opposite number, if you like. I stare down at the corpse, thinking: Shit, I killed this man. He's still clutching the pistol he was shooting at me: a 'Chi-Com', a Chinese copy of a Russian 9-mm weapon. I bend down and grab his wrist, suppressing a shudder at his cold, stiff touch. Bending back his reluctant fingers one by one, I unclasp the pistol from his hand, and unbuckle the holster. I figure that I might as well take it as a souvenir. It may come in useful: these gook pistols are more accurate than our Colt .45s. There's a bullet lodged in the chamber. If his pistol hadn't jammed, perhaps it would be me lying there dead instead of him. I extract the bullet; later I fix it to a lanyard and wear it round my neck as a lucky charm.

We've cleared up the area, and now we're moving out on a new patrol. The point man has just entered the trees when I hear a shout. 'LT, over here!' There's a young Vietnamese lying doggo in a gully. Presumably a straggler from last night's firefight. He's not dead; I can't tell if he's wounded or not. He might just be asleep. He's lying face down. For all I know, he may be concealing a grenade or some other weapon, waiting for us to drop our guard. I've got him covered with my CAR-15, watching for any sudden move. '*Chieu hoi*,' I say – nudging him with my foot. For a moment nothing happens. Then he rolls over; and, as he does so, I see that he's lying on a rifle. In these situations you can't risk a delay. I've already begun firing when I see the look of terror and the hope of pity in his eyes, and I know that I've made a mistake. It's too late. He's dead.

For a long time afterwards I can't clear my mind of the expression on his face. He was only a boy, frightened and alone. It's a lousy feeling to have killed someone who wasn't trying to kill you.

16

Day 43 (323 days short): 18 September 1967

It's early evening, twenty-four hours after the firefight. We're back at the bivouac after another day out on patrol searching for NVA stragglers. The prisoner that we captured confirmed that an entire NVA company had been dug in by Highway 19 waiting for the convoy. Apparently they had been involved in three previous ambushes.

I receive an order to report to the temporary helipad. It seems that I'm being flown back to An Khe to receive a medal. Not just any medal, but a Silver Star, the American equivalent to the British Military Cross, awarded for 'exceptionally valorous action'. I'm told that it's the highest honour you can receive in the field without the personal authorization of the President.

The colonel is due to receive the same award. He flew by chopper into the thick of the fighting. The third guy to be decorated with the Silver Star is the one who chased the enemy soldier down the road and eventually caught him. Several other men are to receive lesser decorations.

The helicopter arrives with the evening rations. We climb aboard.

We fly out to An Khe, where we are billeted for the night. I'm tired and filthy. I shower, change into fresh fatigues, and head for the officers' club, where I down a few beers before wandering back to my billet and dropping into exhausted oblivion. The next morning I try to smarten myself up for the presentation. I shave and comb my hair. At the last moment I remember to pin my lieutenant's bar on to my helmet. I have a brief, rueful memory of a picture of myself dressed in my blues. A world away.

There's a full battalion parade, with a band playing 'The Stars and Stripes'. The divisional commander, a four-star general, has flown out to make the presentations. The first I see of him is when he emerges from a tent and steps up on to a podium. He begins by making a morale-boosting speech. Then he climbs down to inspect the troops drawn up on parade. Finally we're invited to step forward one by one to receive our medals. When my turn comes, and the general reads the citation, I'm so proud that I can hardly see through the mist in my eyes. 'Lieutenant Abraham's gallant action is in keeping with the highest traditions of the military service,' the citation concludes, and 'reflects great credit upon himself, his unit, and the United States Army.' I step forward smartly and salute. Then the general pins the Silver Star on my chest. 'Fine work, Lieutenant.'

I don't consider that what I did was brave. I just did by instinct what I'd been trained to do. There wasn't time to think about anything but the task in hand until afterwards.

After the presentation I'm flown straight back out into the field. There's no let-up, no night on the town. Shame about that: I'd have liked another night on the base. I'd have gone to the officers' club and drunk myself into a stupor. But the men are pleased to see me again, which is some small consolation.

Apparently when I'd flown off to the base there had been some concern that I might be moving on to take up another command. They like having me back. We're comfortable with each other now.

After a month out in the field my platoon has been ordered back to An Khe. For the next few weeks we'll be rotating between different duties: one week guarding the perimeter, the next week on road patrol, the next week on standby as a ready reaction force, which means that we have to be prepared to be picked up by chopper at fifteen minutes' notice. You've got to keep your kit by you at all times.

My platoon has been given a relatively cushy assignment, guarding four bridges on Highway 19. Our job is to defend them from possible ambush. The highway is an important supply line to the remote bases in Kon Tum and Dak To, and the bridges are the most vulnerable points for our transports. There are bunkers at each, manned permanently by units in rotation.

I put a squad on each bridge. I've been allotted a jeep, so I spend my whole day driving up and down the highway between these bridges. It's a fairly populous area, so there will be plenty of girls around to distract the men. I know that they will appear as soon as my back is turned. I can't stop the inevitable, but at least I can protect the men from being invalided out of the field after contracting the venereal diseases endemic in Vietnamese prostitutes. I issue each squad with a ration of condoms from the quartermaster's stores. There's a lot of ribaldry about 'government issue', but I can live with that.

I warn the men not to relax their guard. Some of these prostitutes are enemy sympathizers. Phil told me about one guy who invited a girl into his bunker. The two of them relaxed and smoked some dope together. Then she left. A few minutes later a bomb exploded in the bunker. I was told that you could hear him screaming inside, but by the time they got him out, the poor sap was dead.

For weeks now the whole battalion has been preparing to move north, where we'll be securing an area around a new airstrip to be built near Tam Ky, on the coastal highway south of Da Nang. Day after day we sit around, waiting for the people at the top to get organized. Then we begin the move north, guarding firebases at each stage. The sound of the big 175-mm guns is awe-inspiring. Every time the artillery opens up, it makes me jump. At night they fire H & I every hour, on the hour. There's not much chance of hitting anything, of course, but perhaps it terrorizes the opposition. The scale is different, but it's the same principle as Charlie taking pot-shots at our patrols from the other side of the valley. It keeps us on our toes.

I've spent much of this dead time with Phil Schwarz. Although he must be half a dozen years older than me, we've become friends – as much as you can become friends with anyone in this place. While we wait for our new orders we spend hours talking, what Phil would call 'shooting the breeze', smoking, playing cards. Being a platoon leader is a lonely job most of the time, so it's great to be able to compare notes with someone who's shared the same experience. As Phil talks, my perspective changes: he's obviously less concerned with winning the war than getting his men out of here alive.

One evening the pair of us are sitting on a firebase with nothing to do, just waiting for the sun to go down. This is the first opportunity we've had to discuss our lives back home. Like most people, Phil is intrigued by how an Englishman comes to be serving in the Army out here, and asks me about my background. I tell him about my family, and about Debbie, and show him the photos I keep with me always. In return he produces a picture of his wife and three young children, standing around a barbecue. In the foreground is his youngest, a little girl of five years old with ribbons in her hair, grimacing for the camera. I can't help thinking how difficult it must be for him to be separated from them for so long. It must be strange, being a father. I can't imagine what it is like. Having a family makes him seem much older than the other guys, and I wonder if he sees us as boys.

I ask Phil what made him decide to enlist. 'I know why I'm here,' I say, 'but I'm not married. Why are you here?'

Phil stares out into the hills beyond the perimeter. He frowns. 'My father', he begins, 'is a very patriotic man. He was just a kid when my grandparents brought him to the USA from Eastern Europe back in the 1930s. He worked hard to lose his accent and turn himself into an all-American boy, though he never really succeeded. He served in the Army towards the end of World War Two, and he was very upset that he never saw any action. When my mother died, he became even more intensely loyal. It was hard for him, raising my elder brother and me on his own, as a first-generation immigrant. He was so proud of us – "Young Americans", he called us. He raised us in the belief that America was God's own country, and that we had a duty to defend it from the forces of Communism. When the call came, he thought we should answer it. He expected it of us, and I guess I wanted to give him something back, something in return for all the sacrifices he'd made. And I believed all that Kennedy shit, too. "Ask not what your country can do for you: ask rather what you can do for your country." I don't feel that way now, but I did.'

'What happened to your brother?' I ask. 'Is he out here, too?'

Phil takes a long time to answer, and the longer the silence lasts, the more I dread what he will say. At last Phil speaks. 'He was,' he says. 'He was killed just before I arrived in-country.'

*

I'm walking with the rest of my platoon across an open field. Around the edge is an embankment with a path running along the top. Through a gap in the embankment about ten yards wide I can see another small field, then woodland on a ridge beyond.

This area is what we call 'hot' – very hot. It seems that the enemy is present in strength: maybe a whole NVA company. Somewhere up ahead D Company came under heavy fire earlier today, and was forced to withdraw after taking a lot of casualties: twelve dead and sixty-seven wounded. We in B Company have been flown into the area to attack the enemy from the opposite side. Of course, nobody knows exactly where the enemy is at this stage. My platoon is acting as point for the rest of B Company, probing towards where we think the enemy must be dug in. Phil is in charge of the second platoon, a few hundred yards behind us.

As we approach the gap, we come under machine-gun fire. The platoon scatters, heading for the shelter of the embankment on either side of the gap. As I run for cover I can see several men down already. I dive behind the embankment to the right of the gap. One of my squad leaders is here, Sergeant Price. Most of the others are scattered along the embankment, on both sides of the gap. A few men are still in the open, crawling towards the embankment. We're caught in a killing zone.

Lying on our sides, keeping our heads low, Price and I try to sort out what to do next, shouting to be heard over the din. A frontal attack across the next field – directly towards the machine-gun fire – would be suicidal. To the right, the embankment simply returns round the field, with open ground beyond. Only on the left is there some cover that we might be able to work around to reach the enemy positions from the flank. But that means crossing the gap, where there's no cover at all from the deadly machine-gun fire.

While we're discussing all of this, Phil runs forward to join us, making use of the meagre cover provided by the right-hand wall of the embankment. He's come forward because he wants to know what the hell's going on up here. He asks me what his platoon can do to help. The three of us are squatting on our heels behind the embankment; I'm facing back towards him and he's looking over my shoulder towards the enemy positions.

Just then another machine-gun opens up from a different angle. We're caught in the line of fire. I see Price go down, hit in the face. I'm screaming at Phil, and he's trying to reassure me when suddenly his head explodes with a pop, splattering me with blood and brains. His decapitated body drops to the ground, blood gushing out of his neck. I'm so horrified, that I don't register what I'm seeing. I realize afterwards that he must have been hit by a rocket-propelled grenade. Lumps of gore stick to my skin and my fatigues. I wipe my face with my sleeve, trying to overcome the nausea rising in my gullet.

Get out of here! I dash across the gap, keeping very low to the ground, bullets flying past my ears. As soon as I reach the other side, I hurl myself down behind the embankment.

The radio operator is here. I'm speaking to the company commander, trying to keep the panic out of my voice. His calm authority reassures me. He's organized air support; it should be here at any moment. But he can't see what's happening from back where he is, so I'm going to have to guide the aerial fire on his behalf. Meanwhile I brief him on the situation up here. I tell him that Phil is dead.

A few minutes later we hear the sound of an approaching Chinook. This particular one is the type known here as 'guns-a-go-go': it's stuffed with ammunition, and its firepower is simply awesome. Within thirty seconds it can pepper an area the size of a football field with thousands of rounds two inches apart. The huge chopper passes overhead. I'm speaking direct to the pilot over the radio. I tell him to open up when they reach the woodland. The Chinook begins firing. Bullets rain down in a torrent, cutting the woods to shreds. The noise is appalling. It's hard to believe that anyone hiding there can survive this onslaught.

The Chinook hovers overhead for a few minutes, pouring down fire on the woodland below. Then, its deadly load exhausted, it turns and speeds back past us towards Da Nang.

Meanwhile I've improvised a squad of a dozen or so members of my platoon for an attack on the flank of the enemy positions. As soon as the Chinook has gone, we start edging forward behind the patches of cover to the left of the embankment, until we reach the woodland. Then we attack the machine-gun emplacements from the flank. But there's no one left alive. The Chinook got there before us.

A few minutes later we've finished pushing through the dense woodland to the other side, to find ourselves on a ridge. The flat land below is where D Company must have been when they were attacked. We take up a defensive position on top of the ridge, until other platoons from B Company make their way round from the embankment behind us, sweeping along the base of the ridge to the edge of the plain. They've discovered a network of tunnels down there. It seems incredible to think that there could be such a major fortified position here on our doorstep, so close to the coastal highway and the huge Marine base at Da Nang.

We stand down, watching the men below getting ready to investigate those tunnels. You don't want to go charging into those places, because you never know whom you might meet down there.

I stroll along the ridge, trying to get a better view. I walk past a tree and glance down. Just below my feet there's a machine-gun nozzle, slowly turning towards the GIs gathered in front of the tunnels. For a moment I can't take in what I'm seeing. I'm standing on top of a bunker! I could easily have fallen right into it. I whip out a grenade and lob it into the bunker from above, shouting to my men behind to take cover as I dive to the ground. 'Fire in the hole!'

The grenade explodes. Smoke pours out of the bunker. Just to make sure, I get to my feet and empty two whole magazines through the brushwood roof at my feet.

My men come scurrying up to join me. We fan out and move along the slope, discovering and dealing with another bunker tucked into the hillside.

It's weird. There must have been more than a hundred NVA soldiers here an hour ago, and now there are just twenty bodies. Where have they gone?

The choppers are swooping in, collecting soldiers and taking off again. I'm standing in line with my men, waiting our turn. I'm just starting to relax. One of the medics briefs me on our casualties. One of these is poor Price. It's astonishing that he's still alive, really: the whole of the top right-hand side of his head was shot away. You could see his brains when they stretchered him off. I learned later that he lost an eye, but he recovered.

Then it occurs to me what this mess is all over my fatigues. I'm filled with revulsion, frantically trying to wipe it off. I get the shakes, and suddenly I'm all choked up. I squat down, my face in my hands, my shoulders heaving. The men turn away, embarrassed. In my mind is that picture of Phil's wife and kids, standing round the barbecue. I can't get that sweet little girl's face out of my head. Why him? I keep thinking; why him, and why not me?

They've put me in for another medal, a Bronze Star this time, with a V for Valour.

17

Day 92 (274 days short): 6 November 1967

We're out on patrol, hacking our way through dense undergrowth. You can't see more than a few yards in any direction, except straight ahead and behind.

Like most of the other guys, I'm clutching my rifle with both hands, scanning the undergrowth on each side as we move forward cautiously. There have been intelligence reports of enemy activity in the area, but we've not seen anything yet. In an effort to hurry along my men I've moved up towards the front of the patrol. There's a man three or four yards ahead, then another in front of him, and beyond I can glimpse the point man wielding his machete.

Today we're operating in company strength. We landed a few hours ago on a ridge about a mile back. My platoon has been sent out as point. The rest of the company will wait at the LZ until we signal them that we've secured a new location. It's late in the afternoon, and we're heading for another hilltop only a few hundred yards off, where we plan to make a night bivouac.

The hill is the most prominent landmark for miles around, an obvious place to rest up for the night. We've begun to climb a steep incline, so there can't be more than a few hundred yards to go now. I'm thinking about the evening ahead, once we've secured the perimeter: the chance to rest, to eat a hot meal, maybe some post to read and letters to write.

Machine-gun fire spits out at us from almost point-blank range. Ambush! The three men in front of me all go down, one after another. I feel the shock as my CAR-15 disintegrates in my hands, followed by a series of sharp pains, in my left wrist, in my right side and under my left armpit, then a tremendous blow on the helmet that knocks me backwards on to the forest floor. I lie there stunned, while bullets shred the undergrowth, punctuated with orange-red tracer. My head is full of noise and confusion.

As the seconds pass I force my brain to recover. I've been hit in several places. My head is ringing. My wrist hurts, and there's a searing, burning pain in my side. But I'm alive. *I'm alive, Goddammit!*

I explore my wounds with my fingertips. My wrist and my head are badly bruised. My hip is soaked – but, thank God, it's only water. A bullet must have passed through my canteen. I'm bleeding a little from my sides, but nothing vital seems damaged. I'm OK for now.

'Yankee, you die.' A gloating voice floats across the bodies of our men.

I can hear groaning behind me, and the drumming of AK-47 fire from my left. Jesus Christ, what a mess! I've got to get out. Don't think about your wounds. Just get out of here.

I'm not going to get far without a weapon. As machine-gun fire passes overhead, I crawl towards one of the bodies lying a few yards off. It's Lombardi, who arrived in-country only last week. He's dead, lying on his back with arms outstretched, staring up into the canopy, a look of excitement on his face. There doesn't seem to be a mark on his body. Nearby is another dead man, whose face is a sickening mass of gore. That must be Radzek, I think. I prise an M-16 from the outstretched hand of the third dead GI, who clings to it in a death-grip. As it comes free his head rolls towards me in a look of reproach. Oh, Jesus, it's Newton: a sweet-natured, funny guy. He depended on me, and I failed him. I led him into this trap.

I know what I have to do. Attack the enemy: if you can penetrate his line, he can't shoot at you without the risk of shooting his own men. This must be the classic L-shaped ambush: the enemy machine-gunner facing towards our patrol and soldiers armed with AK-47s lined along one side, to give them a clear line of fire. Just the same as we'd do it. We've walked straight into the ambush. How deep? I wonder.

I check the M-16 magazine: full. Very carefully, I crawl into the undergrowth on my left, where I'll be out of the machine-gunner's direct line of fire. The enemy must be on either side of me now. I unclip a grenade, pull out the pin and hurl it into the undergrowth to my left. As soon as it explodes I'm on my feet, charging back down the hill, scattering automatic fire as I run. The first thing I see is a dead man in NVA uniform. I load another magazine and start moving cautiously back the way we've come, away from the machine-gun, rolling up the enemy line. Every few seconds I hear another burst of machine-gun fire from behind, and the drum of automatic weapons up ahead. There's a distinct difference between the buzzing of our M-16s and the slower hammering of their AK-47s.

I can see another NVA man now, only about five yards away, peering towards the left where we must have passed him a minute before. He hasn't seen me. I take careful aim and fire; he drops. When I reach him he's still alive, so I pump him full of bullets. He thrashes around, then lies still. I move on down the line.

A few yards further, another enemy soldier suddenly stands up out of the undergrowth and starts firing up at me. I hit the ground, fast. I toss a grenade in his direction, and it explodes in his face. Automatic fire sprays wildly across the canopy as the man falls, his hand still on the trigger. Then it stops. I climb to my feet, and move forward.

'LT!'

I spin to my left, weapon ready to fire, and there's a man who was behind me on the patrol. He looks scared, but otherwise OK. I gesture to him to advance alongside me a few yards to my left, so that we can comb the line together; that way we're less likely to find ourselves passing a concealed NVA man who might suddenly pop up and shoot us in the back. Another few yards. I crouch down low and see a dark helmet outlined against the sky. The shape is . . . one of theirs. I lob another grenade. When the smoke clears, the outline has disappeared. I advance warily. There's no body, nothing. The GI is looking across at me. Did I imagine it?

I can't hear any more AK-47 fire. Have we cleared the line of their ambush? We've reached the bottom of the incline; the machine-gunner is still firing blindly down the tunnel behind me. I'm anxious about getting shot by my own men, who must be somewhere up ahead. Crouching down with the other guy, I shout, 'This is 2/6. Is anybody there?'

A friendly voice shouts back, 'LT, is that you?'

I've made contact with the rest of my platoon. I tell them to hold their fire because we're coming in, and a few seconds later we're crouching in a hollow with several of the other guys. Everything's in chaos, with nobody quite sure what's going on or what to do. I organize the retreat; we move stealthily, because there's still a chance that the machine-gunner may spot us through the trees from his elevated position. After a quarter of an hour or so we reach the original LZ, where the rest of the company is still waiting and wondering what the fuck has been going on down below.

My wounds are beginning to hurt as I relax. Lying on a stretcher I receive emergency medical attention from one of the medics. He tells me I've been hit in six places: a glancing blow on my wrist, the bullet that went through my canteen, another that hit my entrenching tool, a bullet that split in two on hitting the hammer mechanism of my rifle, one half entering my body under the left armpit and the other passing through the flesh on my right side; and, finally, a bullet pierced my helmet in the front and found its way between the steel exterior and the fibreglass lining out of the back. 'You are one hell of a lucky fucking bastard,' the medic comments.

Captain Matthews is standing next to the stretcher, urgently expecting my situation report. He's already organized air strikes; jets are in the air, heading in this direction. He holds up the map for me to examine; we study it together, and I tell him as precisely as I can the location of the enemy. I reckon that an NVA company had decided to bivouac on the same hilltop, and that when they heard us coming they must have sent out a patrol to improvise an ambush. We walked straight into it. Matthews radios a map reference to the nearest firebase. Seconds later the first shells start flying overhead, making the ground shake when they explode. Then the jets come streaming in and start strafing the hill opposite with cannon-fire. By this time I'm fading fast. I must have been put on a helicopter, but I don't remember anything about it. The next thing I know, I am waking up in a hospital bed.

I learned afterwards that our ordnance pounded the enemy positions late into the night. The attack was so fierce that a boulder as big as a room was thrown clean into the air, and when it fell it crushed five NVA men beneath it.

The next morning our mortar platoon began mortaring the location, though by now any NVA who remained must have been dead or wounded so badly that they were unable to move. In the intervals between firing faint cries could be heard coming up from the valley where we'd been ambushed. Our guys held their fire for a moment to listen. Eventually they could make out the words: 'Please don't shell me any more.' A patrol was sent out to investigate, and among the corpses they found a guy, lying naked in his own blood, almost sobbing with fear. He was a man from my platoon, one of those behind me when we were attacked. He'd been too badly wounded to move, and when the NVA came he was terrified of being discovered and shot. He decided to lie doggo and pretended to be dead. They'd taken all his equipment and stripped off his clothes, without realizing that he was still alive.

I was awarded a Purple Heart for wounds received in action. It's a great big slab of gold metal. Back in the days of the American Revolution the medal was made of solid gold, the idea being that many of the wounds received in action would leave a soldier permanently disabled and unable to work, so if necessary the medal could be sold for its face value and would fetch quite a handsome sum. Nowadays they're just made of some gold-coloured alloy. Times change.

I'm back in the field after only a couple of days in hospital. I'm sore, but as long as I move carefully I'll be all right. The nurses have given me some spare dressings for my wounds. Right now it's just after dawn; I'm sitting on the damp ground, resting my back against a cold grave in a derelict cemetery, trying to write a letter to Debbie that won't alarm her too much. I think she must know that I'm holding back a lot of the truth from her most of the time. All around are the sounds of the jungle awakening: birdsong of every kind, hooting and whistling in the trees, and small creatures rustling in the undergrowth.

This is an eerie place, especially in the early morning before the strengthening sun burns off the early-morning mist, which hangs in clumps around the graves. It's an abandoned cemetery in the middle of the jungle, obviously very old. The map doesn't show anything else for miles around: not even the smallest hamlet. We stumbled across it on patrol late yesterday afternoon, and, since it was near the location that I'd been ordered to make for, I thought we might as well camp here for a change. There's a little stone wall running around it, which forms a natural perimeter and provides some protection, as well as these graves, stone mausoleums like the ones you sometimes find in European cathedrals, some of them bulging at odd angles as tree-roots force their way up through the soil. Creeping plants of every kind have invaded the cemetery, climbing across the boundary wall and now threatening to smother the graves and their long-dead occupants under a thick blanket of green. There's a sense of decay, of these proud structures surrendering to the irresistible vigour of the jungle. I remember the crashed C-130 we found a few days ago, its huge bulk already disappearing beneath the vines, like the corpse of a whale on the ocean floor. I picture the American bases, at An Khe and elsewhere, crumbling into disrepair, until at last they are obliterated altogether, lost monuments of a vanished civilization.

We have a new guy with us on patrol today, a forward naval observer. The intelligence boys have had word of enemy movements in this area, and he's been sent out with us to provide back-up. Not just him, of course: somewhere over the eastern horizon is the South China Sea, and out there is a big warship, steaming on a course parallel to the shore. She's armed with three pairs of twelve-inch guns, huge fuckers with barrels more than thirty feet long. Each throws a five-hundred-pound shell. Apparently the shell casings are large enough for a man to stand inside.

The naval officer – a lieutenant like me – outlines the advantages of naval bombardment. One is the ability to call down fire in foul weather, when aircraft would be grounded – though ironically the weather is perfect today. Another advantage is that naval guns can target positions inaccessible to conventional artillery.

The point squad has made contact with the enemy, apparently located in a network of bunkers and tunnels in a cliff about eight hundred yards ahead. I move forward carefully to talk to the squad leader, instructing him not to let the men take unnecessary risks or advance any further towards the enemy. Then I give the co-ordinates of the estimated enemy position to the naval observer, who radios them through to his waiting ship. Forty-five seconds later, the first salvo passes overhead in a deafening screech, like a whole squadron of jets flying at treetop height, followed by explosions heavy enough to make the ground shake. It's an unbelievable thrill to be able to call on such big boys' toys. I'm just an ordinary second lieutenant, yet I can command broadsides from a warship ten miles offshore.

After half a dozen salvos we call off the bombardment and move forward to investigate. The cliff-face is pockmarked with holes. The bunkers are empty. We find an entrance to the tunnels, and a volunteer team goes in to investigate. Half an hour later they emerge, with the news that the enemy has evacuated the entire complex. It's my duty to see if they've left anything behind that might be of intelligence value. I enter the tunnel system reluctantly. I always feel claustrophobic underground; I can remember caving in the Mendips when I was a schoolboy and having to be taken out after a panic attack. This isn't so bad, but I'm pleased it doesn't last long. The only thing

I find down there is a forgotten AK-47, which I've taken for my own use to replace my lost CAR-15.

I'm riding with one hand on the side of the chopper, the other stretched out into the emptiness, air rushing past my face, one foot in front of the other on the skis, like a tightrope walker. Looking down, I can see the jungle sliding past, more than a thousand feet below. This is one of those choppers equipped with speakers for 'psy-ops', propaganda broadcasts to the civilians below – but we're not on one of those today. Instead, Jimi Hendrix blasts out from the loudspeakers, drowning even the throb of the blades. Seven choppers, maintaining perfect V formation, heading into battle. It's beautiful.

I'm posing for a photograph, squatting next to a bomb as big as I am. I've tried, and I can't get my arms round it. We found it during this morning's patrol. An unexploded thousand-pound bomb, a real monster, one of the 'daisy-cutters' they sometimes drop from a B-52 to clear an area for a new LZ. When you see one of these fuckers detonate, it's like witnessing an atomic explosion: a vast mushroom cloud, and a shockwave that flattens everything within fifty yards or so, and causes extensive damage for a further couple of hundred.

I've been on the radio to the company commander about the bomb. He's ordered me to deal with it. We can't leave something like this where it is, otherwise Charlie will cut it open and use the explosive against us. The others have all cleared off, leaving Schroeder and me alone: we're the bomb-disposal squad. There's something darkly comical about the situation. I can't help aiming a kick at the bomb, rather as you might take a prod at a sedated lion. Of course, what I'm doing is daft. If it were to explode now, we'd be vaporized; they wouldn't be able to find even the smallest piece of me to post back home to my parents.

Schroeder and I keep kidding and fooling about. We're supposed to wait a full fifteen minutes for the others to get clear, but we decide to give them a little scare by detonating it before they've reached the designated safe distance. I dig out some C-4 plastic explosive and slap about half a kilo on the nose cone and about the same amount on the tail. I run a piece of detonator cord between the two, start the fuse, and then we make for the nearest cover, a rocky outcrop about a hundred yards away. It's a matter of pride with us both that we walk, not run. We take shelter behind these rocks, far too close to such a big bomb. The seconds tick past . . . then KA-BOOM: the world turns upside down in a deafening roar, as both of us are thrown to the ground. The air is full of smoke; it's hard to breathe. Schroeder looks as if he's just come down a chimney – and I suppose I must, too. Gradually the smoke clears. I'm laughing so much that the tears roll down my face.

After I'd been in-country three and a half months I was due for some R & R – rest and relaxation. At the end of my last patrol I returned to LZ Baldy, a semi-permanent base where I was able to wash, shave and put on a completely fresh uniform. I felt wonderfully clean, cleaner than I'd ever felt before. Then I flew out to China Beach, a military resort attached to the huge Da Nang base. It stretched for miles, with big waves rolling in all the time I was there. I was amazed to see guys in the water surfing, as if we were in Hawaii.

Just inland from the beach there were rows of identical wooden huts on stilts, as spick and span as any chalet back in America. It was a marvellous feeling to climb the timber steps outside and walk in, to see rooms with beds and mattresses and sheets, and to be able to lie down in comfort. After so long in the field, this seemed almost sinful luxury. Even better, we could do what we liked – sleep late, stroll down to the beach and swim, catch a movie, or write some letters. It was like a dream. A few miles outside the resort men were being blown up by booby-traps; here we were playing ball or downing beers in the officers' club.

Soon after I arrived I bought some civilian clothes – just a shirt, lightweight trousers, and slip-on shoes – and changed into them; it was a huge relief to feel normal for a few days. By a happy coincidence I ran into an old friend, Jerry McAffee, whom I'd known during basic training and Officer Candidate School back in the States, so he and I were able to spend much of the next few days hanging around together. It felt almost like being at home. But I couldn't relax fully. It was hard to shed the alertness you need to maintain all the time on patrol.

Outside the base is the bustling town of Da Nang, a noisy place packed with soldiers and heavy traffic. I wander into the town for a brief look, but I don't stay because I know it isn't a particularly safe place to visit in the evenings. That doesn't stop plenty of the other guys, though.

A little shanty town has sprung up by the edge of the base, full of shacks and open stalls, a bit like some of the sad places you find on the Native American reservations. But this is a bazaar where everything is for sale – including, of course, sex. There's a particular 'house' where several of the guys I know have already been for some TLC from pretty Vietnamese girls. I try to stay away from it, but the thought of it keeps playing on my mind. I feel that I will be laughed at if I go back to the platoon without having had it away at least once, so on my last night I succumb to temptation and head off there with the others, telling myself that this may be my last time ever.

There's a topless go-go dancer on a raised platform swaying to loud rock music, and lots of girls in skimpy dresses hanging around the bar. The lights are a garish red and green: stop, go, stop, go. I walk in, dressed in my civilian clothes. The guys are all laughing and kidding each other. I order a round of drinks, shouting to be heard above the pounding beat. I perch on a stool watching the dancer, her face impassive as her hips thrust forward and back, her arms held high over her head, offering her small breasts to us. A girl appears on the stool beside me and starts touching my arm. 'You like boom-boom?' she whispers into my ear. I lean over and ask how much. She quotes me a price: it's ridiculously cheap. OK, I say, and she slides off the stool, beckoning me to follow. It's only then that I see how little she is. I rise to my feet and pick up my beer, carrying it with me. She leads the way through a beaded curtain and along a corridor to a tiny room, just big enough to slide in alongside a single bed. A single naked bulb casts a dim red light over the girl's flesh. She undresses. I sit on the bed and slip off my shoes. Like a fool, I haven't brought any protection with me. I take a last swig of my drink. She's naked now, splayed on the bed, hardly bothering to disguise her indifference. As I lower myself on to her I have the disturbing sensation that I'll crush her tiny body beneath mine.

I'm sitting in the resort cinema with my friend Jerry, munching popcorn, our legs over the seats in front. Up on the screen, Paul Newman is starring in a western called *Hombre*. He's white, but he's been brought up by Apaches, and the other passengers in the stagecoach cast him out. They soon want him back again when they are menaced by bandits. They're crossing a baking desert. The *hombre* has a gun. He starts stalking one of the bandits. He creeps up and fires – and I dive under the seat, popcorn flying. Jerry assures me that everything's OK. I come out, feeling a little wobbly, but when they next start shooting I have to hide again, and even when the firing's finished I feel too upset to stay.

18

Day 114 (252 days short): 28 November 1967

There is a strange atmosphere in the platoon when I get back from R & R. I wanted Bruce Schroeder to cover for me while I was away, but the feeling among my superiors was that he didn't have enough experience, so they brought in another senior sergeant from outside. I didn't agree, but I accepted the decision, and I assumed that everything would be fine. It wasn't fine. When I get back from Da Nang, I find that the sergeant is dead.

Captain Matthews briefs me on the incident before I fly out to join my platoon. It seems that the sergeant has been killed during a firefight. They were out on patrol, stumbled across some gooks, and started shooting. That's when he was hit. The worrying thing was this: he'd been shot in the back of the head.

The Military Police investigated, pulling in members of the platoon and cross-examining them one by one. But if anyone can explain why the sergeant has been shot from behind, they're not coming forward.

Matthews warns me to be on my guard. But I'm not anxious. I know these men: I trust them, and I feel that they trust me.

Nobody says anything to me about what happened until a week or so later, when I'm alone with Bruce Schroeder in a foxhole one night. Then he begins talking, as if I've introduced the subject and he's replying to my question.

'That sergeant guy, he wanted us all to be heroes. He was full of shit about storming the enemy emplacements, as if this was some fucking World War Two movie and he was John Wayne. He wouldn't listen to anyone else. It was like he'd been waiting for the moment to lead some Goddam death-or-glory charge. There wasn't any firefight. We ran straight into enemy machine-gun fire. There were two guys down already, and that stupid bastard wanted us to make a frontal assault. I told him it was suicide. He started waving his gun at us, shouting that we were cowards, that he'd shoot us if we didn't move. So . . .'

There's a pause. Schroeder turns and looks at me in the darkness. 'He wanted to die.'

Going back out into the field again is tough. It isn't so much the ever-present danger, the fear that you could be killed at any moment, because that had never really left me in Da Nang. It's more that, after four days of clean clothes, fresh underwear, sheets and hot water, I had felt like a civilized human being again. Now I am back to being an animal: filthy, sweating, aching, and always tired because I never get enough sleep. I think the smell gets to me as much as anything – a sort of heavy, musky smell that never leaves you out here. We call it the 'gook smell'.

We're in the Central Highlands, on a search-and-destroy patrol. Thirty-four men, strung out in a line, hacking through the jungle, day after day. It's still the monsoon season, so you're either soaked to the skin from the outside or dripping with sweat from the inside, moving forward one pace at a time, scanning the jungle around you, rifle held at the ready. Boring, repetitive work – but you have to keep concentrating, because a single lapse can be fatal. One step on the wrong place, and it's goodbye for ever. All of us are alert to the possibility of an ambush. We know that the enemy is around, because earlier today we found a campfire, the embers still smouldering.

Keep concentrating. It's like fishing. People think that fishing is relaxing. It isn't. I remember fishing when I was a boy. I'd stare at the float until the whole world shrank into that orange tip with the black stripe poking from the surface of the water. I had to be ready to react at any moment. If I let my mind wander, the chances were that I'd be too slow to respond when the float dipped and I'd miss the bite.

I'm in my usual position, two-thirds of the way back. The radio operator is behind me. I'm assuming that Charlie is watching us much of the time. If he can identify the officer in charge of the platoon, he'll be able to pick me off with a sniper bullet. They always go for the officer, the same way they head straight for the command post when they attack an LZ.

For the same reason I make three other guys carry maps and compasses, and the men behind them carry dummy radios. When I need to consult the map, I say, 'Right, guys, maps,' or pass the word along the line to the others. All four of us will be looking at the map at the same time, though the other three will be acting as decoys.

The point man has spotted something. The men halt, crouching. I make my way forward. The point man shows me a trip-wire stretched across the trail. Then he moves back to the others. I lay down my captured AK-47, then get down on my knees and start tracing the wire into the bushes at the side of the trail. Very carefully, I peel back the undergrowth – and there it is, hidden among the bushes: a grenade. The wire is wrapped round it to keep the handle in, like a temporary pin. I steady myself on my knees and toes and reach out towards it with my right hand. This is the dangerous moment. In one firm movement I clamp the grenade with my fist. Then I unwrap the wire with my other hand. When it is free, I lob the grenade into the trees. It explodes harmlessly, about thirty yards off the trail. There's a flutter of birds taking to the air, and a hooting noise from some animal in the canopy. A few leaves and twigs drop out of the trees. Within a few seconds everything is quiet again. I signal the patrol to move on.

Later that day the point man spots a hut to the left of the trail, about fifty yards off. It looks deserted. I ask Schroeder what he thinks we should do. There's clear ground between the trail and the hut, which makes me a little uneasy. I tell Schroeder to take a squad and approach the hut from further back down the trail, while we keep watch from here. It'll be more work, because they'll need to cut their way through the undergrowth, but you can't be too careful. Twenty minutes later Schroeder and his squad reach the hut, and check all around for booby-traps before wrenching open the door. It's a rice cache; I can see from here the grains spilling out through the entrance. The hut is stuffed with rice three to four feet deep, several tons of it. This is what the VC live on most of the year. They store these caches when the rice harvest is ready, then live on them throughout the rest of the year while they're operating in the area.

I don't need to tell Schroeder what to do. His men tear off the whole front of the building. With their entrenching tools, they start spreading the rice over the ground outside, where it will spoil as soon as it gets wet. Then they burn the hut to the ground with a Willie Peter grenade.

That night we set up an ambush outside our defensive perimeter. At dusk a squad leaves the camp for a spot I've designated about half a mile up the trail. We know that Charlie is nearby, and I feel there is a good chance that he may come sneaking up the trail towards our bivouac. The hunch turns out to be correct. The enemy walks straight into the ambush, and we kill three and capture one injured man before he can escape.

We're still in the Central Highlands, but we've moved into a more populated area. What we're trying to do is make it secure. The enemy has thoroughly infiltrated this region, so that many of the villages have become VC strongholds, with ammunition dumps, weapons caches and food hidden inside walls or tunnels. It's become impossible to distinguish combatants from civilians. The Army reckons that the best way to deal with the problem is to clear out the area altogether, relocating the villagers to a more secure location.

A new guy has joined the platoon to help us, a Vietnamese. His name is Nguyen, pronounced 'new-yen'. Some of the men seem unable to manage that, so they call him Joe. He's what the Army terms a 'Kit Carson', named after the famous Indian frontier scout, one of the enemy soldiers who've surrendered and turned in their weapons, then retrained to fight with us. Our planes drop leaflets all over the countryside encouraging the enemy to defect, and sometimes they do. The main job of these Kit Carsons is to act as interpreters in our dealings with the local population.

Right now we're rounding up the people for resettlement in a more secure location. Low-flying planes broadcast a message through loudspeakers, ordering everybody to assemble in their villages for evacuation, and warning that anybody remaining behind afterwards is liable to be shot. We're going into villages and gathering the local population into one spot, where Nguyen explains what is going to happen. Then the villagers are airlifted out, while we stay behind to burn the village and destroy the crops.

*

We're entering a village. There's a lot of shouting, with panicked animals careering around under our feet. My men are urging the villagers towards a field, where the choppers are due to come and take them away. Perhaps understandably, some don't want to leave. 'GI, you number ten,' sneers one old woman, as a grunt takes her by the arm. One squad goes from hut to hut, making sure they're empty before moving on. We've learned to be cautious; some of these villages are booby-trapped, even though people carry on living there. Sometimes enemy snipers are lurking in what we call spider holes: pits concealed under matting or some other camouflage. You walk past, then suddenly one of those bastards pops up behind you and starts shooting.

A barefoot little boy comes running up to McLellan carrying a can of Coke, holding it from below like an offering. 'Hey, GI, ten MPC.' He's asking for military payment certificates, which the Vietnamese seem to be able to exchange – God knows how, since they're supposed to be restricted for our use only. McLellan fishes in his pocket and hands the boy a note, smiling. He reaches for the can; as he takes it, the boy pulls his hand from underneath, and something falls out of the bottom: a grenade. Jesus! There's no pin: only the sides of the can have prevented the lever from springing up and detonating it. The boy has disappeared into one of the huts. Everyone starts shouting. Too late, McLellan grasps what's happened. The grenade explodes in a roar of dust and flame.

McLellan's lying on the ground screaming, and two more men are down. The others have taken up a defensive position around the injured. I'm so angry, I want to hit out. There must be someone in that hut who gave that little boy the grenade, someone who extracted the pin while jamming it into the can. Without any further prompting, one of my men walks across to the hut and sprays the inside with bullets. Then he unhooks a grenade from his webbing and hurls it through the entrance.

After the smoke clears I count two bodies inside the hut. I tell my men to burn it down.

The medic is administering emergency first aid to the wounded. He tells me that we need to get them out of here fast. McLellan's obviously not going to make it. Some of the villagers are howling, and I can see Nguyen looking at me anxiously. There's a murderous atmosphere in the platoon. I've got to do something fast. I tell Schroeder to take four of the most reliable men and hurry the villagers out of the way, while the rest of the platoon carries on combing the village for any more hidden VC. Meanwhile I get on the radio and order immediate transport for the villagers and the wounded. Ten minutes later the choppers arrive.

That evening we're pulled out of the field and flown back to the LZ. Nguyen sits beside me in the chopper; I've noticed him sticking close to me ever since the incident in the village. Some of the men have been muttering about 'fucking gook traitors' – as if Nguyen might somehow have been responsible for what happened. That's crap, of course. He's particularly vulnerable because he hasn't any kind of weapon to protect himself with. Many Americans, officers as well as men, are wary of the Kit Carsons and don't allow them to be armed.

I've decided I've got to make a gesture to show that I trust him. I give him my captured AK-47. He knows how to use it, of course, because before he defected he'd been using the same weapon against us.

Later I find myself talking to Nguyen about what happened to McLellan and the others. I find it so difficult to understand what the villagers think of us. Here we are, risking our lives for their sake, yet so many seem content to stand by while our boys walk into trap after trap. Are we wasting our time? Are they all VC at heart, I ask him, or are some on our side and some on the other?

'You know what Ho Chi Minh say?' asks Nguyen. I shake my head. 'The people are like the little fishes in the sea. They swim with the current.'

Schroeder reports that we're going to have to rearrange the squads again. Yet another guy is leaving before his time. This one shot off his big toe while on guard duty in a foxhole. Claimed he'd been cleaning his weapon and discharged it by accident. We both know he's done it deliberately – but what are we going to do? Court-martial him? The way guys like him see it, no kind of punishment could be worse than staying out here. Lieutenants are always grumbling about these 'million dollar' wounds, wounds serious enough to get the 'victim' flown home. They're a bloody nuisance.

We're back out in the hills. We've made camp for the night, and I'm fooling around with my new rifle. I say 'new', but really it's an old-fashioned M-1 – a bolt-action sniper rifle with telescopic sights. I drew it from stores to replace the AK-47 I gave to Nguyen.

Up here around dusk you can often see the odd lone figure or small group of two or three enemy soldiers moving around in the distance. Usually you'll get just a fleeting glimpse of someone moving along a trail in the jungle, or the occasional silhouette showing up over a ridge. They know they're pretty safe at a range of eight hundred yards or more, because an M-16 bullet probably wouldn't even reach that far, and the M-16 certainly isn't accurate at that range. But with this little baby, it's another matter. I lie around scanning the jungle through my scope and taking pot-shots at anything I see moving, just for the fun of it. It's only target practice; I can't tell if I've hit anybody, not in this cover and the fading light. Occasionally I'll shoot a tracer round to see how close I'm getting to the target.

*

Usually you can't see more than a few yards into the jungle, but up here in the hills you sometimes find yourself in a high place that gives you a more distant prospect, maybe from a ridge or over a valley. I'm looking out over the treetops now, across to the other side of a valley. There seems to be something moving along a parallel trail on the far side, perhaps a kilometre or so from where I'm standing. From the way they're moving I'd say that they don't seem to be aware of us. I stare at them through the scope on my rifle. I count three Vietcong and – Christ! – two American prisoners, hands tied behind their backs, staggering slightly as they try to keep up with the pace. They're wearing tattered grey flight-suits: downed airmen.

I pull out the map and plot their likely route. It seems to me that, if we move quickly, we may be able to intercept them some kilometres ahead. I call the squad leaders together, and explain what I'm intending to do. I tell them we'll be setting out at once, moving as fast as we can without showing ourselves. Occasionally we catch a glimpse of the VC through the trees.

Three hours later we're in the position I've identified on the map, though I can't be sure that we've reached it ahead of the VC. Then we hear them coming. I hastily deploy the platoon in the usual L-shaped ambush. Fortunately the squad leaders know what to do and are prepared for this order. Every man is in position and well hidden when the enemy comes into view: first a gook point man, then the two tottering Americans, and two more gooks following behind, just as I'd seen them through the scope. I've instructed the machine-gunner facing back down the trail to hold his fire, because otherwise he might hit the prisoners.

The gooks walk on into the ambush. When I give the order, my men open fire from the side. All three gooks are down within seconds. Under this weight of fire there's no danger of any retaliation, and as we emerge from cover it doesn't take long to establish that all three are dead. The airmen seem terrified when the firing begins, and make pathetic attempts to hide, but once they understand that they're being rescued they burst out sobbing, they're so relieved. We untie them, and give them food and drink. They're in poor shape: pale, gaunt, covered in sores and bruises, their filthy flight-suits bedraggled. It's hard to get any sense out of them: they're almost hysterical with relief. They keep hugging us, which is a little embarrassing. Gradually their story emerges. Two months before they bailed out from a Phantom hit by anti-aircraft fire, and they've been prisoners ever since.

It's raining again. The patrol is moving through thick jungle. Trees and bushes encroach on the trail from either side, so that each man has to brush through them as he passes. Rain collects on the leaves, and streams down on our heads and shoulders. I'm up near the front of the line. As I push past yet another trailing branch, a green snake launches itself at me out of its perfect camouflage, hissing. I flinch, turning my back, and the viper glances harmlessly off my poncho on to the muddy ground, where it writhes furiously for a minute, and then is gone. 'Typical of this fucking country,' says one of the men, laughing. 'Even the wildlife is hostile.'

19

Day 120 (246 days short): 4 December 1967

After a while I came to the conclusion that it was pretty stupid to be carrying a single-action rifle: if caught in an attack, an automatic weapon might mean the difference between life and death. I went back to carrying an M-16.

In early December I transferred to the weapons platoon. It was a promotion in a way, because it meant that I no longer had to go out on regular search-and-destroy patrols. The weapons platoon stayed with the company commander and the executive officer, defending the company CP and providing local support for the other patrolling platoons. This was still out in the field, of course, on a temporary LZ, moving whenever the company moved into a new AO. I'd been leading patrols myself for nearly four months, and after this sort of time it was normal for lieutenants to transfer to slightly safer duties as these became available. Perhaps four months doesn't sound very long. But then platoon leaders were the soldiers most likely to be targeted by the enemy. I heard somewhere that the average life expectancy for a platoon leader in a firefight was thirty seconds.

The weapons platoon was equipped with 81-mm mortars, M-60 machine-guns and M-72 lightweight anti-tank weapon (LAW) rocket-launchers. Some of these were too heavy to lug around on patrol, and the main function of the weapons platoon was to protect the company CP and the executive officer, rather than tramping up and down all day in the boonies. Of course, it wasn't completely safe by any means. There was the ever-present danger that the CP might be attacked, particularly at night. During the day the main danger was from the odd sniper. Since I was now responsible for its defence, I divided the platoon into three squads, and sent two out each day to patrol the immediate area around the perimeter, while one remained behind with the heavy weapons.

Though I knew that I'd be a lot safer in my new job, I felt a pang at leaving my old platoon. Several of the men told me that they were sad I was leaving, and Schroeder tried to transfer to the weapons platoon with me, but Captain Matthews wouldn't allow it. Of course, I would still be part of the same company, so I'd see the men of my old platoon regularly as they came in and out of the CP – but I would no longer be responsible for their safety. I'd commanded that platoon for almost four months; in that time it had won a reputation as one of the safest and most efficient in the battalion. I was proud of that. I spent my last few days breaking in a new lieutenant who'd arrived to take over from me. At first I had him watch what I did; then, after a couple of days, I allowed him to take charge while I watched him. I decided that he seemed OK. When the patrol returned to the CP, I reported to Captain Matthews that I'd formally handed over command to the new guy and was ready to assume my new duties.

I was already familiar with my new sergeant, who had been with me at Fort Dix, but it was harder for me to get to know the other men of the weapons platoon. There was not so much for me to do, and therefore less opportunity for me to show myself worthy of their command. On patrol the lieutenant needs to look out for the men, and the men need to look out for the lieutenant. You're more dependent on each other. However, it was a lot less strenuous in the weapons platoon, and even comfortable in its own way. When, as was often the case, we set up a company LZ near a river, I was able to walk down and take a swim-bath. This seemed an astonishing luxury after three sweaty weeks on patrol without a wash or a change of clothes, my underwear rotting on my body.

A week or so after I took command of the weapons platoon, the company moved, together with the rest of the battalion, to LZ Colt, a semi-permanent firebase. It was almost the end of the winter monsoon, when the rain was at its heaviest. The temperature dropped dramatically, down to the mid-fifties. This seemed freezing after the temperatures we'd become used to, often well over 100° Fahrenheit in the middle of the day.

I'm sitting behind the .50-calibre machine-gun, one leg on either side of the breach, having my picture taken. The .50-cal is set up in an open sandbag bunker, facing out from the perimeter. I'm interested in guns of all kinds, and this is a chance for me to try something different. It's just a bit of fun, really. There's not much variety here on LZ Colt, hanging around on top of this damn hill, so you grab your entertainment wherever you can.

This is one hell of a gun. When equipped with armour-piercing rounds, it's capable of penetrating a tank. Gripping the two handles at the rear and firing it, you feel an awesome sense of power. Yet it's easy to use: it moves freely on its supporting tripod, and there's little recoil. There are no sights; you just look along it and fire, adjusting your aim by watching the tracer rounds. One man on his own can operate it quite easily, feeding in new belts from the ammunition cans here in the bunker. It's also much slower than a conventional machine-gun, firing only about two rounds a second.

Right now B Company is responsible for defending the LZ, and I should really be at my platoon command post. Each platoon in B Company is defending a different sector of the perimeter. The artillery company stationed here permanently defends the battalion CP at the centre of the firebase.

I'm still sitting here passing time with the .50-cal when the sun goes down. Just as it's getting dark, we start to receive incoming rounds. At first it's no more than sniper fire. By now I'm used to this, and it doesn't worry me unduly. Given our position on the top of a hill, we should be protected from rifle fire unless we expose ourselves above the perimeter defences – although by sitting here in this uncovered sandbag emplacement I'm putting myself at risk. Then the first mortar bomb detonates, and another, followed by two or three more every half-hour or so. I hate mortars because there's not much you can do to protect yourself against them, unless you bury yourself deep in a heavily reinforced bunker.

I can't see where the fire is coming from. I try popping off a few rounds here and there, hoping for lucky hit. The tracer looks much brighter and bigger in the dark. Suddenly the gun gives a tremendous buck and explodes in my face.

I lie on my back, stunned. My arms and legs are bleeding in several places; my fatigues are hanging in tatters, my face is scorched; I can smell cordite and singed hair. It hurts like shit – but so far as I can tell I'm not badly injured, thank God. I'm trying to work out what's happened. It felt as if some giant had grabbed the gun and given it the most almighty shake, then dropped a grenade between my legs. The .50-cal is wrecked. Though it seems like a million-to-one chance, I reckon that an incoming round must have come straight down the cone-shaped barrel and exploded the shell in the breach, scattering shrapnel straight at my body, only inches away. Fortunately the barrel must have taken most of the blast, and the jolt threw me backwards, otherwise I'd probably be blinded by now.

I need to be back at my platoon command post, co-ordinating the perimeter defence in this sector. It's a substantial bunker, about fifty yards off. But I can't just limp over there. If I stand up now, I'll be an easy target against the sky. I start wriggling across the LZ on my belly, the occasional bullet whizzing overhead. The pain in my arms and legs intensifies.

I make it to the bunker OK. The medic examines my injuries and removes whatever shrapnel he can see, then applies field dressings. I'm lucky: they're only flesh wounds. Five minutes later I'm wearing new fatigues and ready for action. I assess the situation with the platoon sergeant. It seems that none of my men has seen any movement out there. There's certainly no indication of a serious attack on the LZ in the sector of the perimeter that we're guarding. Sporadic fire comes in. I report on the radio to Captain Matthews. The consensus seems to be that Charlie's just playing a game with us. That's happened often enough before, and we've become accustomed to this type of harassing fire. Charlie likes us to keep our heads down. I order the guards in the foxholes to stay alert, and request regular flares every quarter of an hour in case sappers try to penetrate the perimeter. Typically they come in squads, perhaps eight men in loincloths crawling through the wire, rifles over their shoulders, dragging satchel charges behind them. These are canvas bags packed with plastic explosive. They'll infiltrate the base and head for the command post at the centre, which is all too obvious, with its prominent radio antenna. Once there, they'll pull the fuses, then hurl their satchels into the CP. That will be the cue for the base to be overrun, once the

CP is destroyed and all our main communication is down.

Night falls. Hours pass. By midnight we're still receiving the odd incoming round, and returning fire periodically whenever we can see flashes to aim at. I'm at the platoon command post on the perimeter with the sergeant and a few others. My leg wounds are bothering me, but not badly enough to make me want to undertake the risky journey across the LZ to the aid station. And my duty is here.

Without warning, several large explosions detonate inside the base, one after another. That doesn't sound like enemy artillery. I chance a look out of the bunker, and see flames and smoke pouring from the battalion CP. The bastards are inside the wire! It's a terrifying feeling – as if one moment you're in a locked and bolted house, aware that there is a prowler outside, then suddenly you sense that he's in there with you.

The radio's crackling, but nothing's coming through. We're on our own.

The others crouch down inside the bunker, behind the sandbags, facing out towards the wire. But I think: No, this is shit; Charlie's inside the perimeter and he could easily sneak up behind us and lob a grenade in here, or even one of his satchel bombs. We could be trapped. It's safer to be in the open.

Grabbing my M-16, I duck out of the side entrance of the bunker and crawl round the back, facing towards the battalion CP. Outside is chaos. Fires are burning around the CP, with the occasional explosion still going off. I can see charging black figures silhouetted against the flames. Bullets are coming in from all directions, from inside as well as outside the base, ricocheting off rocks and thumping into the sandbags. There's a very high risk of being hit by friendly fire. I put my head down and wait. If I stay here, I can defend the bunker, and keep in touch with the guys inside. If I crawl further away, I'll be completely on my own.

There's no point in firing unless I have something to fire at, and there's a danger that I might shoot one of our own men in the confusion. I stay put, rifle at the ready, expecting gooks to appear out of the darkness at any moment. Eventually the firing begins to die down.

Captain Matthews comes through on the radio; the operator crawls out from the bunker with the handset. It's as I feared: the battalion CP has been knocked out by the sappers. The colonel, the battalion XO and the battalion sergeant-major are all dead. But the LZ now seems to be secure. I send out a patrol to make sure.

By two o'clock in the morning the firing's stopped. We remain on alert. At dawn we begin the body count.

It's late morning. I sit cross-legged, eating my lunch of C-rations. I'm thinking about the corpses we buried this morning. Not our guys, of course – their bodies are being flown home in body bags: I'm thinking now about the enemy. It was our job to 'police up' – to pick up the dozen or so gooks littered around the firebase and load them on to the back of a pick-up. They are driven across to the edge of the LZ and tipped into a newly dug pit, where a bulldozer quickly covers them with earth.

It was strange how small they were. Even the biggest of them was no taller than a child. Some had the faces of old men, but it was hard to judge their true age, because out here most people look much older than they really are. Others seemed to be only teenagers. I picked up one of the sappers, a boy in a loincloth, and I was startled to find how light he was. Some of the other guys were flinging the bodies on to the pile, but somehow I couldn't do that. I laid him carefully in the back of the truck.

He was a soldier. He deserves a little respect.

Another wet morning on the firebase. Rain drumming on your

helmet and streaming down your poncho. Water dripping down your face, coursing down your neck, splashing up your ankles, running down inside your sleeve as soon as you lift your arm. Mud everywhere. Everything you touch gets muddy: your weapon, your clothes, your mattress, your letters. Letters weeping in the rain, forming sad puddles in the brown earth.

The chopper delivered the mail a few minutes ago. A sackful of hope, a flimsy link to home. It's my job to distribute it. Even when there are letters for me, I make sure everyone else in the platoon has theirs before I sit down to read my own. One from Debbie, full of plans for our wedding, a thousand years from now. And another from my mother, with news of all the family. News from outer space.

'LT, I think you'd better talk to Adams.'

Another filthy, sodden scarecrow. Surely I don't look like him?

'I think he's had bad news from his wife. It looks like a dear-John.'

Dear John, I don't know how to say this . . .

Dear John, I've been thinking so much about us . . .

Dear John, You'll always be special to me . . .

Adams is sitting on a stump, knees out wide, head down and swinging dangerously. A big, wide, clumsy man, with a smile like a sunburst. Except that he's not smiling now. His helmet hangs on a stick, filling up with rain. Water runs down his forehead, forming a curtain over his eyes.

I get my speech ready. It's not the end of the world, you know. They often change their mind. Anyway, there are plenty more fish in the sea.

'Adams . . .'

'Fuck off, LT.'

'Adams, it may not be as bad as you think.'

'Leave me alone.'

I leave him alone, and go in search of the chaplain.

The worst part of it is being stuck out here. It's not just that she's left you. It's that you can't do a fucking thing about it. You can't even get down on your knees to plead.

Later that day, I'm trying to clean my gun when I hear an explosion not far behind me. My first thought is that we're under attack. I jump up and look round – and then I see the mess behind the jeep, and I know at once what's happened.

On top of this jeep is an anti-personnel, anti-tank recoilless rifle. Calling it a rifle is misleading: it's really an artillery piece. The shell comes out of the muzzle at the front, the blast comes out of the back. And it's one hell of a blast. We've all been warned that it can be lethal up to twenty feet away.

It seems that Adams loaded the rifle and stood with his stomach pressed up hard against the back. He wouldn't have been able to reach the trigger from there, so he rigged up a piece of string to the trigger mechanism. When he pulled the string, his body was literally blown apart.

It's my duty to collect the pieces, a leg here, an arm there, something horrible hanging from a bush, trailing in the mud, draped over a hooch. They are scattered a remarkable distance across the firebase. It takes time to find all of him; I don't want to leave any bits lying about. Everything stuffed into a polythene bag, even the head, which I pick up by his thin brown hair. I remember how the water streamed down his face like tears.

Two days ago B Company made a combat assault into new territory. There haven't been any ground troops patrolling in this area until now. We established a defensive perimeter, then settled down on this new LZ where we plan to stay at least a week, while the first search-and-destroy patrol sets out. My men dig pits for the mortars, to protect the mortar bombs from being hit by stray rounds and exploding. There's another reason for digging these pits: to provide a piece of level ground for the baseplate. If the mortar isn't level, none of its calibrations will read accurately.

I'm out with a squad on a local patrol. The idea is to try to sweep the immediate surrounding area, to discourage night attacks on our camp.

We're approaching a tiny hamlet of perhaps half a dozen huts. The men are very tense because we heard some shooting as we were setting out. There's a body lying on the ground near one of the huts. A baby is crying down there somewhere. Before we start moving in, I make the men wait while I radio for support from another squad. When they arrive, I take my squad right round to secure the other side of the hamlet before I feel it is safe enough to go in. All this time we can hear the baby crying.

I'm getting close to the huts now. There are more bodies. We explore the huts one by one, but we don't find anyone alive until we reach the hut with the baby. The howls get louder as we approach, until they drown all other sounds. I'm the first to look inside. There is the screaming baby in a primitive cot. A few feet away is the naked body of a teenage girl. There's a pool of blood between her legs, and more around her head, where half her face has been blown away.

There are ants feeding in her skull. A cockroach scuttles across her belly and away down her thigh.

I feel my gorge rise. My stomach heaves, and I turn away quickly. I vomit on to the ground outside the hut, trembling with horror. Another guy looks into the hut and I hear his shocked exclamation. I rinse my mouth out with water from my canteen. Then I pick up the baby and tell the men that we're leaving.

I've been on the verge of tears all day. My heart feels as if it is going to break at any moment. I don't know what happened back there in that hamlet. I don't suppose I'll ever know. Jesus, that poor girl!

I dare not cry in front of all these brave men. I manage to steal a couple of minutes alone in my hooch to let my emotions out.

I keep asking myself: Why am I doing this? And wondering: Could there possibly be an honourable way out of here?

As of today, I have 228 days remaining before I'm due to go home. I've started to dream about it. I picture myself striding off the plane, dressed in my smartest uniform, Debbie waiting for me behind the barrier.

I'm afraid of what's happening to me. I'm trying to hang on to the important things, but I feel myself going cold inside. I can't feel things the same way any more. This lousy war is fucking me up.

I take out a picture of Debbie and hold it in front of me, trying to remember the sound of her voice. I feel so very, very alone.

Christmas morning. A very weird day. The chopper brings us an unlikely visitor: Santa Claus! Complete with white beard and red tunic – and presents. There's a case of beer from Uncle Sam, and parcels from our families, including a miniature Christmas tree from my mother, complete with Christmas decorations: tinsel and coloured glass balls to hang from the tree, and a star to put on top. Strange to see something so delicate in this brutal place. My mother's also sent me tangerines, nuts and sugared almonds.

I'm trying to read a letter from some friends of my parents back in York, Pennsylvania: a nice old couple. They tell me how much they appreciate my efforts to quell the Communist tide. There was a time when a letter like that would have made me proud. Now I don't feel anything.

*

1.40 a.m. on LZ Shortie, on the night of 6/7 January. I'm asleep in my hooch.

An explosion drags me awake. Shots, shouting, the incongruous sound of a whistle blowing. I stumble out of the hooch, grabbing my pistol. Outside is pandemonium. Flames blaze up from one of the mortar pits. Scurrying figures show up fleetingly against the light. I'm crouching low to avoid the crossfire. Someone blunders into me in the darkness, knocking me over. A grunt. By the time I'm on my feet again, he's gone. Then a sudden whoosh of flame, and one of the hooches catches fire. A flame-thrower! I fire at where I think the gook holding it must be, but a few seconds later there's another whoosh, and this time I see a GI caught by the flame. It's Ramirez, one of my men. He starts screaming and rolling on the ground. I fire again, and shots come whistling past my ear. One of our guys cowers in his foxhole; I scream at him to get up and fight, or I'll shoot. Yet another whoosh, and I have a momentary image of the horrified faces of two men in a bunker as flaming death sweeps towards them. Gunfire coming from every direction. More shouting, and another explosion. Then I hear the company commander's order to cease firing. A flare goes up, illuminating a scene of carnage: scattered bodies, several of them blackened, and burned-out hooches. The enemy has gone.

The next day, after coming under mortar attack from the valley below, we call down air strikes. There seems to be a lot of Charlies in this area. Ten minutes later Phantoms screech low overhead, strafing the enemy positions with cannon. Then they carpet the valley with napalm. We line the perimeter and cheer as the jungle below erupts in fire and black smoke. It sure makes a guy feel good, knowing that all this stuff is at our disposal. I'd feel very nervous if Charlie had such sophisticated weapons to use on us.

After the jets have gone, we send two platoons down into the valley. A while later they call in to say that they've found dead and wounded gooks all over the place. They're bringing back some prisoners.

The choppers are coming to take us out. We're abandoning the LZ. One of the men nails a sign to a tree-stump: 'In memory of Private First Class Raul Ramirez, K.I.A. 7 January 1968'. I leave the Christmas tree below the sign, still loaded with its fragile decorations.

20

Day 153 (213 days short): 6 January 1968

Now that I was with the weapons platoon and spending most of my time at the CP, I became friendly with the company executive officer, another lieutenant, called Bob Trimble. He'd been a bit sceptical of me when I joined the company back in August, but I guess I must have improved in his eyes as the months passed. Bob was a wag: a lanky guy from Hawaii, with thinning curly hair that he imagined made him look like Michael Caine, and round gold glasses that gave him a misleadingly studious appearance. He liked to tease me about being English, often throwing in expressions like 'smashing', 'jolly good show', 'listening to the wireless' and being 'on a sticky wicket'. He had found out from Army records that my real name was Tom, and from then on always called me 'Thomas'. It was all water off a duck's back so far as I was concerned, and we became firm friends. He didn't have a girlfriend back home, so I suggested he write to Debbie to see if one of her flatmates might oblige (her friend Anthea was now writing to

Bruce Schroeder). Bob wrote her a facetious letter, describing himself as 'Thomas's flatmate'.

> I think I should describe myself for your lucky roomy. I'm about four feet three inches tall, with funny glasses, my skin is a slight hue of green, and I'm losing my hair! And I have a slight hunchback, but it's hardly noticeable unless you look for it . . . Your roomys will probably fight tooth and nail for who is going to write to me, so have the survivor send me a picture . . . If not, I'm going to offer myself to Sophia Loren or Twiggy (ugh!).

I don't think that any of Debbie's flatmates ever took up his offer.

By late January the weather was becoming muggy. I was nearly half-way through my tour of duty, and had begun to count the days I had remaining in Vietnam. This was an almost universal habit. When you were approaching the end, you were said to be 'short'. Guys who were short became noticeably twitchy, and were often excused the most dangerous duties, such as ambush patrols. I was hoping that I might soon be transferred to a posting in the rear, away from the action and the ever-present danger. There were said to be six rear-echelon jobs for every one in the front line. Certainly there seemed to be plenty of 'pogues' serving out their tours of duty in big bases like An Khe or Bien Hoa, unloading supplies or carrying out essentially administrative functions. If I'd ever looked forward to being in action, I'd certainly had enough of it by now, and I would have been quite happy to serve out the rest of my tour sitting behind a desk somewhere.

In the more immediate future, I was looking forward to my second period of R & R, coming up in mid-February. As was normal in such cases, I'd be leaving my sergeant in charge of the platoon. This time I was allowed to leave Vietnam altogether. I flirted with the idea of spending the four days with Debbie in Bangkok, but when I weighed up the expense and the travelling time, I decided to head for Hong Kong, which was only a two-and-a-half-hour flight from Saigon.

On 20 January we left LZ Colt, and for the remainder of the month we were kept perpetually on the move, making a series of combat assaults into new locations, never staying in any of them for more than one night. I was pleased, because the constant activity kept us busy and made the time pass more quickly. Gradually we moved further and further north, until by the end of the month we were only twenty miles south of Hue, not far from the DMZ. There were plenty of rumours about what we would be doing next, but by now I had learned not to speculate. It was better just to do what you had to do, and to wait for the next order.

On the anniversary of my commission, I was automatically promoted to the rank of first lieutenant. I was now entitled to wear a silver bar on my shoulder, rather than the gold bar of a second lieutenant. Within the Army, promotion was linked to time in-service, rather than to performance. There was no immediate change in my duties, but at least it meant that I could hope for a staff job in due course. Whatever happened, I would remain a lieutenant; on a first tour a lieutenant could not hope for promotion to captain.

On 31 January 1968, as the Vietnamese celebrated the lunar New Year, the enemy launched a massive offensive against towns and cities throughout the South, penetrating the very walls of the US embassy in the heart of Saigon. Our intelligence had failed to detect the build-up to this surprise attack, which became known as the Tet (meaning New Year) Offensive. It was a profound shock to the American public, which over recent months had received repeated reassurances from President Johnson and his

Army commanders that a successful end to the war was near. Americans back home were horrified to see television footage of diplomats and embassy guards engaged in what looked like a last-ditch defence. Up near the DMZ, the NVA overwhelmed ARVN forces defending the city of Hue, famous for its pagodas and palaces and known as the 'Venice of Vietnam' because of its moats and canals. The capture of the old imperial capital was an important symbolic victory for the enemy. Afterwards the North Vietnamese troops and their Vietcong allies carried out the most terrible atrocities, murdering thousands of the city's civilians.

At the time, we soldiers out in the field knew less about what was going on than the average American sitting in front of his television back home. Much of this I learned only later, when I had access to newspapers and television on R & R. When B Company, in common with other Cav units, was sent in by helicopter to positions west of Hue and ordered to sweep towards the city, we didn't know that we were being sent in to relieve the Marines, who were engaged in fierce fighting in an attempt to retake the city. If we thought about it at all, we assumed that this was just an operation like any other.

We were now operating on battalion level, deployed in line formation, so for this purpose the weapons platoon operated like any other in the company and, indeed, the whole battalion.

We made a combat assault into paddy-fields some miles to the west of Hue, not yet within sight of the city. The winter monsoon had returned with a vengeance, bringing torrential rain and much colder temperatures. Low cloud cover made helicopter movement difficult and air support impossible. As soon as we landed we came under fire, and from then on every paddy, every patch of woodland was fiercely contested.

I'm wading across an open rice paddy. The water sloshes lazily at my feet. I'm keeping my eyes fixed on a small area of woodland about a hundred yards ahead. It's late morning, humid and hot; the sun has briefly broken through the cloud, though I can see another line of grey coming in from the east, from the direction of the sea.

My platoon is spread out around me. Perhaps we should be spread out further. A couple of men lag behind. All of us are alert, expecting action at any moment. We've been involved in firefights every few hours since we began the advance on Hue a few days back.

The air is still; there's no sound apart from the gurgle of water around my boots. None of the men are talking. Then I hear a faint 'ploop', and another, and another. I shout the warning, 'Mortar attack!' Almost at the same moment there's an explosion in the paddy, filling the air with shrapnel and mud, and droplets of water, like a sudden squall of rain. I start running towards the trees, trying to keep low as further mortar bombs explode nearby. There's an explosion behind me, and I feel a sharp pain in my back, just below my pack. I lurch forward to the woodline.

By the time I reach the trees the mortar attack has finished; I wasn't counting, but there were probably no more than half a dozen rounds. I could tell from the size of the explosions that this was a light, portable mortar. Most likely a hit-and-run attack by a small group; they'd probably packed up and gone before we even reached the tree-line. The sergeant sends out a squad to explore the woods in any case. Meanwhile we assess the situation. It seems that the two men behind me didn't make it.

I'm lying on my face. Someone removes my pack. The medic has peeled back the shirt of my fatigues. He extracts a lump of shrapnel lodged in my flesh just to the left of my spine. Luckily it was almost spent, so it hasn't penetrated very deep; and because mortar rounds are red-hot they tend to be sterile, so there's little chance of infection. He cleans the wound and applies a field dressing. Within half an hour I'm back on my feet and we're moving forward once more.

The weather was closing in again as we continued our advance towards Hue. Progress across the sodden ground was difficult, and the enemy continued to put up stiff resistance. We didn't know it then, but we were following the same route that the NVA had taken in their surprise attack on the city. Most nights Charlie tried to infiltrate the defences of our bivouacs. By this time my leave was imminent, and as the cloud cover increased it became touch-and-go as to whether I would be able to get out when the moment came. On my last night in the field I did not sleep at all, as the enemy repeatedly probed our perimeter. Early the next morning we came under mortar attack, and just as this finished a supply chopper arrived. I climbed aboard. As it rose into the cloud, I caught a brief glimpse of the city, now only about five kilometres away. Great plumes of smoke were rising from several different fires.

Twenty-four hours later I was looking down on another city as our plane made the steep descent into Kai Tak airport. On board were fifty or sixty officers, all scrubbed and dressed in crisp khaki uniform with before and after hats, each with a roll of notes tucked into his pocket. A planeload of testosterone, ready to rock 'n' roll.

I'd spent the previous evening with four other guys (two of them from the Cav) at the officers' club at Long Binh, where we'd drunk a skinful of beer over an increasingly riotous poker game. Just as on my last R & R, it felt almost decadent to wear clean clothes and sleep in a bed with sheets, and to eat proper food – to feel like a civilized human being again. After months of enforced abstinence, we were determined to paint the town red together – even our morning hangovers could not discourage us. I'd already decided to stay at the President Hotel in Kowloon, and the other guys agreed to come along, too. Money was no object as each of us was carrying thousands of dollars – accumulated savings from more than six months' active service, since out in the field we'd had nowhere to spend our money. We filed off the plane in a group and walked towards the terminal. But I had to separate from the others at Passport Control, where there was one queue for British citizens and another for everyone else. In one line, hundreds of American servicemen, all raring to go; in the other, me.

On the other side I found a smartly dressed RAF lieutenant of about my own age waiting for me. His name was Dick Steed; he was stationed here in Hong Kong. It seemed that my godfather, now an air marshal back in England, had detailed Dick to take care of me during my stay and to show me around. He had an official RAF car outside. I explained about my three friends, and Dick agreed to drive us all to the hotel. It was a strange and not unpleasant feeling. For the past few years I'd been a foreigner in America and in the American Army; now these Americans were the foreigners in a British colony, passengers in an official RAF car driven by a British officer.

Dick dropped us off at the President, where we took the entire top floor to ourselves, each occupying a penthouse suite. At Dick's suggestion we decided to treat ourselves to some handmade civilian clothes. Within the hour, shirtmakers, suitmakers and cobblers had begun to arrive. They measured us up and departed, promising delivery the next morning. In the meantime we headed for the nearest bar. The rest of the day passed in a blur. I do remember that evening, when we arrived at a Kowloon nightclub. We decided we wanted it to ourselves, so we paid the mama-san to close the club to anyone but the four of us. All the girls gathered round the honeypot. We were like a bunch of spoilt rock stars, with no indulgence too much for us. That night we took the girls back to the hotel in a fleet of cabs.

The next morning there was a tap on my door at a disgustingly early hour. It was Dick Steed. I beckoned him into the now rather seedy hotel room, and he waited while I dressed hastily in my khaki uniform, somewhat crumpled from last night's excesses. Then I walked out with him, a little unsteadily, and climbed into his car. He told me that we were headed for the Gurkha base in the New Territories up near the Chinese border, where the commander was a personal friend. We took the scenic route, and by the time we arrived I was beginning to feel human again. It was disconcerting to step out of the car in an American uniform and return the salute of an Asian wearing the uniform of the British Army. I was shown around like a visiting dignitary, and before we left I was made an honorary member of the Queen's Own Gurkha Rifles.

I spent the next few days sightseeing with Dick, carousing with the boys – and shopping. I had all this money burning a hole in my pocket, and there seemed no reason in the world not to spend it. In one of the huge Hong Kong department stores, where everything appeared to be so cheap, I bought lots of things I didn't need – naff purchases, huge canteens of gold cutlery, that sort of thing. I arranged to leave all of it with Dick for onward shipment back to America. By the time I left Hong Kong, I had spent every cent I had on me, thousands of US dollars. I had to borrow some cash from Dick to tip the chambermaid.

I didn't mind having blown so much money in such a short time. It was worth it, just to experience the sense of freedom after so many months in the field.

It was only after a day or two in Hong Kong that I began to pick up a sense of what the rest of the world already knew was happening in Vietnam. Back in my hotel room that same afternoon as our visit to the Gurkha camp, I watched with incredulity a television bulletin about the brutal house-to-house fighting in Hue. We hadn't even been told that the citadel had fallen to the enemy. This was my first glimpse of the war as it appeared to the outside world since my arrival in Vietnam. I was dismayed by what I saw. Our view on the ground was that we were on the brink of victory, yet according to the television reporters we were on the verge of defeat. Were we fooling ourselves? I found it very confusing.

That night I spoke on the telephone to Debbie. I'd written in advance asking her to be sure to be around on that day to take my call. I was very nervous beforehand. When she answered the phone, I was so excited that I could barely think what to say. She sounded as if she was feeling nervous, too. It was more than seven months since I'd last heard her voice. Of course, we'd been writing to each other every few days, so there wasn't much news to catch up with: it was the contact itself that was so precious. She cried a little, and I found myself longing to take her in my arms. The call lasted over an hour. It was very hard to say goodbye at the end. I found myself repeatedly assuring her that I would take care of myself and promising to come back safely to her at the end of my tour – as if I could promise any such thing.

The following night, my last night in Hong Kong, I telephoned home. I spoke to my parents and to my sister Pat. It was another very emotional conversation. I hadn't grasped until this moment how anxious my mother had been about me. She sounded almost desperate. I tried to calm her with a series of platitudes. Things were not so bad as they appeared; the press tended to sensationalize the danger; I was through the worst now, and there was every chance that I would soon be moving to a post in the rear. And so on. The conversation unsettled me. The more I tried to reassure her, the less convincing my answers seemed. I was dreading the thought of going back to Vietnam. And, of course, I didn't know then what was about to happen.

I'm sitting on the bed in my hotel room, my passport in my hand. There's a knock at the door. I don't answer it. I hear a voice asking, 'Bud?' and then, after a pause, footsteps fading away down the corridor.

I've been agonizing about this most of the night, and I still haven't decided what to do. Now I've hardly any time left: minutes maybe, half an hour maximum, before Dick arrives to drive us back to the airport. And by then it will be too late.

For perhaps the hundredth time in the past twelve hours I get to my feet and walk to the window. There's a spectacular view over the harbour to Hong Kong island. Down there, millions of people are going about their everyday lives, with nothing more to worry about than the next week's rent. How I envy them!

It was my mother who dangled the terrible temptation before me. After I spoke to my parents on the telephone last night, she called back a few minutes later. I knew without asking that my father wasn't listening in: maybe he had known that she was going to call me back and had deliberately absented himself to avoid an argument, or maybe she was calling me without his knowledge; I don't know. She went straight to the point. I didn't need to go back to Vietnam. The United States Army had no jurisdiction over me. I was in a British colony; I had my passport; I could take a cab to the airport and catch the next plane back to England. She pleaded with me. I owed it to Debbie not to go back. Most of all, I owed it to her. She thought she would die of grief when she lost Rick. If she lost me, her life would be over.

She began to weep. I tried to comfort her, though I was so stunned by the possibility she'd raised that I didn't know how to react.

I told her I'd sleep on it.

Of course, I didn't sleep. I've been tossing and turning all night long, thinking it over this way and that. *I don't have to go back!* This amazing thought has never occurred to me before – perhaps the idea was half formed in my mind, but I hadn't allowed it to take shape there. The possibility is so enormously attractive. There's no risk involved. I'd be free in England; there's no danger of being extradited. It's like a condemned man being offered a full pardon, if only he will sign a little piece of paper.

I turn away from the window and walk back to the bed. There's my passport staring up at me. Take it, and go!

If I don't go back to Vietnam, I can never return to America. A whole side of my life will be gone for ever. How much does that matter? I can marry Debbie and settle down in England. No problem. What else do I need?

Desertion. That's what it would be. A dishonourable end to my military career, breaking the trust put in me by the Army. It sounds bad, but I can live with that. It's one thing to be puffing out your chest at Fort Benning. It's quite another thing to be struggling through the mud in the pressure-cooker heat of Vietnam. Somehow all those words – duty, honour, loyalty – have less resonance out there.

I suppose the war hasn't turned out as I expected. Most of the time we're not fighting a clean fight, one man against another, in a trial of strength and courage. It's all booby-traps and snipers on one side, air and artillery strikes on the other. High tech against low tech. And, in the middle, the Vietnamese people, who don't seem to care one way or the other.

All that trudging around in the jungle seems so pointless. We spend weeks making an area secure; and then, the moment we move out, the enemy moves back in.

Nobody I've met out here cares about defeating Communism

or any of that shit. Everyone just wants to survive through to the end of his tour.

I'm English, Goddammit. It's not my war.

Then I think about some of the men who haven't made it: Phil Schwarz, his head disintegrating in front of my eyes; Price, his jaw blown away; McLellan, his life leaking away into the dirt, a look of astonishment still on his face. And so many others I've seen suffering and dying. I owe it to them to go back.

There's another knock at the door. I hold my passport between my thumb and forefinger as if weighing it, my teeth clenched. Then I drop it into my bag. 'I'll be with you in a minute,' I shout.

I flew back into Da Nang through torrential rain. All the choppers were grounded. I managed to cadge a ride up towards Hue in the back of a truck, part of a heavily guarded supply convoy: a slow journey along a cratered highway, its surface awash. Visibility was down to ten yards or so: I could barely see the lights of the truck behind. The rain drummed down relentlessly on the tarpaulin cover. As we approached Hue I could hear the sound of heavy fighting. The convoy swung west off the highway before it reached the city, then halted at what seemed to be some kind of depot. Half-naked men started unloading the trucks in the rain, water streaming down their faces and their bare torsos. I jumped out, splashing my way through the mud and chaos, stopping to ask anyone who looked like they might know for directions towards my unit. Half an hour later I was on my way in an armoured personnel-carrier (APC) to my battalion CP.

Reporting for duty, I found that I'd been reassigned to D Company, which was short of an experienced lieutenant. I never did go back to the weapons platoon; I suppose some other lieutenant took over. I was a bit pissed off about the change, but I didn't make too much of it; it was normal for lieutenants to be shifted around like this. My new company commander, a tall, white Midwesterner in his late twenties, briefed me on my new command and the tactical position. The battalion had reached the outskirts of Hue, within sight of the citadel, but we were still meeting heavy resistance and had yet to link up with the Marines. The weather prevented us from calling down air support, and the generals had forbidden us from using heavy artillery within the city limits in the forlorn hope of preserving the ancient citadel from destruction. All technological advantages over the enemy had therefore been neutralized. Supply was a problem: everything needed to be trucked in, so priority was being given to ammunition and C-rations. Hot food and all other luxuries were suspended. Later that day another APC drove me along one of the many tracks leading into the city to join my new platoon, slipping and sliding in the mud.

I found the platoon in the western suburbs of Hue, a jumble of ramshackle, single-storey shacks with corrugated-iron roofs and only the occasional more substantial building lining muddy avenues and narrow alleyways, many backing on to the intricate waterways interlacing the city. Plenty of these were in ruins; the streets were littered with burned-out vehicles and corpses. We were conducting house-to-house searches: one man would take up position to provide covering fire while the others entered the building and flushed out the civilians cowering inside. Only when we were certain that they were not VC would we allow them to return and move on. Once we came across a mass grave of civilian 'collaborators' butchered by the enemy, the bodies sprinkled with lime to speed their decomposition. The killers had been forced to retreat before they could bury their victims.

The enemy could be anywhere – behind a wall pitted by sniper fire, in a darkened, burned-out building, in the sewers. Often the two sides were no more than a few yards apart. The smell of death and burning hung over the city. As we neared the citadel we could hear up ahead the sound of rockets, mixed in with the crack of rifles, the zip of automatic weapons and the staccato drumming of machine-guns. Later, the restrictions on the use of artillery within the city were lifted, and loud explosions could be heard.

Conditions were appalling. Most of time we were up to our knees in mud, shouting at each other through the rain and moving forward only with extreme caution, frequently coming under harassing fire from small cells of NVA or Vietcong. Sometimes, when the cloud lifted, I glimpsed an elegant pagoda standing serenely on the banks of the Perfume river to the south: an incongruous vision of timeless sanity, a weird contrast to the stressed-out madness of everything else that was happening.

After several days of this house-to-house fighting, moving ever closer to the citadel, the moment came when the resistance faded away. The enemy pulled out, fleeing from the city, north towards the DMZ and west towards the Central Highlands. Cav units were ordered to cut off their escape. Once control of the main highway was re-established, D Company was trucked out beyond the retreating NVA forces, and then began sweeping back towards the city, with the aim of mopping up as many of them as we could find. We were forced to use road transport, because all our choppers were still grounded. To begin with, there was no air support for the same reason, though as the weather cleared, our aircraft began to resume their sorties.

The operation turned into a seemingly endless succession of skirmishes with small groups of enemy soldiers who had become separated from their units. Occasionally, however, we encountered the enemy in greater strength.

It's late afternoon. The rain has stopped, and the sky is now almost clear. A hot sun harassing the wispy cloud, drinking the water off the leaves, sucking it up from the ground. We've decided to make camp in this patch of woodland between the paddy-fields, which at least provides some shade. The men are digging foxholes around the edge of the trees and the sergeants are organizing guard duty. Then we come under mortar fire. No hit-and-run attack this time, but sustained and heavy. Like everyone else, I'm flat on the ground, with my face pressed into the soil to avoid the flying shrapnel. We're taking a lot of casualties. Between the explosions I can hear screams and groans, and agonized calls. Medics are bobbing up and down all around. The company commander is radioing for urgent artillery and air support. Though no one quite knows where the fire is coming from.

Then I hear someone shout, 'They're coming!' I look out over the paddy and see dozens, no, *hundreds* of soldiers streaming across the field towards us. These aren't VC: they're NVA regulars in pith helmets, wave after wave of them. It's so weird seeing them out in the open like this, after so many months when they've been hiding from us. I grab my rifle, in a surge of fear and elation. At last! I fire at one of the nearest men, now less than fifty yards away; I see his body jerk, and fall.

Then a heavy artillery bombardment begins, pulverizing their rear positions. They're still coming on, though, and the nearer they get, the safer they are from our artillery. They're firing at us now. A man kneeling behind a tree near me lets out a sudden sigh and collapses. I can hear the rattle of an M-60, then the shockingly loud scream of jet engines as a Phantom passes so low overhead that I duck. Cannon peppers the paddy like vicious rain, dropping the enemy soldiers one after another. Their line breaks, and scatters, running for cover. We're still picking them off as the survivors disappear into the distance.

21

Day 209 (157 days short): 2 March 1968

By the end of February 1968, a month after the Tet Offensive was launched, the enemy was in full retreat from the towns and cities of South Vietnam, back into the Central Highlands and to their safe havens across the border. They left behind tens of thousands of dead. 'I don't see how Charlie can survive much longer,' I wrote to my parents. I didn't say anything about the ordeal I'd just been through. On 2 March, the battalion was pulled back out of the field to Camp Evans, another huge LZ in the Central Highlands, known to us as 'Tent City': hundreds of timber-framed semi-permanent buildings with tent coverings, on several square kilometres of bare earth, devoid of even a scrap of green. A big tanker used to drive around the site every day, dribbling diesel oil into the sand: when compacted, the ground was almost like Tarmac.

Here we could rest and re-organize, introducing new men to bring us back up to strength, to replace the losses we had taken during the fighting in and around Hue. It was an opportunity for me to shower and get into some clean clothes, to start feeling human again. Meanwhile I had been moved up to company executive officer, responsible for administration and logistics, and effectively second-in-command to the company commander. As XO, I would no longer play a tactical role; from now on I would remain behind on the LZ, to organize supplies when the company moved out into the field. It was a huge relief. A week later I received a further promotion, this time to a staff job as assistant battalion security and intelligence officer (S-2). This was a job normally filled by a captain, based on the battalion CP, either at Camp Evans or on the battalion firebase. In my new position I would be a key member of the battalion commander's staff, helping to co-ordinate intelligence and plan operations. It seemed that my days as a platoon leader patrolling out in the boonies, humping packs around in the jungle and making a new bivouac every night, were well and truly over. Thank Christ for that.

I celebrated my twenty-third birthday on Camp Evans. 'I wish we could all go out together to Howard Johnson's for a bite to eat,' I wrote to my parents. I had only twenty weeks of my tour remaining. It really did feel now as if I was getting 'short'.

As assistant S-2, I was on duty throughout the night, monitoring the locations of all the platoons in the battalion and receiving hourly reports of any actions or contacts from each of the companies, so that I could brief the colonel at six o'clock every morning. Then I was off-duty through the day – though not, of course, when the battalion was out in the field. The heat and the humidity made it hard to sleep during the daylight hours, not to mention the everyday bustle on the camp. I found myself tired most of the time. But at least my sleep wasn't broken by the night-time barrage of the big artillery pieces firing H & I.

My new job gave me access to military secrets. Many of the

pieces of paper crossing my desk were marked 'For Modified Handling Only – Do Not Release To Alien Subjects'. It never seemed to occur to anybody that I was an alien subject. The sensitive nature of the job came home to me particularly strongly on one occasion, when I received a secret booklet detailing a proposed new shoulder-launched weapon, code-named 'Davy Crockett'. This carried a small but very deadly nuclear warhead.

The new job also gave me a far better appreciation of the overall strategic situation. Though it was very hard work, I found it absorbing. We were now concentrating on breaking the enemy supply lines that ran from North Vietnam through Laos into the south. In particular, we were preparing for a large-scale assault into the A Shau valley, a remote and inaccessible region near the Laotian border, surrounded by high mountains. The head of the valley formed a main junction with the Ho Chi Minh Trail. It was therefore a key stage in the enemy supply-infiltration route into the area between Hue and Da Nang. NVA forces within the valley were rumoured to include heavy artillery and tanks, and even a few helicopters. Following several weeks of arc-light bombing from B-52 bombers to soften up enemy resistance, we planned a joint assault with forces from the 101st Airborne Division.

But before this could take effect, the Cav was called upon to relieve the Marine base at Khe Sanh, on the old French road into Laos, up near the DMZ. This was the setting for one of the most bitter struggles of the war, followed closely at home by public and politicians alike – especially President Johnson, who had a scale model of the base built in the White House basement. For the previous ten weeks, six thousand Marines and ARVN rangers had been besieged at Khe Sanh by an estimated forty thousand North Vietnamese regulars located in the hills around the base. Cut off by road and totally surrounded, the base was supplied and reinforced by air, often at great risk to the incoming aircraft. After several C-130s had been shot down, they resorted to parachute drops, pushing pallet loads out of the cargo bays as they flew low over the base, though many of these supplies landed outside the defensive perimeter. Meanwhile the hills around were pulverized by more than 75,000 tons of high explosive, dropped mainly by B-52s. Just before our combat assault, our bombardment had levelled the entire top of a hill to provide a flat LZ for our helicopters. Even so, we came under fire as we landed.

The approach to Khe Sanh was an astonishing sight. Wave after wave of helicopters, hundreds of them, flying in over the jungle-covered hills, carrying three Cav brigades – approximately five thousand men. In accordance with SOP the battalion staff flew in several separate choppers, to minimize the risk that we might all be eliminated in one strike. We landed some six kilometres west of the base. My first duty was to establish a battalion CP, from which the colonel could begin to direct operations. Within twenty-four hours we had set up a fully operational tactical operations centre (TOC) some five feet below ground, protected from mortar attack or shelling by enemy howitzers situated on the other side of the border up to 18 kilometres away. Once this LZ was secure, a company was sent forward to test the enemy strength. They made a combat assault on to a hilltop only 2,500 yards from the base, and encountered only light resistance. We suspected that, as so often happened, Charlie had withdrawn the bulk of his forces rather than face the prospect of pitched battle. Cav battalions began sweeping the surrounding hills to clear away the remaining enemy, circumnavigating the entire base over a period of days, making camp at night within a temporary perimeter. During this advance, each battalion would spread out in a diamond shape to sweep a large area, perhaps several hundred yards wide and two or three hundred deep. As part of the battalion staff, I stayed in the rear with the colonel at all times.

It turned out that the NVA had indeed already withdrawn most of their forces before we arrived, so we did not encounter the enemy in the expected strength. Instead we became involved in a succession of minor firefights with small units left behind.

We're advancing on foot up a wooded incline when we come under RPG fire. The whole battalion staff, flat on our faces, grovelling in the dirt. This shouldn't have happened, of course: the point company must have missed an enemy bunker as they swept through ahead of us. But there's no time now for recriminations: we've got to deal with this, fast. The senior staff officers do not know what to do – they have never been in this kind of situation before. So three of us, all lieutenants and former platoon leaders, decide that it's up to us. We don't talk, we don't wait for orders, we just start moving, spreading out so that we can approach the bunker from different directions. The fire seems to be coming from about fifty yards ahead. I move off to the left and begin circling around from the side. We three know what to do: two of us providing covering fire on the bunker as the third advances from tree to tree. We communicate by hand signals. As I come closer, I can see the bunker – just a hole in the ground with a covering of brush: you could easily miss it if you passed by more than ten yards away. The three of us converge on it at roughly the same time. I lob a grenade into the bunker, while the other two stand up and pump rounds into its smoking remains. Afterwards we pull out five bodies.

Within a week of our arrival, the Cav had cleared the hills above Khe Sanh of the remaining enemy forces. We had established contact with the Marines, and had reopened the road. At that moment, the majority of us who were still up in the hills simply turned and walked downhill *en masse* towards the base. As we approached, we flushed out the odd enemy soldier, but we didn't meet any serious resistance. The Marines had cleared a route for us through their defensive lines: roll after roll of wire, with signs of heavy fighting everywhere. My first sight of the base itself shocked me: it felt like something out of the First World War – the trenches at Ypres, maybe. Everywhere was pockmarked with shell craters. The runway was littered with the carcasses of dozens of ruined aircraft. There were no buildings left standing that I could see, just a network of bunkers and interconnecting trenches and tunnels, heavily reinforced with used shell-cases arranged in honeycombs for greater protection. The bunkers had become stinking cesspools, full of Marine shit, and rat-infested.

You'd have thought perhaps that the Marines might have welcomed us with cheers and open arms, but it wasn't like that. It was almost as if they resented our help. It seemed to us at the time that they had been sitting there on their arses, too scared to come out and fight. In subsequent years, I found it absolutely amazing that the history books and the films always seemed to give the Marines credit and to glorify their actions at our expense. For our part, we felt that the Cav had become the ready reaction force for the whole of Vietnam, always flying in to where the action was hottest.

In the second week of April we are pulled back to Camp Evans. A week later we finally make our much-postponed assault on the A Shau valley, without the 101st Airborne, which is elsewhere by this time. The plan is to land wherever we can find suitable LZs in the mountains on the eastern lip of the valley. Unfortunately our intelligence has failed to detect the presence of 37-mm anti-aircraft guns, buried in pits and hidden under brush. As the first wave of our helicopters arrive, they come under fire from these concealed anti-aircraft guns, and from other weapons such as .50-cal machine-guns and even tanks. My battalion is the first to go in.

Our chopper is approaching the lip of the valley. I'm sitting on the bench seat, watching another flight of choppers up ahead. Suddenly one erupts into a ball of flame. Oh, my God, get me down quick! The air all around is patterned with ugly little explosions. Our choppers swoop in low, cutting off the angle for anti-aircraft guns not directly below. The door gunners are strafing the jungle, red tracer lining paths into the green. Another chopper is hit in the main rotor blade and immediately drops straight to the ground, exploding like a bomb. I'm clutching tight on to the frame of ours as the lead pilot seeks out a place to land. There's a clear patch up ahead. The first chopper hovers, ten feet above the ground, the undergrowth flattened by the downdraught. Cavalrymen pour out, hitting the ground and rolling like parachutists, the heavy packs on their backs unbalancing them. Now it's our turn. I jump, and the ground comes up like a fist to hit me. I roll over and look up, just in time to see another chopper get hit in the tail rotor. Once the tail rotor is out of action, the helicopter itself begins to rotate, flinging men out from either side. It's a hideous sight. The damaged machine falls slowly, lashing out like a huge wounded animal. It spirals down until it hits the trees, then explodes with a dying roar.

We lost eight Hueys, four Chinooks and one Crane helicopter in that assault. The first waves suffered the heaviest losses: after the anti-aircraft guns had identified their positions by opening fire, we were able to guide in attacks by helicopter gunships or Phantoms, which quickly neutralized the threat. Once on the ground, we met little resistance. We swept the mountain ridges, then moved down into the valley itself; as usual, the enemy withdrew rather than stand and fight. Within two weeks we had cleared the valley right up to the Laotian border. By this time the monsoon was closing in, and we were forced to evacuate. Logistics would have been impossible in that location without daily resupply by air. Of course, as soon as we pulled out, the enemy walked straight back in.

By mid-May I was back at Camp Evans, where the battalion was assigned to perimeter defence. I was on night shift in the TOC, in case anything happened on the perimeter itself, or at any of our observation points (OPs) dotted around the perimeter. It looked as though we might stay here another three to four weeks; I now had only eleven weeks remaining. 'I am getting shorter and shorter,' I wrote to my parents. I was making plans for my return. My instinct was to fly straight to England to see Debbie, but I was uncertain that this would be allowed under Army regulations. And would this be fair to my family, to my mother in particular, who had undergone such torment while I had been out here? I would be flying over to England for the wedding within a fortnight of my return anyway. It was difficult to decide what was best.

In the preceding few months the Cav had been so busy here, there and everywhere that we'd had little chance to clear out the area immediately around the base itself. As a result Charlie had been able to build up his strength nearby, and we suffered rocket or mortar attacks almost nightly. We got used to these. Generally speaking, the enemy would pop off a few mortar bombs or rockets, then move, for fear of being detected and subjected to overwhelming artillery fire. At such times I was quite pleased to be on duty at night, because it meant that I was alert and conscious during the hours when there was the greatest danger of attack.

*

It's the middle of the night. I'm down in the TOC bunker, writing a letter to Debbie, when I hear rockets coming in. A whoosh, a bump, and then an explosion. And then another. I go outside to watch the fireworks. You might think that this is stupid. I'm safe in the reinforced bunker from anything short of an atomic bomb. But I'm bored. Those 120-mm rockets are big, but they're notoriously inaccurate. Your chances of happening to be within range of the blast of one of these in a base as big as Camp Evans are pretty slim. Unless it's got your name on it, of course.

I climb the steps out of the bunker and walk a few steps into the night. I stand there a few minutes, looking up into the sky. It's hard to see the rockets coming in; they don't leave any trail behind them. The attack seems to be concentrated over on the other side of the base, a good 1,500 yards from where I'm standing. I'm almost disappointed. I fish out a Pall Mall and light it with my Zippo.

Then one of the rockets hits the ammo dump. The first thing I see is a pillar of flame shooting up hundreds of feet into the sky, and an upcurrent of dust and rubble curling towards me, illuminated by the brilliance behind. Then the shockwave rushes past, lifting me off my feet and flinging me back fifteen feet on to my butt. As I lie there dazed, trying to sit up, I'm almost knocked back again by the tremendous roar of the explosion. I'm still reeling from the din when I'm showered with dust and debris. I look around and see, in the light of the fires, many of the timber-framed buildings still trembling from the blast. Ripped tents everywhere, with bunks and bookshelves and desks hurled across rooms and through the temporary walls on to the ground outside.

There are more explosions coming from the ammo dump. It's not going to be safe with all this crap flying through the air. I stagger to my feet and lurch back to the safety of the bunker. Within a few minutes the colonel and other senior staff have arrived, and the bunker is full of frantic activity. Of course we're asking for situation reports from the perimeter, to be sure that this rocket attack isn't the prelude to an attempt on the base. But even if Charlie was planning an attack, I reckon that now he will think it's too dangerous, with all this ordnance going off in every direction. Heavy explosions continue throughout the night.

In early June I transferred to Brigade HQ. I was still on night duty. My new job was to write the intelligence summary for the past twenty-four hours. Usually I'd have a rough draft ready by midnight, get it typed out on a stencil, correct it and then go to press. This left me plenty of time to write letters home. I found the job interesting and I didn't mind working at night, when it was quiet, and when there weren't any senior officers around to harass me. It was just a desk job, really, as different as it could be out there in Vietnam from traipsing around in the field, afraid of what might happen at any moment. Nevertheless I was counting the days until I could go home. 'I am so looking forward to getting out of here,' I wrote to Debbie. I worried about little things I might have forgotten – which hand to use to hold a knife and fork, for example. I had become so accustomed to crapping and peeing on the nearest piece of ground that I knew I would need to make an effort to use the lavatory when I was back in civilized company.

By now I wasn't thinking much about the war, or the men I'd be leaving behind. It was as if I'd switched off that part of my life.

On my last night at Camp Evans, on 2 August 1968, there was a small gathering at the officers' club. The colonel attended and said a few words, presenting me with a silver wine goblet embossed with the brigade crest and inscribed as follows:

To Lt Thomas F. Abraham, Asst S-2
Third (GarryOwen) Brigade
Vietnam 1967–8

Then everyone raised their beer cans and toasted my safe return home.

22

Day 365 (1 day short): 6 August 1968

Another hot morning at An Khe. A group of lieutenants in starched khaki uniforms assembles on the edge of the runway. Some are men I've served with; a few I recognize from the flight out here. Almost exactly a year ago, we disembarked from a C-130 transport on this same runway, looking around curiously, full of anticipation but not knowing quite what to expect. Now we're going home. All those of us who made it, that is. The group is quite a lot smaller than it was when we arrived. We don't need a C-130 for the flight back to Saigon; they've given us a C-147, a much less imposing, twin-engined, turbo-prop transport.

I look around at the others, trying to sense the mood. Most of the guys are smoking. Nobody talks much. It's like the last moment of a big football game: very tense. We're on our way home, but I don't think anyone is going to relax until we've left Vietnam behind for good, until we're on that big bird high above the Pacific.

There's hardly any luggage here on the runway. Most of the guys have an Army-issue duffel bag with a few mementoes and personal effects, and that's all. They've taken back all our kit, though they let me keep as a trophy the Chi-Com pistol I took from the NVA officer in the action that won me the Silver Star. It's been here waiting for me ever since I submitted it, in accordance with SOP. I see that a couple of guys have captured AK-47s that they're taking home with them. I wish I'd thought of that.

I've been here at An Khe three days, ever since I arrived from Camp Evans, waiting in one line after another, as I'm processed out of Vietnam. It's been incredibly tedious. I can't wait to get out of here for good, to get back to 'The World'. I have a momentary thought that it may not be quite so easy to go home. Perhaps I'll be taking a piece of Vietnam with me.

They're ready for us to board, so we walk up the ramp into the hold. There's already some pallets of cargo stowed there. A few lucky ones grab the seats facing in along the edge; the rest of us squat on the floor, among the rollers and strapping.

The ramp lifts to horizontal; they won't close it any further for this short, low-level flight. It's cooler that way, and you get a view out of the back. The engines start up, first one and then the other, and the C-147 taxis down the runway, slowly picking up speed until I feel it leave the ground, climbing steeply as we pass over the perimeter of the base. The plane banks until it finds its correct course, then settles into its cruising altitude: quite low because, like the C-130s, these planes aren't pressurized. Only a couple of hours now until we land at Bien Hoa. Tomorrow I'll be aboard that 707 for Tokyo, then on to Seattle. From Seattle on to Chicago, and then Chicago to Harrisburg, where my parents should be waiting to drive me home. What could be simpler?

I'm deep in a dream about driving my Mustang down the

main street in York, showing off my medals to all the girls, when suddenly I'm interrupted by a loud bang.

All of us are instantly alert. Then the pilot's voice comes over the intercom. We've taken a hit from the ground. The port engine's on fire. We're going to have to make an emergency landing. Ah, shit. After all I've been through, I'm going to die in a fucking plane crash. And all because of some little gook who's taken a pot-shot at the plane flying low overhead and got lucky.

There's no panic as the pilot makes a controlled descent. Everyone takes up the crash position. Those of us without seats huddle together, trying to wedge ourselves in a mass of bodies. The pilot's bringing us down over paddy fields. He's going to make a belly landing. He shuts off the engines just before we touch the ground. There's a tremendous jolt, then a terrifying scraping and grinding as the plane skids along the earth for several hundred yards, chewing up small trees and bushes and bumping over hummocks. The noise is almost unbearable. Every part of the hold seems to be rattling, and the seats are vibrating so hard that it's difficult to believe they won't tear loose. Anything unsecured is thrown about, ricocheting back and forth against the fuselage. Something bashes my head as it hurtles through the hold. I'm gripping the metal frame of the interior, while the rest of my body is shaken helplessly back and forth. Somebody's boot crashes into my back. My eyes are closed. I'm trying to hold on to the thought of Debbie, to block out the fear hammering at the door of my mind. I feel as if I'm going to be sick. I have a nightmare vision of the plane tearing open, and of being smashed to a pulp as I hit the ground at a speed of a hundred plus miles an hour.

But it doesn't happen. We come to a halt on the edge of a rice paddy. I stumble towards the rear of the hold, now littered with debris, towards the sunlight streaming in from the open ramp. I jump down, and move away quickly to avoid the other guys pouring out of the plane. The pilot and the co-pilot appear round the side of the wing; they're both uninjured. Apparently they've radioed ahead with our co-ordinates, so help should be on its way. Someone says that we must form a defensive perimeter. For all we know this area may be stiff with Charlies.

Oh, great. Here we go again. Back in the boonies, only this time with just my captured pistol and a couple of clips to keep the gooks away. One of the guys gets out his penknife and cuts down a stick of bamboo, sharpening the end. I do the same. So that's what we do: we form a ring round the plane armed with makeshift spears, like a bunch of primitive tribesmen. A few other guys retrieve their trophy weapons from the cabin, but of course we've hardly any ammo.

Fortunately no gooks appear before we hear the throb of rotor blades, and a minute later there's the welcome sight of a couple of Chinooks, escorted by a gaggle of Huey gunships, swooping in low over the paddies, flattening the grass and churning the water into a frenzy as they land. We form two orderly lines and begin boarding.

We reach Bien Hoa without further incident. The next day I'm sitting aboard a chartered Boeing 707 on the runway at Saigon's Tan Son Nhat airport, waiting for take-off. The engines roar, and we surge forward, accelerating ever faster until we leave the ground, punching a hole in the sky. A cheer rings round the cabin. Goodbye, Vietnam, fuck off.

I'm in the airport at Tokyo. We're stopping over here for a few hours while the plane refuels before flying on over the Pacific. I've changed some dollars into yen. There's something I've got to do. I find a phone in an empty corridor, and fill it full of coins. Then I dial Debbie's number. Darling, it's me. I'm on my way back.

*

A day later, I'm on another plane, on the last leg of my journey to Harrisburg. We've just taken off from Chicago's O'Hare airport and we're heading out over Lake Michigan. I suppose we're about five thousand feet up; you can still see white horses, and the wake of boats on the lake below.

There are five of us, all still in uniform, sitting towards the back of the plane. We're in good spirits, having enjoyed a bevvy or two while we've been waiting to board at O'Hare. We're travelling on what's called 'military standby': you get a free flight, but you can't book, you just have to wait until a seat becomes available.

A sudden ear-splitting boom, as one of the engines mounted on the tail implodes into the cabin, only a few feet behind where I'm sitting. I turn round in my seat, to see black smoke being sucked out through an ugly hole in the fuselage. One of the hostesses is giving emergency first aid to a man covered in blood. Panic, screaming, a hideous howling as the pressurized air leaks out of the cabin. Oh, God, not again! The plane veers sharply to port, and the hostess is thrown across the cabin. Then we go into a steep dive. I have a vivid mental picture of the pilot struggling with the controls. The cabin is full of junk hurtling through the air and bouncing off the fuselage, as if this was an oversized pinball machine. An overhead locker springs open, spilling its contents over the passengers below. I'm gripping the arms of my seat, teeth clenched, trying to pray in the din.

And then the plane levels off at about two thousand feet. The dive has lasted perhaps thirty seconds. We're still flying with a hole in the tail and the wind is whistling round the cabin, but the pilot has the plane under control, for the moment at any rate. He explains over the Tannoy that we're returning to Chicago, but he can't land with the tanks virtually full. We need to remain airborne until he can dump most of the fuel safely over the lake.

Someone is crying. The passenger who was seated next to the imploded engine is dead.

Further up the aisle I see a man get up from his seat and dash down towards the rear. He starts fumbling with the emergency door. Where the fuck does he think he's going? A hostess comes running after him, and locks her arms around his chest from behind. He's thrashing about, trying to shake free of her. I unbuckle my seatbelt and rise to my feet. There's another man up now, gibbering about a parachute. A different hostess tries to block his way. She looks pleadingly at the five of us in uniform as she tries to restrain the hysterical passenger. We don't need any further invitation. A minute later the situation is under control, both men out cold. Everyone's back in their seats.

We circle the lake for the next half-hour or so as the pilot dumps the fuel. The grateful hostesses bring us a drink. We discuss what might have happened: probably a bird being sucked into the engine is the general view. Then the pilot starts the descent into O'Hare. It's a fairly straightforward landing, though as soon as the plane comes to rest we make an emergency evacuation, all the passengers sliding out down a chute. I pick myself up off the Tarmac and set off to look for the next flight.

Later that same day: we've landed at Harrisburg. We line up to leave the plane. The doors open. I pause at the top of the steps and look down. There they are on the Tarmac: Mum and Dad, and Pat, waving frantically. My mother's trying not to cry. I feel a lump rising in my throat, and my eyes are misty. I follow the other passengers down the steps and, at the foot, step away from the line. There's a moment's pause, and then Mum comes hesitantly forward. I spread my arms wide and hug her tight. I hold her for a long, long time. I'm home.

It doesn't take me long to detect that my parents are a little wary of me. Everything's just a little bit more low-key than I expected. I find out later that they've received a letter from the Department of the Army which has scared them. It warns families that returning veterans must be treated carefully: don't argue with them, don't make any sudden moves, and avoid any loud bangs.

The next day I'm out with my mother in her Pontiac Catalina station-wagon. We pull into a gas station to fill up, and I get out of the car to unlock the petrol cap. Just then another car pulls in. Back then there was often a rubber strip across the entrance to the forecourt covering a wire, which rang a bell in the gas station to alert the attendant. As the other car pulls in, this bell rings: 'Ding-ding, ding-ding.' I dive straight for the ground. Then I look up from my hands and knees, to see my mother's anxious face looking down at me.

Ten days later I've just stepped off another plane. This time I've flown over the Atlantic, changed planes at Heathrow, and flown on to Manchester. I'm dressed in my smartest uniform. Before I go through Customs, I step into the gents and check how I look. I give my hair a final comb. Then I straighten my shoulders, put away the comb, and march out of the door.

I'm very nervous about seeing Debbie again. It's been more than a year. What if it's not the same? Of course it will be the same, I tell myself. You spoke to her only a few days ago on the telephone for over an hour. You're coming over here to marry her. There's nothing to be nervous about.

As I come through Customs and turn the corner, a cheer breaks out. There's a huge banner stretched across the hall: WELCOME HOME! Loads of people waving and yelling, with smiling faces and badges. I'm so staggered that I pause for a moment. I scan the waiting faces for one in particular, the face that's never left me, even in the worst moments. And then a little figure detaches itself from the crowd and runs forward, arms open wide, and the cheering gets even louder.

I'm lying asleep in my hooch. There's nobody on the mattress beside me. Outside, the perimeter has been dismantled; the men of my platoon have struck camp and left in the middle of the night. They've abandoned me. Now I'm alone here in the jungle, without any protection. There's a gook creeping towards me. Has he got a knife? He's stretching out his hand towards me. Just in time, I wake. In one motion I leap off the mattress and pin him to the wall, my hands around his throat. He's trying to wriggle away, but I'm holding him tight, squeezing the life out of him. Something's not right. He's not a gook, he's not even Vietnamese. It's Debbie's father, a look of horror on his face. I'm not in the jungle, I'm in her parents' house, in the guest bedroom. Splashed across the wall is the morning cup of tea he's brought me. It's confusing. I release him, stammering an apology. He looks more concerned than angry. Then it hits me what I've done: a few seconds more and I'd have killed him. I can still see the alarm in his face. He must be wondering if I'm the right sort of man to be marrying his daughter.

My wedding day: St James's Church, Birkdale, in Southport. The peal of bells from the tower behind me. Ladies in hats and gentlemen in tailcoats. I'm dressed in my blues, a row of medals pinned to my chest. Debbie looks beautiful in white, a veil swept back from her face, her blonde hair immaculately bobbed. We stand outside for the photographs, surrounded by family and friends. Behind a heavy police cordon, a small group of protesters chants anti-war slogans, but I don't mind them. I'm back in 'The World'. I survived Vietnam. I still have Debbie. From now on, everything's going to be fine.

PART IV: The Cage

23

But it wasn't fine, of course. Although I came back from Vietnam with apparently nothing worse than a few scars, I had a wound inside that refused to heal. A wound that I received during the mopping-up operation outside Hue.

I thought that I had escaped – but I was wrong. I know that for certain now. My reaction when they locked me up in that police van was the final proof. My body is free, but my mind is still trapped.

After my breakdown, an old friend told me he wasn't surprised. 'It's been a long time coming,' he said. He must have noticed the signs, because I'd never told him about the cage. Nor anybody else – no one back home, that is. I didn't want to talk about it, because I didn't want anyone to think that there was anything wrong with me. I hated the idea of being labelled a head-case, a nutter who needed sympathy and help. So far as I was concerned, I could look after myself.

I tried to conceal what had happened to me in Vietnam for

thirty-two years. I thought I'd done pretty well. I kept a tight lid on it – until that evening when I was stopped by the police.

There had been the occasional outburst before, of course. Close friends have always known that they should keep clear when they see me turn 'white and tight'. But they don't know why. It's as if there's all this violence inside me, waiting to explode. I'm not sure how to explain it. Maybe it's because I'm so angry about what was done to me.

It was being locked up again that tipped me over the edge. I see now that I'd been on the slide for quite a long time, since my business collapsed, or even before. I was drinking heavily, which didn't help. Everything seemed pointless. I felt derailed. It reached the stage when my sole ambition was to get through the day without any interruption or complication.

Then I lost it altogether.

It's six weeks since that night when I attacked Sally with my Vietnam knife, the night the police came to take me away. I'm now living in this bedsit on my own, with nothing, absolutely nothing at all, left to look forward to.

I've started going to the local pub at lunchtime. It's only a short walk from the bedsit where I'm staying. I go early, when there's almost nobody else around, and I've been sitting in the corner on my own. Recently I met this guy there. He's been in the services, too. We started chatting about my time in Vietnam, and right away he seemed to understand much better than anyone else how I feel. I suppose that he must have experienced similar things. When I found out that he was a chaplain, I didn't know what to think. I haven't got much time for God these days. I used to be a believer before I went to Vietnam, but the horrific sights I saw there changed all that.

But there isn't much preachy about this guy. He's just a really sympathetic person. He's helping me to face up to the past. Sometimes I get a bit tearful, but I know it's doing me good. We've met a few times now, and I'm starting to trust him.

He says that he thinks I'm holding something back, something important that I ought to unburden myself of. At first I pretend not to understand what he's getting at. But he persists, and eventually I start telling him about the cage. I find it very difficult. But the more we talk, the more convinced I am that he's right: I need to confront the terrible memories that I've suppressed for so long.

I know that I can't go on as before. I left something behind in that jungle; I must go back and search for it.

Vietnam, late February 1968

We're advancing in company formation over a flat landscape of paddy-fields, interspersed with small clumps of woodland. We're approaching another of these now. It's early afternoon. There's no sign of the sun: just a low ceiling of grey cloud stretching to the horizon in every direction. The weather's been the same for weeks now; everything looks dank and dismal. Though it's not raining right at this moment, I'm still sodden from an earlier cloudburst: soaked through to the skin.

I'm wading through muddy water about a foot deep, my M-16 tucked comfortably under my arm. The platoon's spread out wide; if I look either left or right I can see the next man about twenty yards away. It's as if our normal patrol has been rotated through ninety degrees, so that, instead of moving in a long line one in front of the other, we're alongside each other, like beaters flushing out game.

There's the sudden drum of a semi-automatic AK-47. Bullets are zipping into the water around me.

When you first come under fire, you often don't know where

it's coming from, or from how far away. You don't know whether the enemy's clustered together or spread out. You don't always know where your own men are. In the first few seconds, the most important thing is to find some cover. You have to act on your own. There's no time to organize, even as a squad. Suddenly it's a very private war.

I'm caught in the open. If I stay where I am, I'll soon be dead. I must move quickly. I don't stop to think; I slosh forward as fast as I can towards the woodline, shouting at the others to follow. It's only about twenty yards away. I'm probably heading straight towards the incoming fire, but even if the gooks are concealed among the trees, I reckon that I stand a better chance there than I do out here, without any form of cover. And, if I make it there, maybe I can start to fight back, rolling up the flanks of their line.

Mud flies up as I splash through the water towards the trees. I'm craning forward, trying to reduce the size of my body as a target. As I head for cover I'm remembering yesterday, when we were the ones concealed in the woods, mowing down wave after wave of NVA soldiers in pith helmets as they charged across the open paddy fields towards us. I imagine myself now in the sights of an enemy soldier concealed up ahead. I see my running figure suddenly stop and then collapse, falling face down into the water.

I reach the woodline in a few seconds and hurl myself down on to the damp soil, panting from the sudden exertion. I'm fiercely glad to be alive. But I know I'm not safe yet. At least one enemy soldier still has me targeted; bullets are pinging off the trees around me. I lift my head cautiously and peer out from underneath my helmet. I can see muzzle flashes, and glimpse movement in the undergrowth. Rising to one knee, I empty two or three magazines in that direction. Then there's a lull. I can't see any of our men anywhere. Not a single one. Where the fuck are they?

It's ominously quiet. I would expect to hear the reassuring zip of M-16 fire, and the noise of the other men in my platoon crashing into the woods around me. But there's nothing: not a sound.

My magazine is empty. I eject it. The click is startling in the sudden silence. I'm reaching in my belt for another magazine when an eerie feeling comes over me. Someone is near. I hold my breath, hoping I haven't been seen. I glance up. Five rifles pointing at me, each one held by a black-clad Vietcong. There's no way out.

At first I can't take it in. It's happened in seconds. One moment I was leading the platoon through the paddy-fields; the next I'm on my own, surrounded. Where the fuck are my men?

The Vietcong are shouting at me, the same phrase over and over. I recognize words I've used myself. '*Chieu hoi.*'

I drop the rifle. It's empty anyway, but even if there had been rounds in the magazine I'm completely outnumbered. Almost of their own accord, my hands seem to float up above my head. I get slowly to my feet.

My eyes scan my captors. Four men and a woman. All small and wiry, all similarly dressed in black, with sandals made from those old rubber tyres we call 'Ho Chi Minh racing slicks'. One has round, gold-framed glasses that make him look like a student. An older man wears a conical hat; the rest look young, maybe in their early twenties, though it's hard to tell out here – they could be teenagers. The woman seems to be doing most of the talking. Perhaps she's their leader.

Two of the men approach, while the other three keep me covered. I smell them as they come near. The one with a brutal, stupid face picks up my rifle, while the other – the 'student' – frisks me. He starts searching my pockets, discarding anything that doesn't interest him. He flicks through my wallet, pulling out a snap of Debbie, which he studies for a moment, then drops; the photograph lands face down in the mud. He pockets the wallet. Then he and the other guy remove all my kit, yanking it roughly off me: helmet, webbing, bayonet, canteen and pouch. My dog tag goes in one savage wrench. I see the St Christopher medallion Debbie gave me at the airport disappear into a black-pyjama pocket. The student unclips my watch, then fastens it round his own wrist.

The brutal-faced gook grabs my hands, pulls them down in front of me and ties them together with rough twine, threading it between my wrists in a figure-of-eight, so tight that it pinches. Then he pulls back my elbows and jams a bamboo stick between them, pulling on my wrists. Though it hurts, I try not to show any more than a grimace. He places a lasso round my neck.

I realize with a huge sense of relief that they're not going to kill me. Not yet anyway. I guess that's because they can see I'm an officer from the black smudge on my helmet. Maybe they think they can get something out of me. Usually they kill the enlisted men where they find them.

Then I remember the bodies we've found of our boys after they've been prisoners of the Vietcong, tied to a tree, skinned alive before being shot. My scalp crawls as I try to delete the horrifying picture in my head. Don't think about that now. One thing at a time.

They lead me deeper into the thicket. There's a brief discussion, and three of them – the woman, the student and the older man – leave. The rope round my neck is tied to a high branch of a tree, so that I can't sit down. I stand there like a tethered animal.

I study my two remaining captors, squatting on the ground. The brutal-faced one smokes an evil-smelling cigarette. The other has hair that flops over his forehead, and a chubbier face; now I look at him more closely I can see that he isn't much more than a boy, maybe as young as fifteen. Neither of them speaks to me or looks me in the eye.

I keep hoping my platoon will appear. Where are they? My ears strain for the slightest sound, the click of an M-16 magazine or the pad of a stealthy footstep. But all I hear is the drip-drip of rain sliding down the leaves and falling on to the mud. As the minutes pass, my hope of instant rescue fades, then disappears altogether. This little group of Vietcong seems to have slipped through the net tightening around Hue. The company was spread out wide, and most of the line would have carried on moving forward during our skirmish. I don't know what happened to the guys in the line nearest to me. Maybe they're dead.

It seems like for ever before the other three return. I can't tell where they've been or why. Their faces don't tell me anything. The old man unties my tether from the tree and fastens the end around his waist. Then we all set off: the woman leads the way, followed by the boy and the old man; the one with the brutal face walks behind me, with the student bringing up the rear. We leave the woods and enter the paddy-fields, those same paddy-fields that I was advancing over less than half an hour earlier. A short while ago there were more than a hundred of our troops marching across these fields; now a small band of Vietcong is walking through them quite openly. Just five little black-pyjama'd Vietnamese and one bound Englishman, towering above them.

We keep marching for the rest of the day, following the raised dikes along the edge of the flooded fields until we leave the rice paddies behind and ascend into the hills along twisting trails, eventually entering the jungle. There's the occasional sound of artillery explosions and bursts of automatic fire, gradually fading into the distance. I see no sign of any other soldiers, friendly or otherwise.

At one point it rains hard for about half an hour, the water coursing down my unprotected face, leaving my hair hanging down my forehead. My shoulders ache from the unaccustomed strain of being pinned back, and I soon lose all feeling in my hands.

Although I'm scared to think of what will happen to me, part of my brain is strangely detached. It's fascinating to observe how my captors behave. After so many patrols when you might get a glimpse of a gook in the distance only once in a while, here I am, right in the middle of a VC cell. There's nothing furtive about them: on the contrary, they make no attempt at concealment and chatter away to each other in loud voices, almost shouts. I find it difficult to believe that when we started we must have been only a dozen or so kilometres from Hue.

I try to estimate which direction we're heading in by the position of the sun. The cloud cover makes this difficult. I think we're heading west and a little south, into the Central Highlands and towards Laos. The border can't be more than about thirty kilometres away.

They move fast, much faster than we do on patrol. They don't seem at all anxious about booby-traps.

Nobody speaks to me. If I try to stop for a moment, a gun pokes me in the back and the old man in front reaches round to yank at the lasso round my neck. I don't have anything much to do except scrutinize my captors. At first I thought that the woman was the leader, but sometimes the student seems to be giving the orders. I'm now not so sure that any of them is in charge: maybe it doesn't work that way. Or perhaps I can't read the signs.

I think back to the two American airmen we rescued from a similar small band of VC. I picture some other lieutenant on a routine patrol studying us right now through his scope, plotting my rescue. I know it's only a very remote possibility. But I hope.

The light begins to fail. I find it harder and harder to keep

Soldiers advance with close helicopter support. © Philip Jones Griffiths / Magnum Photos

Combat assault into A Shau Valley, 'Operation Delaware' 1968. This time there is no contact with the enemy as Cav troops land. Note lingering traces of red marker smoke.

© Tim Page / Corbis

With Company XO Bob Trimble, one of the few guys I allowed myself to get close to in Vietnam. He used to tease me endlessly about being English.

Sitting behind a .50-calibre machine-gun on our defensive perimeter. Less than an hour after this picture was taken, the LZ was attacked; the .50-cal was destroyed by an incoming round and I received shrapnel wounds from the resulting explosion.

Out in the field, the washing facilities were primitive.

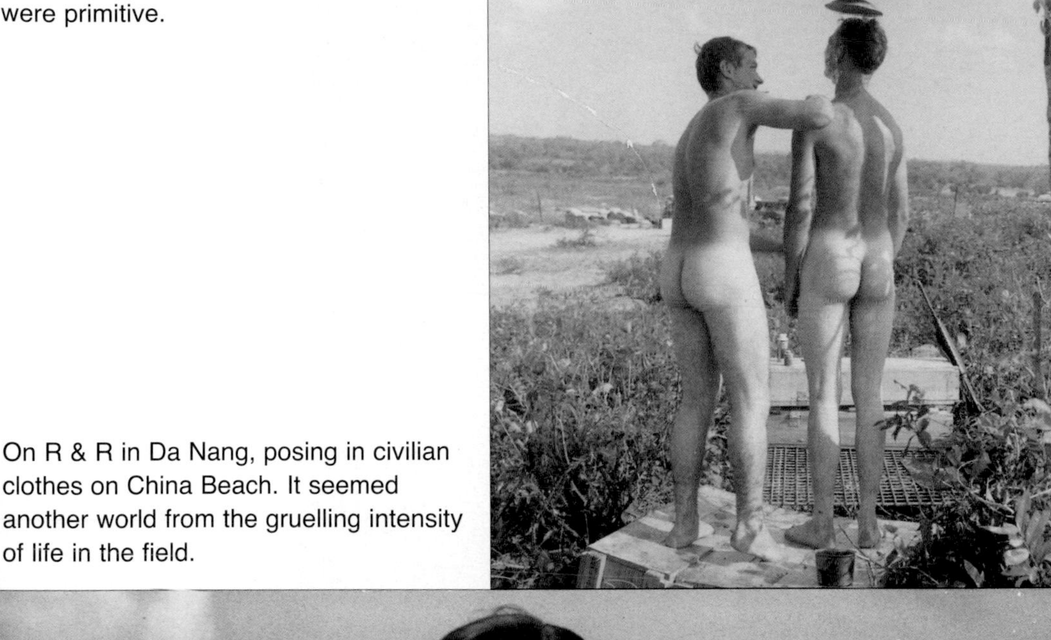

On R & R in Da Nang, posing in civilian clothes on China Beach. It seemed another world from the gruelling intensity of life in the field.

Christmas on LZ Shortie. Beer courtesy of Uncle Sam; tree sent by my parents. A couple of weeks later, this LZ was overrun by enemy sappers wielding flame-throwers, and one of my men was killed.

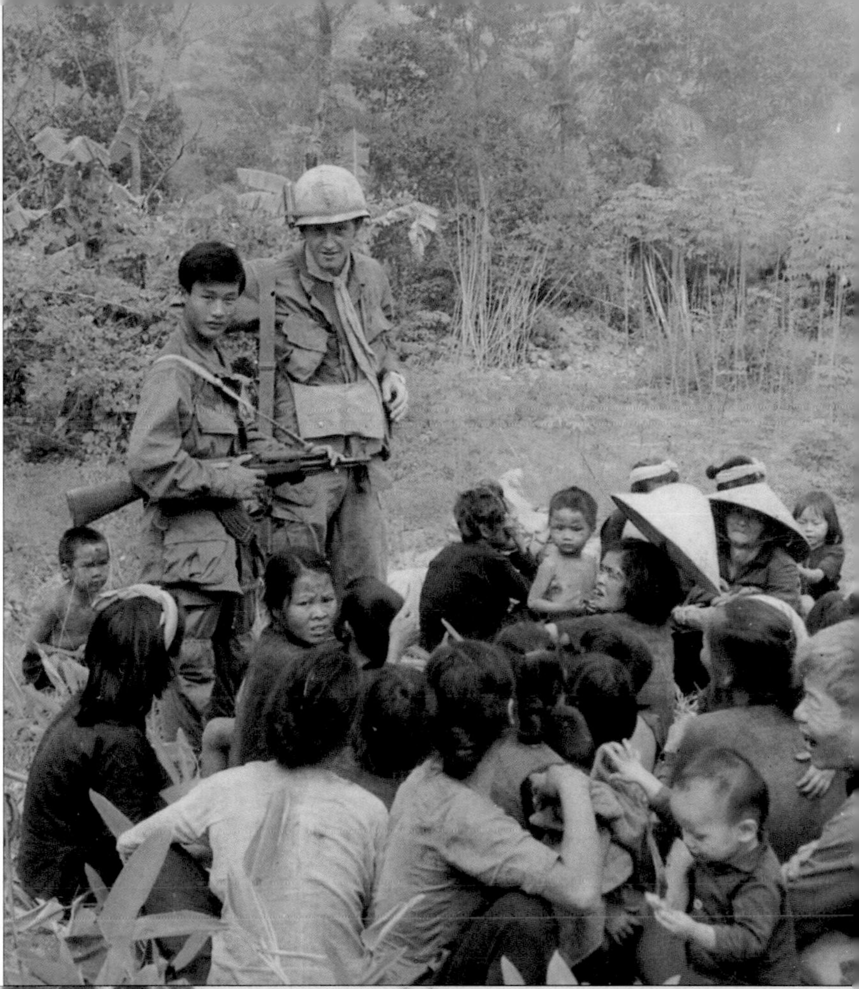

My 'Kit Carson' Nguyen addresses a group of villagers who are about to be resettled. He is carrying the captured AK-47 I gave him.

Some members of my mortar platoon with a couple of Vietcong suspects. Note the shoe in the foreground made from a cut-down tyre: we knew these as 'Ho Chi Minh racing slicks'.

Soldiers advance across a paddy towards the tree line. Photri

With Debbie, the girl who waited for me; our wedding-day in Birkdale, 24 August 1968. I am wearing my 'dress blues'; outside the church a small group of anti-war protesters staged a demonstration.

On the same day, posing with my grandfather Mac.

With my second wife, Sally, at the Vienna Opera Ball in the mid-1980s. Having made a mess of my first marriage, I was all the more determined not to fail a second time.

from stumbling. Out in the open I could walk along quite easily, but even during the day the trails through the jungle are always in shadow; now that the sun is going down I can't see where to put my feet. It's harder to keep your footing when your hands are pinned in front of you, and you can't stretch out your arms for balance, or pull yourself forward on a branch. The earth is wet and slippery, littered with roots, holes and sudden dips or mounds. One hole sends me falling headlong. I can't use my hands to protect my face, so I twist sideways, landing jarringly on my shoulder. I feel a sharp, tearing pain between my shoulder and my neck. The brute and the student pull me roughly to my feet. I wonder what would happen if I twisted my ankle and couldn't go on walking. They'd probably shoot me.

Even when it becomes completely dark, we don't stop. Slowly my night vision shows me where I should step.

Finally we halt by a little hut in the trees. A typical hooch: timber frame, thatched bamboo roof, walls of bamboo and mud. I'm led inside. The old man unties the tether and fastens it to one of the timber uprights. Then he wanders off, leaving me alone with the one with the brutal face. He starts shouting at me. I can't understand a word he's saying. I don't even know whether he's asking questions or simply shouting abuse. I try to tell him this. I meet his eyes. Mistake. He slaps me on the side of the face, very hard. I stagger, dazed from the blow. I can taste blood in my mouth. I can't understand what's happening. This doesn't seem like an interrogation. Surely he's not going to kill me now? More shouting, then a punch in the ribs. I'm reeling around, trying to keep my footing. He picks up a rifle, and brings the butt crashing down on my head, sending me sprawling on my front. My brain swims; stars dance in front of my eyes.

A few final words of what seem like derision, and he leaves, shutting the bamboo door on me and securing it with twine. I feel angry and frustrated. I try to get to my feet, but I find it impossible with my hands tied and my elbows pinned back by the stick between them. I manage to roll over on to my bottom. My head droops forward on to my chest. Water drips off the roof on to the soil outside.

My bladder's bursting, and I can't hold it any longer. Warm pee courses down my leg inside my fatigues, and gathers in a little pool around my feet.

My leg burns. The smell of urine fills my nostrils. My mouth is dry, and I'm longing for a drink. I wonder how long it will be before I start drinking my own pee.

I can hear my captors outside, gabbling away around a wood fire. I'm thinking about what they might have planned for me. You hear so many stories, some of them pretty macabre. Don't dwell on these, Abraham: try to work out logically what's most likely to happen. From what I've heard in talking to intelligence officers, most American prisoners who aren't killed immediately are taken north. So maybe that's where I'm going. I remember hearing that the journey back up the Ho Chi Minh Trail can last up to nine months. They take you in stages, from one holding camp to another, softening you up along the way with regular beatings and a starvation diet. I try not to think too much about what kind of state I'd be in after nine months of that.

I start thinking about torture. All I know about torture is based on old films, Hammer horror movies of victims being stretched out on the rack, and Second World War films like *Bridge Over the River Kwai*. But that's all absurd, surely? I remember being buried up to my neck during officer training. They do that here, I know. We once found a head poking out of the earth, the flesh picked clean by ants. But that's execution – it's not the same as torture, is it?

I'm horribly afraid that they may think that I know more than

I do, and therefore that they may keep torturing me in the belief that I'm holding something back. Should I invent something to tell them? Or should I make it clear that I don't know anything, in the hope that they'll leave me alone once they see that I'm telling the truth?

I'm frantically trying to remember what we were taught about interrogation on OCS. It wasn't the most in-depth part of the training. Don't show weakness; don't make it easy for them. The more you give them, the more they'll take. The less you give them, the sooner they'll give up and leave you alone. But what if this advice turns out to be wrong? It's easier to believe what the Army tells you when you're inside the perimeter. Out here, things look different.

I'm frightened of pain. I'm frightened of my body being mutilated, of being disfigured, of not being able to walk again, or to make love to Debbie. I don't think I could bear to be a cripple, dependent on other people for every humiliating body function. I think I'd rather die.

There's another kind of fear, too: fear that the degradation I'm about to face will strip me of my pride, my sense of self, perhaps even my sanity. I remember seeing a film about a guy who was captured and brainwashed by the Communists during the Korean War. By the time they'd finished with him there was nothing he wasn't prepared to do at their command. They even had him assassinating his fellow PoWs. Afterwards they sent him to America on a mission to kill the President.

'Charlie likes to fuck with your head,' I remember one of the sergeants saying.

What the gooks want most of all is to make you say that they are right and you are wrong. Like everyone else back home, I've seen television footage of pathetic American PoWs somewhere in North Vietnam chanting the party line: how they've come to recognize that this is an imperialist war, that the NLF's political analysis is correct, that Vietnam should be reunited, that we Americans should leave, and so on. I remember feeling desperately sorry for those guys. You could see by the way they spoke in expressionless voices and looked down much of the time that they were deeply ashamed of what they were being made to do.

Those two American airmen we rescued a few months back were in a pathetic state. Each had lost around a quarter of his bodyweight. Two months of imprisonment by the Vietcong seemed to have broken their spirit completely. The pride was gone.

I decide not to look too far ahead. I'm going to try to deal with what's happening now, rather than worrying about what they're going to do to me tomorrow.

The party outside seems to be breaking up; it's time to move on. I suppose this must be just some kind of holding pen. I don't know how long we've been here – perhaps four hours or so? I wish I had my watch. It's still night, though now there's a faint silvery pallor shining through the bamboo walls of the hut: the moon must have risen behind the clouds. Someone's opening the door; the old man and the brute enter and drag me to my feet. My wrists are chafed and sore; there's a horrible throbbing sensation in my hands when I get up. They tether me as before. Then we're on the move again, travelling pretty fast along jungle trails. My eyes have adapted to the dark, so most of the time I'm able to avoid tripping over roots and blundering into bushes. I'm trying to judge how far we've come by estimating our speed, but of course it's difficult to do this when you have no record of time passing.

We've come to an abrupt halt in what seems to be the middle of nowhere. Moonlight bathes the scene in a ghostly glow. The old VC in front of me starts sidling round the edge of the trail, pointing at the ground ahead of where I'm standing, and prodding at some loose foliage with his rifle. I'm looking into a pit six feet deep, filled with punji sticks. He's showing me a booby-trap! It's almost funny. I look into the old man's eyes to indicate that I've understood. There's not a flicker of warmth in his response. Then I follow him round the edge of the trail.

Around dawn we arrive at a ramshackle group of huts, perhaps seven or eight dotted around in the trees. It's probably an abandoned village; there are plenty in the jungle. I can see by the bars in the windows that this one has been adapted to become a PoW holding camp.

My captors announce our arrival with shouts. A few other men, all Vietcong, appear. There are no other women, and no children. No one seems surprised to see us. A few stare at me with undisguised hatred. I still can't get over how strange it is to see Charlie so close after he has been out of sight for so long.

One man blocks my way. He shouts abuse at me. Then he spits straight in my face. I jerk my head away, and his gob lands on my cheek. I feel it trickle slowly across my chin and slide down my neck. I stare back into his eyes. This man's not just an enemy soldier. He hates me. He hates all Americans. The wild thought enters my head to protest that I'm not American, I'm English – but, of course, that's beside the point. I'm still an officer in the American Army.

The old man unties my tether and hands it to one of these new VC. He and some of his buddies lead me towards one of the huts. There's no door. They push me inside and hurl me on to the dirt floor. Once again, I writhe around, trying to get to my feet, but the way I'm bound makes this impossible. One of them kicks me in the ribs, and they all appear to enjoy this, because there's a lot of laughing. Then another kick, and then another. Oh, God, please stop! I'm rolling around on the floor, trying to protect my head and my genitals. One kicks me in the butt, propelling me forward on to my wrists, sending an electric shock of pain through my body. Even so, I don't cry out, reckoning that would only encourage more kicks. Then they seem to get bored, and most leave. A couple remain, sitting on the ground outside.

I notice that the Vietcong never seem to be without their AK-47s, even when they're at rest. They're always slung round their necks and carried in front of them. I store this thought in case a moment comes when I'm able to grab one of their weapons.

Meanwhile I examine my prison, trying to take my mind away from my aching shoulders, my bruised ribs, the sharp pain in my butt, the burning pain in my arm muscles, and the throbbing in my wrists. The inside of the hut is like millions of others in Vietnam: a single room about twelve-foot square, with a straw roof that slopes down from the centre to join the walls, with probably an overhang outside. The doorway is so low that the average American would have to stoop when he enters. There's no smokehole; inside is that pungent, acrid smell typical of Vietnam, an amalgam of human, animal, spicy cooking, opium and marijuana. It makes me feel slightly sick. The floor is just dirt. Light streams in through the open doorway.

I must have dozed for a while. I'm groggy with lack of sleep.

My men are outside, sweeping through the village. The VC lie face down on the ground, their hands tied behind their backs. I recognize the student and the old man. One of my guys holds the protesting woman by the arm, trying to restrain her. Another kicks open the door of my hooch, his finger on the trigger of his M-16. He scans the inside, but he can't seem to see me. I'm trying to call to him, but he can't hear because of the noise of the woman screaming in his ear. I hear choppers landing, and shouts as the patrol leaves. Then the brutal-faced VC appears in the doorway of the hut, and I know that he's going to start kicking me.

I wake suddenly, just as one of the VC guards raises his leg to kick me again. When he sees me open my eyes he thinks better of it and wanders off.

I twist my head to look out through the open doorway. Still no sun, but I can tell that the day is well advanced. Maybe midday?

A new man has arrived, a North Vietnamese Army officer. He's wearing NVA uniform: pith helmet, olive-coloured jacket with breast pockets, flashes on his shoulders, with pips presumably indicating his rank, armed with a pistol in a holster. I get the impression that he's their equivalent of a captain. The Vietcong obviously defer to him. He speaks to them in peremptory bursts. They don't salute or click their heels, but you can tell from their body language and the way they reply to his commands that he's their senior. A man of about thirty, I think: thick lips, wide, flat nose, sunken cheeks. Perhaps a hint of petulance in his manner. Certainly a sense of expectation.

One of his first orders to them is to get me to my feet. Two of them grab the pole between my elbows on each side and yank me up. It's agony, but I try not to cry out. The way I'm tied compels me to lean forward, but I force my stiff body to stand up as straight as I can. He walks round until we're facing each other. Like the others, he's a small man, so I'm looking down at him.

Then he speaks to me for the first time: 'What is your name? What is your rank, and what is your unit?'

To my astonishment he speaks perfect, educated English. I almost smile: he could be an Oxford undergraduate. Is this a good sign? There's no menace in his voice. I've been taught that it's OK to give an enemy interrogator your name, rank, serial number and date of birth, so I give him my name and rank. Then, because the patch on my fatigues makes it obvious anyway, I add, 'First Cavalry Division.' I'm longing for some food and water, but I don't want to show any weakness at this stage, so I say nothing more. He has my wallet in his hands, and he's been studying it while I've been giving my replies. He looks up at me as if checking something, then turns and walks out of the hut.

I feel desperately disappointed. This NVA officer seemed as if he might be a civilized man. I hoped somehow that he might help me, at least untie me and offer me something to eat and drink.

The guards push me back on to the floor. They settle down outside again. It looks as though nothing is going to happen for a while. I doze off.

I'm standing in a queue at a ticket-office, maybe at a railway station. I reach the head of the queue, and a uniformed man asks me what I want. I ask for a ticket to York, Pennsylvania. He disappears for a moment, then comes back with a ticket. I see it has a picture of Debbie printed on it. I want to take the ticket, but he demands payment first. I'm a little confused at this point. I try to open my wallet, but my hands are tied and I can't reach the notes. People behind me are becoming restless. The uniformed man starts shouting and waving his arms.

One of the guards is slapping my face and shouting at me. I blink a few times as they heave me up again and lead me outside to another hut a few yards away. The NVA officer is waiting there for me, calmly shuffling some papers. He doesn't look at me. I see that he's taken off his pith helmet. This new hut has a door, and a window – just an open space, with bamboo bars – in the same wall. Inside is a basic table with some papers on it and a chair.

The guards remove the stick from my elbows. My shoulders flop forward. It's an almost unbelievable relief. My hands are untied for the first time since my capture. They're completely numb and the pain of the blood circulating though them again makes me gasp. My wrists have a red chafe mark around them.

I start rubbing them together, but the guards pull back my arms and strip off my shirt, so that I'm naked to the waist. Oh, Christ, this is it!

They drag me towards the far wall, and bind me, crucifixion-style, to the upright posts in the corners. My shoulders are on fire again, and my bruised ribs start to ache. My knees sag so that my weight tugs on my wrists.

The NVA officer has been preoccupied with some papers on his desk, but now he tidies them away and stores them in the desk drawer. Then he strides over to face me again. His features are expressionless, almost bored.

The two guards remain in the background, sitting on the dirt floor, holding their rifles vertically between their legs, smirking occasionally and chattering amongst themselves.

The officer lights a cigarette with a silver-coloured lighter, and starts speaking quietly, almost casually, telling me that, if I co-operate and do as he asks, things will go more easily for me. I signal some kind of acknowledgement by nodding. Smoke from his cigarette drifts into my nostrils. It's one of those filthy local brands, but I find myself longing for a drag.

'Are you married?' he asks.

I'm thrown by this question. I've been expecting him to pump me for military secrets – not that I have any, but maybe he doesn't know that. At the very least I've been expecting him to ask about the number of men in my platoon, and in my battalion, the name of my commanding officer, that kind of thing. I've been considering how much I should tell him, and when. But not this kind of personal question.

'How many children do you have?'

I wasn't ready for this. If I tell him one thing, however harmless, I could end up telling him another, and then another until I'm sucked dry. Be careful, Abraham. Don't give yourself away.

'Where do you live?'

I have a crazy thought that maybe there's an undercover Vietnamese unit operating in the States, and that if I give him this information they may use it to hurt my family.

'How many brothers and sisters do you have?'

Does he know about Rick? No, of course he doesn't. I keep my mouth shut tight.

He is getting annoyed. His voice rises. He tells me that I'm not co-operating and that, if I don't soon, things will go badly for me. He steps right in front of me, so close that I can see the pores in his skin. 'I'll ask you one more time. Are you married?'

I don't answer. Very slowly, he draws on his cigarette. Then he takes it out of his mouth and presses the burning tip to my chest, just below my right nipple.

Even worse than the sharp, searing pain is the shock. I'm completely unprepared for it. I know that if I show any weakness I'm finished, but I can't prevent myself flinching, with a sharp intake of breath. Some of the hot ash sticks to my flesh and goes on smouldering for a few seconds. I can smell my own flesh burning. My stomach is drawn in tight, as if my insides are huddling together for safety. My teeth are clamped so hard together that I can feel my jaws ache, despite the excruciating pain in my chest.

Then I look my interrogator fully in the eye for the first time, and I see something there that fills me with fear. This guy enjoys his job. Oh, God, dear God that I don't believe in, please, please, protect me from this man.

I know that the others hate me. I'm sure they would kill me as disdainfully as they would some animal pest. Perhaps they enjoy having an American soldier to abuse, after taking so much from our side. But I don't think that they take any particular pleasure from my suffering. This man is different. He's a sadist. I can sense his physical excitement at the prospect of inflicting pain.

In my first year at school, there was an older boy who liked to get me alone. He was fat, and rather creepy. I hated him. He'd push me on my front then twist my arm into a half-nelson, digging his knee into the small of my back. It was unbelievably painful. There was no reason for it that I could understand; he just liked to humiliate me, to see me squirm. He'd lean over, so close that I could smell him, and whisper insults in my ear, make me tell him about my home, little details that boys of that age find embarrassing.

One day I'm going to find that fat boy and kick his head in.

Now the NVA officer is shouting at me and asking the same questions over and over. His face is only inches from mine, a blur of gleaming eyes and yellow teeth. I wish my hands were free so that I could push him away. His breath smells sour.

I know I've got to give him something, so when he asks again if I'm married, I tell him, 'No, I'm not married.'

'You're lying! Tell me the truth.'

Then he starts screaming that his cause is right and he'll teach me to appreciate that America is wrong. The words wash over me. I've been expecting a political speech. What worries me is what comes next. He's lighting another cigarette.

He takes a deep drag, expelling the smoke from his nostrils.

'Are you married?'

'No.'

'Don't lie to me!' This time I'm expecting him to press the cigarette against my chest, but when it happens it's still horribly painful. He holds it there so long that I can't help it, I cry out. I feel sweat spring out on my forehead, running down my back, trickling down under my arms.

I don't remember much about what happens after that. I may have fainted. I do have a memory of him getting worked up again, screaming 'Filthy Americans' and 'Yankee imperialists'. Then he shouts to the guards. One of them produces a knife and waves it in front of my face, grinning. He starts sawing away at my trousers. Oh, Christ, not that! My heart is hammering so hard that I can barely breathe.

The guard with the knife cuts away the rest of my clothes. He gives me a few deliberate nicks with the knife, but nothing worse, thank God. I'm pinned against the side of the hut, naked now except for my boots.

The NVA officer leans forward. 'We'll make you acknowledge that our way is best.' What the hell does he mean? He strides out of the hut, after a few more words to the guards.

The other guard comes over, smiling. What does he want? He says something to me in Vietnamese. His tone is jovial, like a grown man telling a joke to a small boy. Then he punches me in the face. Just at the last moment I turn aside so that his fist misses my nose and hits my cheek below the eye. My head is knocked back by the force of the blow. There's an explosion in my brain; waves of stinging pain spread out from my cheek. Then his fist crashes into my mouth. More punches follow, smashing repeatedly into my unprotected face. I strain pathetically against my bonds.

At last he stops. My head flops on to my chest. Blood trickles down from my lip. My face stings in several different places. Pain shoots through my head.

I don't want to look at them. I don't want them to see me like this. I close my eyes and drift off into unconsciousness again.

I'm in the science labs at school, dissecting a dead frog. It's pinioned to a board with sharp spikes. We laugh as the schoolmaster demonstrates how to make the frog's limbs twitch by applying electrodes to his muscles. Then everything seems to turn inside out, and I'm the frog, surrounded by huge jeering faces, my arms and legs flapping helplessly as the current flows through me.

*

Towards the end of the day the guards untie me. I'm so numb and stiff that I collapse in the dirt. They strip me of my boots, then each takes an elbow and they frogmarch me out of the hut and away from the other buildings. What's going to happen now? I'm so far gone that I hardly care. I wonder if they've decided to shoot me.

I'm aching in what seems like a thousand different places. Blood has coagulated on my face. One of my eyes is swollen so that I can only see through a watery film. The inside of my mouth is parched. My stomach has shrunk to a tight knot.

They drag me down to a small lake, perhaps a hundred feet across. I noticed it in the distance when we arrived. It doesn't look natural; it looks as though it might have originated as a bomb crater, or a series of bomb craters. Perhaps a couple of the big thousand-pound bombs from one of our B-52s. There's a cleared area of thirty yards or so around the lake, where I suppose all the trees have been flattened by bomb blasts. The lake is an opaque green, bloated by the monsoon rains. It could be three feet deep or a hundred; there's no way of telling. The water seems thick, and greasy; there's something disgusting in the sound of it slurping against the bank.

I'm still not sure why they've brought me out here. Perhaps now I'm going to be shot? I can't think why they've taken my clothes otherwise. I'm still too dazed to be frightened. My brain is fuzzy and my vision is blurred, but an object on the bank of the lake is taking shape. A cage, maybe three feet long and the same height. A kennel? A pig-sty? I haven't seen any animals about. It's made of bamboo, strapped together with some form of binding. Everything in Vietnam's made of bamboo. Attached to the top is a pole, ten or twelve feet long. In my bewildered state, I wonder vaguely what it can be.

One side of the cage forms a simple door. It stands ajar. As they drag me towards the cage, I realize with a sickening jolt that it's for me. I struggle, but I'm too weak to resist. The guards bundle me inside, laughing and jeering, and secure the door with twine. There's not enough height to stand, so I squat awkwardly, like a captured animal being put on display.

They push the cage towards the water. I'm rolling around helplessly inside. I clutch on to the bars as it slides across the mud. Surely they're not going to drown me? A splash, and I feel the lukewarm water rising around my crouching body as the cage sinks. Panicking, I grab the bars above my head with both hands. As it slowly sinks deeper into the water, I'm forced to crane my neck to keep my face above the surface. A few seconds more and I'll be dragged under. I'm sucking in air as deeply as I can. How long can I hold my breath? I imagine the moment when I can't keep from breathing out any longer, expelling a mass of bubbles, trying and failing not to breathe in again, the shock of water flooding into my lungs, looking up and seeing the light fade behind a fog of green.

But it doesn't happen. When almost all the cage is underwater, they rest the pole on a simple tripod and wedge the end to hold it there. After a few insults, they leave me.

The sound of voices recedes into the distance, to be replaced by the buzzing of cicadas and the croaking of toads. The sky is darkening. As the night thickens, the air fills with mosquitoes. They dance around my face. I duck under the water when they become intolerable, but within a second or two of surfacing they return.

I'm getting cold. I start rubbing my body to keep warm. One small consolation is that the water soothes the cigarette burns.

My neck is already aching from the strain of keeping my face above the surface. I'm so thirsty that I can't resist gulping a little water, though I know I shouldn't. If I catch dysentery now, I'll probably die. I mustn't drink any more.

Think. Try to think. What's happening to me?

I can't see the village from here. With my face only just above the water, I can't even see the guard who walks around the lake every hour or so, though I know when he's near. I hear his footsteps, and the jangle of his rifle against something hard. A button? A belt? I hear the match strike when he lights a cigarette, and I smell the tobacco burning. I hear him cough and clear his throat, I hear him swallow, I even hear him breathe. There's a whiff of woodsmoke in the air, and I catch a glimpse of the odd spark shooting up into the sky from the direction of the village. Occasionally a burst of excited conversation reaches me across the water. As the night wears on, this dies away.

But there are other sounds, a rustling on the bank, and then a plop as something slides into the water. Rats. Out here they don't wait until you're dead. You get rats on the LZs that crawl into the hooches and bite sleeping soldiers' faces.

A few seconds later I hear something climbing on to the cage, its claws scuttling on the bamboo. I bang the top of the cage with my arm, uttering a primitive cry of aggression. The cage rocks and my face ducks below the water; from under the surface I hear the crawling thing drop off the cage and swim away.

My biggest fear is snakes. There are any number of different kinds of snake in this fucking country, and plenty of them are poisonous. I've seen them swimming around in lakes like this, and in rivers, too. They wriggle in a sinuous motion, only their heads above the surface, tiny eyes glinting. I try to tell myself that there's no reason for a snake to bite me, but somehow not being able to turn round and see them swimming towards me is very disturbing. Being naked doesn't help, of course. I'm also worrying about leeches. I've seen leeches in the paddy-fields up to five inches long: great black slugs that stick their teeth into your flesh and drink your blood. Out on patrol we burn them off our hands with cigarettes. But I haven't got any cigarettes. I try to protect my penis between my legs. I shudder at the thought of a leech crawling up my anus.

In the middle of the night, I find to my disgust that there are leeches trailing from my neck. I rip them off, tearing my skin as I do so.

The worst thing is not being able to stand or sit straight. At first it's no more than uncomfortable. Gradually my body begins to ache, and as time passes the ache swells into the most intense torment. I writhe within the confines of the cage, like a fish suffocating in a net.

Pain works in different ways. There's the sharp pain that comes from an immediate assault on the body, like being burned with a cigarette or hit by a bullet. It's excruciating, but it doesn't last. That kind of pain is a warning that you are under attack; after a while the body provides its own anaesthesia. If it becomes too extreme, you pass out. It's the same with a beating. The first few blows are painful, but after a while you hardly notice them.

The most unbearable pain is the kind that persists, that the body doesn't protect itself against. It's usually less dramatic, but worse by far because it doesn't fade. The pain builds slowly but inexorably; there's nothing the body can do to confine it, to isolate it, to block it out. Slowly the pain becomes so great that it invades your mind. There is nothing else you can think about. Even worse than the pain itself is the anticipation; you know that the anguish will intensify; your body and your mind fill with fear.

When they drag me out again the next morning I can't stop shivering. My body is so stiff from having had to crouch all night that I'm unable to stand. The guards are shouting at me and kicking me. They seem more threatening than before, and I feel more vulnerable. Eventually I stagger to my feet, and they start urging me back towards the huts, prodding me in the back with a rifle to make me walk faster. I know that something bad is about to happen, but my overwhelming feeling is one of relief at being out of the cage. My body still aches all over, but somehow it's not so bad now that I can at least attempt to stand straight. It occurs to me that I'm very tired.

They lead me to the same hut as yesterday, and tie me spread-eagled as before. After a while my interrogator arrives. His tone is sarcastic. 'So, how are you feeling this morning?'

I don't bother to reply. I'm still shaking from the cold.

'Perhaps you'll be more co-operative today, now that you know what's ahead of you?'

Still I don't say anything. What can I say? I stare past him at the tree I can see through the window. If I concentrate hard enough on the tree out there, maybe I can ignore what's going to happen in here.

'OK, let's try again. Are you married?'

He reaches into his pocket. Here come the cigarettes. I feel an adrenaline rush of fear. He taps out a cigarette for himself and holds it between his fingers as he offers the pack to the guard, who hastily takes one. The NVA officer flicks open his lighter and lights the guard's cigarette before lighting his own. The ritual seems to last an age. Then he turns back to me. 'Do you understand?'

I don't reply, so he asks the same question, louder this time, and when I still don't reply he presses his cigarette, almost languidly, against my chest. He doesn't stub it out; he just holds it there as it burns through the skin into my flesh. Though I've tried to prepare myself, the pain still comes as a shock. I tremble, determined not to groan. He gazes at me with faint amusement, as if to indicate that my efforts are pointless. I am completely at his mercy. He can do anything that he likes with me, anything at all.

He withdraws the cigarette and takes another long drag. I watch the tip glow red as the air passes through the burning tobacco. Then he presses it back against my skin.

'Do you understand?'

What the fuck does he mean? Do I understand what?

'Yes, I understand.' My throat is so parched that my voice comes out in a crack.

'That's good. I'm going to teach you that you Americans should leave us alone. Do you understand?'

I nod.

I've been trying to work out a strategy for dealing with his questioning. It's obvious by now that he's not really interested in my answers, at least not for their own sake. He's not writing anything down. Anyway, why the hell should he care whether I'm married or not, or where I come from? I think it's like splitting a log. Once there's a crack, once I give him something, even the smallest detail, he'll be able to insert a wedge, and then he'll keep hammering away at that until he's split me wide open.

I don't want to let him into my life. If I start telling him about my home, my family, about Debbie, he'll be over the threshold, able to trample all over everything I care about, to foul everything I love.

I know that I may not be able to hold out if the pain becomes too strong. In that case I will have to start giving him some answers. I must steel myself not to care about anything he says. Or perhaps I should lie to him, invent a cover story to hide behind? The trouble is that I'm not sure I'd be able to keep it up during the worst moments.

I decide to hold out against giving him any information for as long as possible, and then, if it becomes too painful to resist any longer, to provide him with what he wants in scraps.

*

'I'm glad you've decided to co-operate with us. It will make things much easier for you. So, where do you live?'

I don't reply.

He asks me the same questions as before and, just as before, I don't reply. He starts off softly, but after a while I can sense him getting worked up. The strange thing is that I know he likes getting angry, that it turns him on. He's anticipating the moment when he can hurt me again. I stare very hard at the tree.

When he's really mad, he barks out an order in Vietnamese. One of the guards scampers across the room towards me, lifting his rifle butt, and clubs me in the jaw. I taste blood, and spit out pieces of broken tooth.

'Do you see now why you Americans should go home?'

I can't make any sense of what he's saying. Of course I want to go home!

'So, we'll start again. Are you married?'

'No, I've already told you I'm not married!'

'Where do you live?'

I don't answer. I see he's lit another cigarette.

'You are making life very difficult for yourself. Why are you making life so difficult?'

'I don't know.'

'We will win this war, you know that, don't you?'

I don't reply.

'Vietnam will be a much better place when it is unified.'

Silence.

'You know you Americans shouldn't be here, don't you?'

I still don't say anything.

His voice rises to a shout. 'Why don't you answer me? You know you will answer me in the end, don't you? Why are you being so difficult?'

He holds the cigarette against my skin.

*

I lose track of time. It seems to me that the torture continues for days: more shouting, more cigarette burns, the occasional punch in the ribs or slap on the face from an enthusiastic guard. My interrogator's face gleaming as he asks the same questions over and over again. I writhe helplessly in my straps. I lose control of my bowels; I should feel ashamed, but I'm beyond caring. My defences crumble. Each session seems to last an hour or so, and then he leaves the hut for a while. The waiting is part of the torture, I know that. I try to rest, though my body is in constant torment. I'm not thinking about anything now except survival. I don't think this guy is going to stop until he has broken me, until he has forced me to submit to him completely, until he can be sure that I will do anything he wants.

Towards the evening the guards cut me down and drag me outside towards the lake. I can't make my legs work, so they just pull me along, one on each arm, my feet trailing behind. The sight of the cage terrifies me. I struggle, but I'm too weak to resist them. They shove me in and tie up the door. One hands me a bowl of sticky rice through the bars. I'm ravenously hungry. I scoop it up with my hand, cramming my filthy fingers into my mouth. After the first mouthful I realize that I mustn't eat too quickly, so I slow down, trying to savour each grain, swilling it around my mouth rather than swallowing it straight away. The guards squat on the bank, laughing at me and chatting to each other.

All too soon I've finished the rice. I feel hungrier than I did, perhaps because this small meal has reminded me how hungry I am. And now I'm even more thirsty. The guards take away the bowl and push the cage into the water. It sinks slowly, until I'm left with only my face above the surface, just as before. And, just as before, the guards taunt me a little before they leave.

The light dies very quickly. Soon it's pitch-dark. I'm cold again.

My name is Tom Abraham. I'm English. I'm an officer in the American Army. I have been decorated for gallantry in the field. I'm engaged to be married. Debbie – oh, Debbie, help me get out of here, please.

My muscles have gone into spasm. My body is a network of pain. Now I have to face another night of agony in this cage. I don't think I can take much more. Another day of this and I'll be as good as dead.

I've got to escape. Think, Abraham, *think*.

I reckon that tonight will be my last chance. I'm nearing exhaustion, and my strength is ebbing. After tonight, even if another opportunity arises, I won't be in a state to get away.

I've been staring at the straps holding the cage together. Now I examine them more closely. They're finely shredded strips of bamboo, wound criss-cross over the joints and secured with some kind of knot, like the strapping you get on wickerwork chairs.

I start trying to loosen the strapping round one of the vertical bars on the side facing away from the shore. Each bar is strapped in three places: top, middle and bottom. I've chosen the middle strap: it's underwater, so what I'm doing won't be so obvious to the guard when he comes round on patrol.

At first all that happens is that my fingernails keep splitting. My skin is soft and wrinkly; my hands feel leaden and clumsy. Every time I move a finger I feel the muscles in my back and in my shoulders shriek. I can't look at what I'm doing and breathe at the same time. So I fumble blindly, with my head craned back to keep my face above the water.

It seems as hopeless as trying to dig up a Tarmac road with my bare hands. But at least it gives me a distraction, something to take my mind off the pain.

I'm deliberately not thinking too far ahead, taking one thing at a time.

Then I try something different. The straps are composed of hundreds of strands. I start picking these, peeling them away one at a time. Once I loosen the strap slightly I'm able to push in my thumb and work on them from the inside. It's still a daunting task, but I haven't much else on tonight.

It all has to be done by feel: I can't see anything underwater. By now several of my nails have split and my fingertips are bleeding. As I peel away more and more strands, I keep testing the strap to see if it's weakened. Eventually it snaps. I've done it! The sense of triumph fills me with exhilaration.

Once the first is broken, the rest of the strapping quickly unravels. Now the bar is only fixed top and bottom. I push it as hard as I can, but I can't bend it enough to force my way through. I'm going to have to unpick another strap. I begin working at the bottom one. It's down by my feet. I have to duck my head under the water to reach it, then come up again for air. I daren't thrash around too much in the cage in case I attract the guard's attention. But I must work quickly.

Finally the strap breaks, and I unravel the rest. Now I can loosen the bar. I lever it forward until I'm sure there's enough space at the bottom for me to squeeze out.

This is the most excruciating moment of all. I'm terrified that my work will be discovered before I have a chance to escape. But, though I long to be out of the cage, I make myself wait until I'm calm.

I decide that I must slip out of the cage and swim underwater, right across the lake, surfacing silently on the far side so as not to cause the slightest ripple that might be noticed by the guard. Thirty yards? Forty? It's not going to be easy. I'm a good swimmer, but even on peak form I'm not certain I could swim that far underwater. After what I've been through in the last few days I'm not sure that I can swim at all.

Fortunately we're in the monsoon period, which means that a thick layer of cloud blocks out any light from the sky. The moon hasn't risen yet, thank God. There's no light from any of the huts. It is so dark that I can barely make out the near bank, only a few feet away.

Around midnight, there's a torrential downpour. It rains so hard that it hurts. The lake explodes under the impact of falling water. I turn my face up to the sky, close my eyes and open my mouth, while the rain drums into my grateful throat. Then, abruptly, it stops.

Time passes, with no more sign of the guard. Perhaps he's gone to sleep.

It will be dawn in four or five hours. By then I must be concealed, as far away as possible.

I practise breathing deeply for several minutes, while I steel myself for what I am about to do. I am Lieutenant Thomas F. Abraham of the 1st Cavalry Division. I'm a good swimmer. I'm going home to Debbie.

When I'm ready, I duck under the water and slip out under the bar.

24

I'm underwater, one hand holding the edge of the cage. My heart races. For a moment I hesitate, combating a mad impulse to slip back inside.

I begin swimming. It's a slow start. I don't dive or push off from the cage, because I mustn't make any disturbance on the surface that could be seen by a passing guard.

I'm moving through total darkness. Water bubbles in my ears. I try to swim in a straight line, but it's easy to become disorientated when you can't see anything. I'm petrified that I may lose my way in the murk and surface back near where I started. Or come up at the feet of some waiting guard.

My fingertips touch mud. I must have reached the shore. I come up as slowly as I can, like an insect pupa hatching out of the surface film. Though I'm gasping for air, I force myself not to gulp it down, just take little sips while I wait to catch my breath, my hands clutching the muddy bank.

I stay like this for a few minutes, only my head and shoulders above the water, shivering a little. I'm straining for any sound. I can't hear anything beyond the usual noises of the jungle at night. Over to my right, in the direction of the village, I can see the glimmer of the evening campfire, and the glow from a couple of lamps. Someone must still be awake.

Straight ahead, the outline of the treetops is visible against the sky. At night there's no way of judging their distance, but yesterday I estimated that they're about thirty yards off. Now it seems much less clear. Between here and there is open ground, which I must cross without being detected.

When I'm as sure as I can be that there's no one nearby, I haul my naked body up on to the bank, moving as quietly as I can. Then I crouch for a moment, dripping and tense, every sense attuned to the slightest possibility of danger. Nothing. I relax a little. I lower myself softly towards the ground and begin crawling, alligator-style, towards the trees. I move very slowly to avoid making any sounds. I try to stop myself shivering, though I'm very cold. Every time a twig or a leaf crackles beneath me I freeze, expecting a shout of alarm, or a gun in my back.

I'm full of fear that I'll be found and taken back to the cage. My mind won't yet admit the possibility of escape.

So far as I can remember from yesterday, the ground between the lake and the trees is mainly scrub. I'm wary of blundering into an unseen obstacle, or falling into a hole, or even a booby-trap, so I move carefully, only one limb at a time, as if climbing a vertical rock face. The earth is wet and slippery. My body is bruised and aches in a hundred places – but I haven't time to think about that now. Branches tear against my unprotected skin, soft and wrinkled from spending so much time in the water. I'm starting to get dirt inside the wounds from the cigarette burns. Sometimes my trunk is off the ground and I'm walking on my palms and my toes; sometimes I'm flat on the ground, slithering across the cold, damp earth. My fingers are already bleeding from my struggle to unpick the cage bindings; soon my elbows and knees are, too.

I'm trying not to leave a trail. Although the ground is wet from the monsoon rain, there's plenty of undergrowth. I don't think my tracks will be too obvious. Though of course I can't be sure, because I can't see anything.

I'm halfway to the woodline when I hear something moving behind me. There's a rustle of foliage, lasting two or three seconds. Is it a guard? I stay utterly still. Another rustle. Pause. Then another, nearer this time. I'm wondering whether to make a run for it, when a loud laugh echoes across the water from the direction of the village. The rustling stops. I hear no further sounds. An animal, then.

There's more light now in the sky, casting the faintest of shadows on the ground. The moon has risen behind the clouds. Good for me; good for them, too.

It seems to take an age for me to reach the safety of the trees, but I guess it can't be more than a quarter of an hour. The undergrowth is thicker here, and I slither through it, heading for the deepest area of darkness. I'm tiring, and the muscles in my arms and my thighs are burning from the exertion, but fear drives me forward. I don't have a plan. I just know I've got to get away from those huts.

I'm not really thinking at all. I'm no longer a rational, civilized being. Terror has peeled all that away. I'm just a frightened animal who's escaped from his cage and dreads being caught.

This is thick, triple-canopy jungle, the kind a platoon would normally expect to hack through with machetes. I'm moving beneath the lowest canopy. The vegetation is actually thicker from waist level up than it is down on the forest floor, so in many ways it's easier to move along the ground than it is upright – though it means ploughing through a layer of dead leaves often inches thick. Trailing plants brush across my skin, scraping my face, my neck, my arms, my stomach, my penis – and my thighs, my calves, my feet. I push my way through ferns and under banana plants. I hear a rattle of leathery leaves above, and look up: against the lighter sky I see a dark shape moving, high in the canopy. A flying squirrel, maybe.

As I crawl through the undergrowth, I start thinking about the animals that live here in the jungle. Right now I'm not so concerned about the big ones, the tigers and the elephants: you're unlikely to come across those so close to human habitation. I'm much more worried about blundering into something like a monkey, which might start whooping and howling, loud enough to raise the alarm for miles around.

The jungle is full of small sounds, of rustling and sighing; I tense at each one. All my senses are alert for the possibility of sudden danger. My biggest fear is of being bitten by a bamboo viper. Those bastards like to rest in bamboo stalks, or other bushes or branches of trees, a few feet above the ground. If you brush against one, the viper will strike at you. And, of course, they're poisonous.

A prickling sensation on my arm makes me shudder. I hold it up to the dim light, trying to see what it is. An ant. I brush it off, relieved. But it would be easy to put a hand or a foot down on something that might bite or sting me: a poisonous spider or a scorpion, or even one of those venomous centipedes and millipedes that you find in the jungle here. I've heard of a soldier being killed by a sting from a scorpion that crawled into his boot at night.

Being naked and defenceless makes these creepy-crawlies seem much more threatening. When you're standing upright and wearing thick boots, they don't seem much to worry about. But when you're lying on the ground naked they're a lot more formidable. A snakebite or a scorpion sting now might well make the difference between survival and painful death.

Somewhere near here is the valley I've heard described as the most poisonous place in the world. Perhaps I'm in it now.

I keep crawling forward, negotiating the occasional obstacle: the largest being a fallen tree. I contemplate climbing over it, but in the end I reckon that would be too risky, so I wriggle my way around, sliding my body through the lichen-covered, fractured gap between the trunk and the stump, scraping my sides as I pass.

After perhaps an hour, I can no longer see the lights of the campfire. I've probably not gone more than two or three hundred yards into the jungle, but I decide not to move any further. I might end up going round in a circle and find myself crawling back into the village. Besides, I'm exhausted. I need rest. I haven't slept properly for more than seventy-two hours. I curl up, hugging myself to keep warm.

I'm inspecting the guard outside the White House. Like the men, I'm in 'dress blues', full dress uniform: blue serge jacket with yellow and silver epaulettes, blue trousers with gold stripes, shiny leather boots, peaked cap pulled down over my forehead, white gloves, and curved steel sabre with ebony grip at my side, in a gleaming nickel-plated steel scabbard. My medals hang proudly on my chest. Suddenly I'm aware of a commotion over by the railings. I march down to investigate. It's my mother, pleading for me to come home.

My father stands beside me on the airfield Tarmac, wearing his RAF squadron leader's uniform. He has his hand on my shoulder. I'm dressed in full flying gear: leather jacket, boots, goggles pushed up on to a leather flying cap. Beside us is a Mosquito, its twin propellers powering away, the noise smothering any conversation. It's a winter evening: time to go. My father tries to say something to me, but I can't hear what it is. I smile, wondering whether to embrace him. We shake hands awkwardly. Then I climb into the cockpit. He goes on waving as I taxi down the runway. It occurs to me that I don't know how to fly.

But it doesn't matter, because now I'm with the boys in my platoon, riding in a chopper. It's a combat assault. The chopper swings in low, and we pile out on the edge of a village, weapons at the ready. There's some firing. We run for cover. There seems to be some movement in a nearby hut; I unclip a grenade and lob it through the door. The grenade explodes. When the dust clears, we rise, fingers poised on our triggers, and advance towards the hut. I enter first, and it's a shock: the hooch is my ruined home. I'm filled with a sense of foreboding. I can see legs protruding from some debris. I kneel down to investigate. The horror is complete: lying under a mass of wreckage are the bodies of my family.

I wake with a start, and sit up. Grey light struggles down through the leaves, filling the jungle with shadows. Early dawn. Mist hangs off the edges of the branches. Uprooted trees lean at fantastic angles; innumerable creepers trail from every branch. Everything is wet and still. It's cold; I'm shivering.

There's a sudden commotion as a parrot flies up from the jungle floor a little way off. Danger! I plunge deep into the undergrowth. I hear the crunch of leaves: not far away. I'm lying full length on the ground, peering up through the foliage. Somehow being naked makes me feel more exposed. I grub down even lower in the undergrowth. Another sound, closer this time. Maybe it's just an animal? Silence. Has it gone? Then another sound, very close. I'm holding my breath. The muscles in my stomach clench. Suddenly he comes into view: Vietcong, a man about my age. He stands motionless, listening, sniffing the air. I can tell from his expression and the way he's carrying his rifle that he suspects something. Did he hear me? He scrutinizes the jungle floor in front of him. Then he looks up, searching the foliage ahead. His eyes skim over the place where I'm hiding. I try not to breathe. I feel a bead of sweat course, very slowly, down my spine. He's finished his sweep; now he looks back towards me. He knows I'm here! He advances another few paces, his rifle pointing straight at me. He must spot me at any moment now.

A shout echoes through the jungle. He looks away, in the direction it came from. Then he turns back and looks towards me. Another shout. Reluctantly, he turns again, and begins to walk away. Relief courses through my blood. He's about ten yards off when suddenly he spins round, shoulders tense, rifle ready. He scans the jungle one last time. Seconds pass. Then he turns and moves off, disappearing from my sight.

I lie still, not daring to move. Gradually the jungle comes to life again. Birds arrive and start singing. A small rodent darts around the forest floor, lifting its nose in the air and sniffing every few seconds. Something unseen swings through the canopy above. A passing patrol of ants decides to march across my arse. Still I don't move.

When I'm sure he's gone, I start crawling again, in the opposite direction from which he came. I figure that he'd been following my trail up from the lake. He can't have been sure of my tracks: otherwise he wouldn't have abandoned the trail when the call came. They must have found the cage empty by now. That thought makes me smile briefly. But I must get further away from them as soon as I can. I'm still weak, and very tired. I'll put some more distance between us, and then I'll find a place where I can rest until dark.

I crawl another hundred yards or so. Every inch is an effort. The air is heavy and humid; I'm already sweating. Then I rise to a crouch, so that although I'm still under the canopy I'm moving on the balls of my feet rather than on my elbows and my knees.

It's not exactly comfortable, but it's a huge relief to be up off the ground. I start shuffling forward, my bent knees stinging from the scrapes they've received.

I've reached a bamboo thicket. The stalks stand well over head height, in places as tall as twenty feet, and close together. It's impenetrable without a machete to cut back the bamboo. Even if I could force a way through, I would leave an obvious trail. I start to work my way round the edge of the thicket. There's no telling from where I am how big it is; on patrol I've come across them hundreds of feet in diameter.

Each second, I expect Vietcong to loom up in front of me. I can't get over the feeling that this is their jungle: that they belong here and I don't.

It begins raining again, a few drops at first and then a torrential downpour. Water crashes down from the canopy, drenching me, washing away the muck clinging to my body. Rivulets form in the earth around my feet, which sink into the muddy soil. I stand up straight for the first time in two days, stretching my arms in the air; there's not the slightest risk of being seen through these vertical sheets of rain. The sound is deafening. I turn my face to the sky as the water cascades through the trees, funnelled from one leaf on to another. It's a delicious feeling, like being under the most powerful shower. I can't resist shouting out loud, knowing nobody can hear me.

The rain slows and then stops. I crouch down once more to stay hidden. The jungle is steaming; the sound of droplets fills the forest. A tree frog with bright red eyes appears, clinging to a leaf.

It's time to be moving again. I resume my shuffle.

Another half-mile or so on, I stumble across a trail. I've seen enough of these to feel sure that this is one of the routes the Vietcong use regularly. It could be my way out: it's bound to lead somewhere. But not today: I'm almost exhausted. I start searching nearby for somewhere to rest. I don't want to go too far away from the trail in case I can't find it again: these trails are hard to see until you're right on them. But I don't want to be too near, either. I can't shake free of the fear that they'll find me while I'm asleep.

About twenty yards further I find a place to lie low, a moss-filled hollow scooped out of the roots of a huge tree, its trunk thirty feet round. The roots project like giant buttresses; the trunk soars up out of sight. Some of these trees can be over a hundred feet tall; I've seen them from the air, towering over the middle canopy. This hollow faces away from the trail. It's a good hiding-place: if I conceal myself in here, I can't be seen unless someone pokes his head right inside. There's shelter from the rain, and some protection from wild animals, too.

I remember one of my men being grabbed by a tiger. There was no warning. We were hacking through the jungle – typical triple-canopy jungle, just like this – on a routine patrol. I was in my usual position towards the rear, when bang! the tiger came crashing through the undergrowth about twenty yards ahead. He seized one of the men by the arm and disappeared into the foliage on the other side of the trail, carrying the GI in his jaws as if he were no heavier than a mouse. The whole thing was shockingly quick: perhaps two or three seconds from first to last. Some of the other men started firing blindly after the tiger, until I shouted at them to stop in case they hit our man. We could hear him screaming, not far off. Three of us left the trail to investigate, moving cautiously. About thirty yards away the huge beast was lying dead. Beside him was the GI, his arm hanging in shreds, terrified but alive.

It's no good thinking too hard about things like that. If an animal's going to get me, it's going to get me. I've no means of defending myself.

I'm going to spy out the land around if I can. Quietly and

carefully, I climb the tree. I pause once I'm above the lower canopy, about thirty feet from the ground. Even up here the vegetation is so thick that I can't see very far. I can't even see the trail. Toadstools and flowering plants grow in crevices. I look up towards the middle canopy, another fifty feet above my head. Weak and groggy as I am, I don't think I can make it that high. I climb back down to the ground.

It suddenly occurs to me that I'm ravenous. There's a banana tree nearby, though sadly no bananas. It must be the wrong season. I've tried nibbling the stalks in the past when we've been out on patrol, and found them quite tasty, a bit like celery. I rip some down and nibble hungrily at them. Where the big leaves join the stem, there's a bowl that has filled up with fresh water from the earlier rain; I cup my hands together and scoop out several handfuls to drink. I feel refreshed, though still very tired. I lower myself down into the hollow until I'm sitting on the ground, back against the tree-trunk.

A snake winds its way across the forest floor, ignoring me.

I take stock of my physical condition. I'm exhausted and filthy. I still ache all over. My flesh is raw in several places, particularly my knees. My jaw is bruised and painful. The wounds on my chest are leaking yellow pus. Umpteen parts of my body ache or sting. But I'm OK; I don't think anything's broken; I haven't got gangrene or fever. If I can get out of here soon, I'll be fine.

I pick away the dozens of ticks that have attached themselves to my body while I've been crawling through the undergrowth. If you don't pull them off they burrow their way into your skin. There's a huge bull leech hanging from my right thigh. I try to rip it off, but it's so slimy that it's difficult to get a grip. I'm trying to squeeze it when a jet of blood squirts out more than a foot – my blood. Eventually I scrape it off with a sharp bamboo stick.

I huddle into a ball to keep warm. I wrap my arms around my

body and tuck my head down, like a child. I'm going to sleep now. I need to be awake at night, the normal time for the Vietcong to be on the move. I reckon that if I'm awake, I'll be able to hear them coming. Tomorrow I'll take the trail that I hope will lead me out of here.

I wake suddenly, the noise of an explosion ringing in my ears. Was it a dream? The light has faded; it must be evening. Then a whirr, and another explosion rocks the forest, not far off. Harassment and interdiction: I recognize the characteristic sound of our 105-mm howitzer shells. Glory hallelujah! So there must be a firebase within the twelve-kilometre range of those howitzers. Not too far off: but, alas, I don't know which direction they're firing from. Another whirr, another explosion, closer this time. Fuck! I've escaped from the enemy only to be killed by an American shell. Oh, perfect. I crouch deeper in the hollow, protecting my head with my arms.

But the shelling stops almost immediately. Peace soon returns to the forest. Animals and birds start moving again. I poke my head out of the hollow and peer around me. No sign of the enemy. All the time, I'm listening for unusual sounds. Nothing. When I'm confident that nobody's about, I climb out of the hollow. I'm a little cold, and I rub myself to warm up. I walk over to the nearest banana tree, scoop out handfuls of water and drink until I'm satisfied. Then I break off some stalks and nibble them.

The dark deepens. I can hear a wild hooting from the canopy; I've no idea what that can be. Soon it's night. It becomes colder, and I start shivering again. I snuggle into my hollow, hugging myself to keep out the chill.

An hour or so later, I hear something big moving through the jungle, leaves crunching, and a shuffling sound, as if some heavy creature is dragging itself across the forest floor. The shuffling stops. A moment later, the crack of wood splitting, seemingly right outside the hollow. A heavy, musty smell. I hear the crashing of a branch being pulled down from a tree. I try not to breathe. More shuffling; I can feel the movement through the earth. Gradually the sounds fade into the distance. I relax.

The moon comes up, illuminating the small patch of forest I can see from the hollow. It's like watching television in the dark. There's no sign of the mystery beast.

I remember stories I've heard about the Montagnards, the people who live in the forest. They aren't on our side or on Charlie's; they aren't even Vietnamese. Occasionally we'd come across them on patrol. It was eerie: nothing would be said, and we would just pass by, as if nobody was there. Probably they saw us plenty of times when we didn't see them; they were always very wary, and of course the jungle was their home. They hunted with spears, and bows and arrows. You'd hear stories of bodies found face down in the forest, arrows in their backs: whole squads ambushed and wiped out. NVA units and Vietcong cells, too. Back at the LZs I heard talk of Montagnard cannibals. The jungle is a creepy place.

I'm dozing in my hollow. Suddenly I'm alert. Something's happening, I don't what. Then I hear voices. They get louder. It must be Vietcong coming down the trail. I shrink back into my hiding-place. I can hear them continuously now. They're chattering away. One of them is singing, a weird ululating sound I've heard in villages. It's amazing to hear them making so much noise. When we were out in the jungle at night we moved as silently as possible.

They seem to have stopped. What's happening? I can hear movement near the hollow. They must have left the trail. Why? It doesn't feel as if they're searching for me. Someone very nearby is talking to others further away, and laughing. Suddenly I get a powerful whiff of cigarette smoke. I see his feet, right outside the hollow. Black trousers and rubber sandals: I could almost reach out and touch them. Then a familiar splashing sound. He's having a pee! I can smell it.

The splashing stops. I can hear a rustle of clothing, and see his feet move as he shifts his weight slightly. He drops the cigarette. All the time he's talking to his friends. Then I hear him stroll back to join the others. Their voices gradually fade as they move off down the trail.

I climb out of my hide. There's the stub of the cigarette, still burning. I pick it up and take a drag, drawing the smoke deep into my lungs. It has a strong, acrid taste, a bit like a French cigarette, which makes me cough slightly. Holding the tip between my forefinger and thumb, I take another deep drag, the last one possible, and feel the rush course through my bloodstream. Then I let the stub drop.

I decide to have a pee myself. The scent of urine is very strong. I realize that I'm like a dog, marking my territory.

I settle down again in the hollow.

I'm spreadeagled naked against a wall, bound head and foot. My interrogator blows smoke in my eyes. I glare back at him. It's Lieutenant Raab. He steps on my foot, grinding his heel into the toe of my boot. I look down and see that my boots are scuffed. I feel a sense of rage, knowing how long it's taken me to polish them. Raab tells me that I'm improperly dressed. The guards cut me down. Raab makes me do fifty push-ups. I'm being punished because I'm not an American.

Now I'm creeping away. The CO shows me a place where I can hide, under the bed. I crawl in there and wait, hardly daring to breathe. I hear someone approaching. Don't let them find me! Then a torch shines in my face, and slowly the beam traces all over my body. I hear mocking laughter.

*

The sun's streaming into my eyes. I blink, and look away, dazzled. I feel the warmth on my skin. Then I turn back, keeping my eyes down. A beam of sunlight descends from the canopy into the hollow. Other shafts spear down on to the jungle floor, punctuating the dark shadow. The first sunshine I've seen for weeks. It must be a good omen. Mustn't it?

I climb stiffly out of the hollow. It's a warm, muggy morning. The air is utterly still. There's nobody about. On the ground is the cigarette stub from last night; casting about I can see signs of where the gook left the trail.

I hear a snuffling sound, not far off. It doesn't sound like anything threatening. I crouch down behind a bush and wait. The snuffling comes closer. A few minutes later, a pot-bellied pig waddles into view. I've seen plenty of them in the jungle: they're semi-domesticated, and the Vietnamese let them roam until they're ready to eat.

It occurs to me that I'm very hungry. I'm not looking at an animal any more: I'm looking at ham sandwiches, fried bacon, roast pork. I start salivating. I decide that I've got to catch this animal and eat it. How do you kill a pig with your bare hands? Catch it first. I wait until the pig wanders towards me, then make a dart at it, arms outstretched. To my surprise the pig is quicker. I find myself hitting the ground empty-handed, like a full back failing to tackle a wing three-quarter in full flight. The pig disappears into the undergrowth, squealing.

Then it dawns on me what a risk I've taken. I'm furious with myself. Hunger has made me reckless. I strip off some more banana stalks and munch them. I'm still ravenously hungry. What else can I eat? A large slug labours along a leaf in front of me, leaving a trail of slime. I pick it up and examine it closely. I lift it towards my open mouth, and then hesitate. Can I do this? Fighting down revulsion, I pop it into my mouth. It tastes . . . disgusting. It's too big to swallow, so I'm forced to chew it. The sensation of biting into slug is vile; some unmentionable liquid squirts out into my throat. Struggling to overcome nausea, I swallow the little pieces of slug; each squeezes down my throat like a solid piece of fat. Then suddenly I retch, vomiting from deep inside. Those little pieces of fat reappear in my mouth, and I spit them out. I'm bent forward, breathing deeply, dribbling.

When my stomach settles, I rinse out my mouth with water and nibble some more banana stalks. I find some bamboo shoots and eat these, too. But I can't get rid of the foul taste in my mouth.

It's time to get going. I've decided which direction to take down the trail by looking at the sun, whenever I can catch a glimpse of it through the canopy. So far as I could tell, the band of Vietcong that captured me were heading west most of the time, so I reckon that my best chance of escape lies in trying to make my way back east. Of course, my choice could be wrong. None of the jungle trails is straight; just because this stretch points the way I think I should go doesn't mean that it won't double back around the next corner. If I've made the wrong decision, I could find myself walking directly into the arms of my captors. I wonder if they are still searching for me.

I've been following the trail for perhaps two hours. I reckon it must be mid-morning by now. I'm moving very cautiously, stopping every few paces to listen for the sound of anyone coming. Nothing so far. I keep my eyes peeled for booby-traps. Every half-hour or so I check my direction against the sun: I seem to be heading roughly the right way.

I hear the throb of an approaching helicopter. The United States cavalry, coming to my rescue! I run down the trail, trying to find a piece of open ground where they can't fail to spot me. I catch a glimpse of the helicopter hovering overhead, above the canopy, only two or three hundred feet from the ground. I start jumping and waving, trying to attract their attention. Surely they can see me? It's so tantalizing: throbbing fills the air and I'm so close I can read the markings on the chopper. I'm desperate at the thought that they may fly off and leave me here; I start shouting at the top of my voice, abandoning all caution. Then I'm aware of a commotion in the jungle to my left. An instant later a huge animal comes charging through the undergrowth, clearly terrified by the din. A buffalo! It heads blindly towards me, bowling me over, and disappears into the jungle to my right. For a moment or two I lie stunned; by the time I'm back on my feet, the chopper has gone. The throbbing of its blades slowly dies away. I sink to my knees, trying and failing to resist the tears boiling up inside me. Will I never get out of this place?

Three or four hours later, open patches of sky begin to appear ahead. I'm reaching the edge of the jungle. I'm even more wary, now that there's less cover. The jungle thins, then gives way altogether to a thin band of scrub. Beyond I can see a field of elephant grass, standing more than head-high.

I find a tree to climb, and shin up twenty feet or so until I can see over the grass. On the other side are paddy-fields; in the distance I can see several clusters of huts, and beyond them mountains. The air is still; the moment quiet. I've no idea where I am. Nothing looks familiar.

I consider what I should do if I see a villager approaching. I decide to stay hidden. Many are sympathetic to the Vietcong. The people who live round here must know that there's a VC holding camp only five kilometres or so back down the trail. I can't bear the thought that I might have come so far only to be recaptured and taken back for more torture.

Even if not enemy sympathizers, Vietnamese peasants may nevertheless be hostile to American soldiers: plenty of them have had bad experiences during the war. Villagers often shout abuse at us as we pass through. Or they might be frightened by an approach from an American soldier; I've seen that, too, when an old woman starts screaming with fear at the mere sight of us. Either way I might be betrayed, deliberately or otherwise. And, of course, I have no clothes on.

Anyway, I don't look like an American. I probably don't even look human. My body is covered with wounds and sores; my hair is wild and tangled; I have the best part of a week's growth of beard.

So I wait for a while, perched comfortably over a fork in the tree. I wait and I watch. And I hear it first – a faint swishing, like the sound of wind in the trees. Then I see the elephant grass rippling. Somebody's coming – lots of people. My heart begins to pound. Could this be what I've been hoping for? How many times have I deployed a platoon on just such a manoeuvre, the men spread out in a long line, moving cautiously through the grass? Is that a radio operator's aerial I can see poking up through the grass? Or is it the enemy, an NVA unit or even a VC search party still hunting for me? A familiar helmet bounces into view, then another, then another. At last! A pulse of joy surges through me. Thank you, thank you, whoever you are up there!

They seem to be heading along a trail that leads this way. As usual, they're moving very slowly; I guess it might take them another ten minutes to get here. I start thinking about all the things that might still go wrong: I might be recaptured at the last moment, the patrol might be ambushed, they might turn round and head in another direction, leaving me behind. Please, please, God, don't fail me now! I'm so excited, I can't bear to wait. I drop down out of the tree, and scamper into the long grass along the trail towards them.

A terrible thought stops me in my tracks: how do I know they won't shoot me? If I come running at them, waving my arms, they're likely to shoot first and ask questions later. I force myself to wait by the trail for their arrival. I'll stand here and show myself, making it obvious that I'm not an enemy soldier.

The wait is excruciating. My eyes are fixed to the trail ahead. I keep thinking that I'm waiting in the wrong place, or that they may turn back before they reach here. I glance round every few seconds, expecting to see VC rifles pointed at my bare back.

Then the point man appears round a corner in the grass. As soon as he sees me, he drops to one knee in the firing position, shouting at the others to take cover. His voice is cold and determined. I raise my hands above my head. My knees tremble.

He orders me to advance, keeping my hands high where he can see them.

'Don't shoot,' I plead, as I walk forward. 'I'm an American officer.' My voice is shaking, damn it. I haven't spoken for – how long? 'I'm an American officer,' I repeat, more distinctly this time, as I approach.

When I'm about twenty feet away, he orders me to stop and wait there. His eyes are wide. I can see he's just a kid: nineteen, maybe. He passes the word back down the line for his lieutenant. I stand naked with my hands raised, sweat dripping down my forehead.

A moment later, the lieutenant arrives from the rear of the platoon. He looks perplexed. The two of them approach, still covering me with their weapons. I begin to relax. I can see from their patches that this is a Cav patrol. The lieutenant looks awfully young and green; I suspect that he's only just arrived in-country. For the first time I feel self-conscious about my nakedness. I wonder whether to salute, and decide against: I think an informal introduction is probably more appropriate in the circumstances. 'My name's Abraham,' I tell them. 'I'm a lieutenant in the 5th Battalion of the 7th Cav. I've just escaped from the Vietcong.' It sounds fantastic, I know, especially delivered in an English accent. The situation is so ludicrous that I almost laugh out loud. I'm aware of the rest of the platoon gawping at me in the background.

At first they're suspicious. It's a little unusual for a jungle patrol to come across a naked and dishevelled man with a British accent who claims to be an American officer. But I don't care. I've all the time in the world to prove who I am. Slowly, I lower my hands, without any prompting. I've made it! The relief is so great that I almost break down into sobs. I shiver. I'm very tired and my heart is full, but I'm determined not to break down in front of these men.

The lieutenant decides that he's going to treat me as if I am who I claim to be. 'For God's sake, get this man covered up!' he shouts.

Some of the men start rooting around in their packs for spare kit, and within a minute or two I'm dressed in fatigues, like all the others – though still barefoot and unarmed.

One of the men offers me his canteen. I drink greedily. Another produces a couple of cans of C-rations. I fumble with the opener, dropping it. The guy gently takes it from me and opens the cans himself. Then he hands them back, one at a time. Dry biscuits and cream cheese: delicious. Chipolata sausages and beans: heaven. I use the little plastic spoon provided to wolf them down.

I give the LT my serial number, and he relays it over the radio, calling up a transport to take us out of the field. The platoon has cleared an LZ a mile or so back, so the chopper will pick us up there.

The other guys are sitting around on the trail and relaxing. One tears open a packet of Camels and taps one out for me. I take it gratefully, but I can't prevent myself flinching when he snaps open a lighter. He looks startled. I mumble an apology; then I take his proffered lighter and hold it to the tip of my cigarette. I draw smoke deep into my lungs and hold it there for a moment, then expel it through my nostrils. This feels like the best moment in my entire life. The GI tells me to keep the packet; he has plenty.

We head back down the trail. I walk with the LT, making conversation as we go. We talk about everyday stuff, the issues officers in the field face daily. He doesn't ask me about what I've been through, and I don't press the subject, taking my lead from him. I know that I'll remain under suspicion until the intelligence boys have given me the all clear. I can tell that the men in the platoon are a little wary of me.

It seems extraordinary to be strolling down this trail, chatting to the lieutenant in a desultory way about routine matters. For the past few days I've been terrified almost all the time. I've been concentrating solely on survival. It's still intensely vivid in my mind; by contrast, what I'm doing now doesn't seem real. I feel as if I'm playing a part in a film.

I start noticing the way the men act. It's weird to observe how watchful they are, to begin to see the country as they do once more. Four days ago I was marching this way with a band of Vietcong, marvelling at how they moved across the landscape so openly. While I was their prisoner I might as well as have been in North Vietnam, for all the precautions they took to keep themselves hidden. For the past two days I've been on the run from them, hearing them laughing and singing in the jungle, watching them from my hides. Now they've become invisible again. Has it all been a dream? I slip my hand inside my shirt and carefully touch the cigarette burns.

An hour later we're at the battalion firebase, where the LT passes me over to the intelligence officers with a heavy-handed attempt at humour. 'He seems fairly plausible, but you never know – he's a Limey.' There's a debriefing that lasts only half an hour or so; they ask me about the village where I was held, and what I saw while I was there, and that's all. I'm a little bemused – though of course I'm relieved it doesn't last any longer. They don't seem at all suspicious of me, or want to know the details of my interrogation at the hands of the NVA officer. I suppose my story has no strategic or intelligence significance. Afterwards I get some perfunctory attention from the medic, dabbing my wounds with iodine. 'Jesus, LT,' he says, 'you been smoking in bed?' By chance I run into the point man who first spotted me. He avoids my eye, looking embarrassed. I get the impression that they all want to be rid of me.

That evening I'm flown back to Camp Evans. I'm given a billet for the night and issued with a complete set of new kit. It's wonderful to have a hot meal, to sleep in a warm bed – with sheets! – to be able to take a shower – with soap! – and shave. I feel like an American soldier again. I go to the bar that night and drink half a dozen cans of Budweiser. There are a few guys around I know vaguely, but no one asks me about my capture, and I don't tell them. I just want to forget all about it.

The next morning I report to my company commander as ready for duty. 'Glad to have you back, Abraham,' he says. 'Delighted to find you alive.'

I found it disconcerting that the other men in my unit didn't really want to know what had happened to me. They all crowded round when I arrived, of course, and a few said how pleased they were to see me back. I'd been listed as MIA (though as yet this listing hadn't even reached the battalion HQ); most of them had assumed that they would never see me again. But once I'd explained the outline of my story nobody was very interested in the details. Out in 'Nam you kept yourself to yourself; curiosity was a liability. So many people there had been through so much that one more tale, however extraordinary, didn't seem particularly important. Even while I was still marching barefoot through the elephant grass, I had decided not to talk about it unless pressed. And nobody did press me.

Nor did anyone press me when I came home at the end of my tour. After our wedding Debbie and I returned to America by sea, honeymooning on the old *Queen Elizabeth*. I served out the remaining five months of my three-year term of duty in the Army as a training adviser in Oakdale, just outside Pittsburg and not so far from my family home. Afterwards we stayed on in America for a couple of years, but Debbie was never happy there, and in 1971 we came back to England by sea. Our first daughter was conceived in mid-Atlantic, and two more daughters were born over the next few years as I began to carve out a career in the textile industry.

So far as my family was concerned, Vietnam was in the past. Like most of the guys serving out there, I'd had a policy of glossing over anything unpleasant I'd witnessed in my letters to Debbie and my family. I didn't want to worry them unnecessarily. Time and again I would write that things were looking up, that I was far from the front line, that any danger had been temporary, and so on. When I got back, I found it difficult to disabuse them of this fantasy, and I thought that perhaps it was better not to do so. Very few people back home wanted to know the reality of the war. The brutality, the suffering, the terror: all these were subjects too gross for discussion in small-town America, let alone suburban England. Why bring it up now? Why not just get on with life?

Civilians tended to react to the war in one of two different ways. One group, often consisting mainly of older people, wanted to hear about the war as a noble and patriotic struggle for freedom. That might have been the way I felt when I joined the Army, but it wasn't quite how I felt when I left. I went along with people who talked that way, but I didn't have the heart for it myself.

The other reaction was hostile, or even contemptuous: 'What did you want to go and do that for?' I'd have to stop myself getting riled by people who reacted like this. Sometimes, when I found myself with some idiot going on about the war, I'd get up and walk out.

Nobody wanted to hear about how you might have suffered in Vietnam. If it wasn't distressing, it was embarrassing. Most people seemed to think of the Vietnamese as the victims and of us as the aggressors. I'd expected some recognition for the sacrifices we'd made, but that didn't happen. Looking back, I'm not surprised that so many vets topped themselves in the years that followed.

Among my family, it was almost as if there was a conspiracy to pretend that everything out there had been as benign as I'd described it in my letters, and an assumption that, now I was back, the true nastiness of what had gone on was no longer relevant.

I hadn't mentioned being captured in any of my letters. It wasn't the sort of thing I wanted to put on paper. Somehow I was ashamed of it. There was a sense in which I, too, wanted to put it all behind me, to forget that once I'd been stripped and bound, tortured and abused. The idea of being locked in the cage still terrified me. I had nightmares about being back in the jungle, with Vietcong still searching for me; about being caught and dragged back to the cage. I locked up the memory in a corner of my mind and left it there.

I could never talk to Debbie about any of this. All the time I was in Vietnam I had kept a picture of her in my mind as pure and clean and unsullied by all the filth and misery I saw around me. I couldn't unlock these terrible memories without destroying that picture. I'd wake up sweating in the night – but I wouldn't tell her what I'd been dreaming about.

The psychiatrists say that the strain of keeping it hidden may have contributed towards the breakdown of our marriage. I don't know about that. I do know that over the years I became more and more isolated from her, as I became increasingly absorbed in my work. I would leave home very early in the morning and not come back until very late at night. It was as if I was on the run from something.

Of course the inevitable happened. I started an affair. I told myself that Debbie and I had drifted apart, when the truth was that I had never let her get close to me. We divorced, after thirteen years of marriage.

I met Sally at a trade fair in Frankfurt. We were part of a group that hit the town one evening and ended up at a disco late at night. As the others gradually peeled off and went to bed, we sat up, and eventually I asked her to dance. They were playing some corny Barry White song, but it didn't matter, because we only had eyes for each other.

Sally and I hit it off straight away, and seemed to understand each other perfectly. We quickly became so close that friends used to joke about it: they'd refer to us as the 'Tom and Sally Show'. I decided that I wanted to spend the rest of my life with this woman, and asked her to marry me. When she agreed, I felt as if I'd been given a second chance of happiness.

But even Sally has never been interested in what happened to me in Vietnam. She's always treated the little I've told her as if it were a story: not exactly a dream, but something irrelevant to her and her life in England, something that happened a long time ago, and in a sense not real.

She tends to make light of it all – perhaps for my sake, so that I don't dwell on it. I think I must have resented her for that. I felt belittled. I used to shout at her sometimes, when I thought that perhaps she was laughing at me. Maybe poking that knife into her ribs was my mad attempt to force her to acknowledge what I'd been through.

And all that did was drive her away. I've lost my wife, my home, and my self-respect. One way and another, being locked up in that cage has robbed me of everything on this earth that I value.

I roll over in my sleeping-bag and tap out another cigarette. Then I flick the lid and ignite the lighter, all in one movement. I've had plenty of practice over the past thirty-five years. I hold the flame to the tip of the cigarette and draw the smoke gratefully into my lungs. It's getting dark outside. Soon another day will be over – another day of doing nothing, going nowhere, seeing no one. I can't believe my life has come to this.

25

It's nearly midday. As usual, I get up late, though I've been awake for hours. Breakfast is a bowl of cereal. I keep the milk outside the window to stop it going sour too quickly. Some days I don't bother to dress, but today I have to go down to the post office to collect my benefit payment. I've shaved and combed my hair. When I'm ready, I pull on my coat, pick up my key, and open the door into the hall. As usual, there are letters piled on the first few treads of the stairs. I walk over to take a look, though there's never yet been anything for me. But this time there is: a large, official-looking brown envelope, with my name and address typed on the front. The stamp reads 'Kingston-upon-Thames County Court'. I tear open the envelope. It's a form of some kind – oh, Christ, it's a divorce petition. On the form, Sally is 'the petitioner' and I am 'the respondent'. There's a statement from Sally. 'I sincerely believe I have done everything in my power to help, support and stand by the respondent,' the statement reads, 'but there is no trust left and the petitioner can no longer remain the respondent's wife. She lives in fear of him and trusts he will not find out where she is living.'

I know that Sally is my only hope. I must make her understand what's happened to me. If I can just speak to her, just spend a few hours with her, everything might be OK again. If I let her go, I'm finished.

But I'm not supposed to contact her. There's a court order forbidding me to do so. And now we're in the middle of a very acrimonious divorce. It's harder for her in a way, because I'm on legal aid and she is having to pay for her lawyers. I've nothing to lose.

I write Sally a long letter, saying how sorry I am for what I've done and begging her forgiveness. It takes me a whole day to write. I tell her that I love her and that, despite everything that has happened, I hope she still loves me.

I send it to her care of her lawyers. I put on paper things that could undermine my legal position, but I don't care. If I don't have Sally, I don't have anything.

I tell her I want us to meet. There's a pub where we sometimes used to go together, and I suggest a date and a time when we could meet there to see if we can sort things out.

I'm very nervous that day. I get up early to travel to London by train. My sister has lent me the money for the fare. I know I mustn't be late, and I end up arriving so early that I have to hang around outside for an hour before going in. She isn't there. I buy a drink and sit down to wait. My hand is shaking so much that I spill some of the drink every time I pick it up. After a while I hear the landlord call out: 'Is there a Tom Abraham here?'

I approach the bar, not knowing what to expect. 'I'm Tom Abraham.'

He hands me an envelope. 'Your wife left it for you,' he announces.

I tear open the envelope and find a formal letter from Sally inside, telling me that she doesn't want to see me, not now or ever. She tells me never to contact her again. I'm stunned.

The locals begin to titter. 'Oho, she's stood you up! Your wife doesn't love you any more!'

I break down and run out of the pub.

I write to Sally again, begging her to see me. I promise to do anything she wants, give up drinking, anything, if she will only have me back.

I know she wouldn't have hurt me so much if she hadn't been so hurt herself.

One afternoon I am writing Sally yet another letter when the telephone rings. It's her! I'm so excited I can barely marshal my thoughts. She sounds strained and distant, but she agrees to meet me on neutral territory. My best man has already offered his house as a place where we could meet, so that's where we go, the very next day. The two of us spend the whole day together, talking, talking, talking. For the first time, I'm able to explain to her what happened to me in the cage, and in the jungle afterwards. It's not easy for me to talk about it, but I manage somehow. I can see that it's registered with her, even though she finds it hard to understand. And, at the end, she agrees to take me back.

Three years have passed. Sally and I have a home together again, a modest little cottage on the outskirts of London. I'm off the drugs now, and I feel more relaxed and contented. When I do get upset, Sally helps me through it.

We're still short of money, but somehow it doesn't seem so much of a pressure. We're happy just to be together once more. The 'Tom and Sally Show' is back on the road.

I don't get flashbacks, these days. But some nights I find myself visiting Vietnam in my dreams. Horrific sights project across the screen of my mind, like grotesque holiday snaps. Here are the severed limbs, here are the skinned bodies sprawling against trees. I watch my buddy's head disintegrate under the impact of an RPG. I feel my disgust as I wipe his scattered brains from my fatigues. I see my interrogator's grin as he slowly stubs out a cigarette on my chest.

What I dread most of all is the moment when once more they will squash me into the creaking bamboo cage and lower it into the lukewarm water.

Then I feel Sally's soft embrace, and my mind is free again.

Glossary

AIT Advanced Infantry Training
AK-47 enemy assault rifle, known over the radio as 'Alpha Kilo 47s'
AO Area of Operations
APC Armoured Personnel-Carrier
ARA air rocket artillery
ARVN Army Republic of Vietnam, used to denote South Vietnamese soldier
Arc-light strikes successive heavy bombing raids

Bird colonel full colonel, who wears an eagle insignia, as opposed to lieutenant-colonel, who wears a silver leaf cluster
Blues, dress blues formal army uniform, worn on ceremonial occasions
Bouncing Betty enemy booby-trap bomb that springs into the air

C-130 large transport aircraft
C-147 a smaller transport aircraft
C-4 plastic explosive
C-rations canned army rations
CAR-15 combat assault rifle
Cav 1st Cavalry Division
CCF Combined Cadet Force
Charlie nickname for the North Vietnamese or Vietcong soldiers
Chi-com Chinese copy of a Russian weapon
Chinook helicopter transport
Chow Army food
Claymore mine US Army anti-personnel mine, often captured by the enemy and used against American troops
Cobra attack helicopter
CP Command Post
Crane large twin-bladed helicopter transport

DMZ Demilitarized Zone between North and South Vietnam

Daisy-cutter thousand-pound bomb often used for clearing new LZs
Double timing marching on the run

FNG Fucking New Guy
.50-cal powerful machine-gun, often mounted on top of an APC
fugas mixture of diesel and napalm
full pack in full combat uniform, carrying all the standard equipment

GI literally 'Government Issue' – used to denote an American soldier
Gook derogatory term for an enemy soldier
Grunt American infantryman
Guns-a-go-go heavily armed Chinook

H & I Harassment and Interdiction artillery rounds fired to deny territory to the enemy rather than being aimed at a specific target
Ho Chi Minh racing slicks shoes made of rubber tyres worn by the Vietnamese
Hooch tent used by soldiers in the field; also Vietnamese hut
Hoochgirls Vietnamese maids
House brothel
Huey UH1-B helicopter

In-country in Vietnam

Kit Carson enemy defector retrained to serve with US forces
KP Kitchen Police, used to denote kitchen duties
Klick kilometre

LAW lightweight anti-tank weapon
LT lieutenant
LZ Landing Zone

M-1 old-fashioned semi-automatic rifle
M-8 US Army bayonet
M-16 US Army assault rifle
M-60 US Army machine-gun
M-72 US Army lightweight anti-tank weapon
M-79 US Army grenade-launcher
MIA missing in action
MPC Military Payment Certificates
Mama-san older Vietnamese woman
Medevac medical evacuation team
Million-dollar wound wound serious enough to necessitate removal back to America

No.1 Vietnamese pidgin for the best
No.10 Vietnamese pidgin for the worst
NLF National Liberation Front
NVA North Vietnamese Army

OCS Officer Candidate School
OP Observation Point

Papa-san older Vietnamese man
Piece rifle
Pogue US military personnel assigned to the rear
Point, point man in the lead, leading man in the patrol
Psy-ops literally 'psychological operations', used to denote propaganda broadcasts from aircraft-mounted loudspeakers
Punji stick bamboo stake used by the enemy as booby-trap
PX literally the Post Exchange – US Army supermarket/bar/cafeteria

R & R rest and relaxation, known colloquially as 'I & I', (intercourse and intoxication)
RPG Rocket-Propelled Grenade
RTO Radio Telephone Operator

S-2 Security and Intelligence Officer
SOP (US Army) Standard Operating Procedures
Short, getting short time remaining of tour of duty
Snoopy small spy helicopter
Spooky helicopter gunship

TACs 'tactical officers', newly qualified lieutenants responsible for OCS training
TOC Tactical Operations Center
Tracer rounds treated chemically to indicate their trail

VC Vietcong, literally Vietnamese Communists, a derogatory term used to denote Communist irregulars
Ville Vietnamese village

Willie Peter white phosphorus grenade
World, The anywhere but Vietnam

XO Executive Officer